W9-AOC-403

The Fundamental Wisdom
of the Middle Way

The Fundamental Wisdom of the Middle Way

Nāgārjuna's *Mūlamadhyamakakārikā*

TRANSLATION AND COMMENTARY BY

JAY L. GARFIELD

New York   Oxford
OXFORD UNIVERSITY PRESS
1995

Oxford University Press

Oxford   New York
Athens   Auckland   Bangkok
Calcutta   Cape Town   Dar es Salaam   Delhi
Florence   Hong Kong   Istanbul   Karachi
Kuala Lumpur   Madras   Madrid   Melbourne
Mexico City   Nairobi   Paris   Singapore
Taipei   Tokyo   Toronto

and associated companies in
Berlin   Ibadan

Copyright © 1995 by Jay L. Garfield

Published by Oxford University Press, Inc.
198 Madison Avenue, New York, New York 10016

Oxford is a registered trademark of Oxford University Press, Inc.

All rights reserved. No part of this publication may be reproduced,
stored in a retrieval system, or transmitted, in any form or by any means,
electronic, mechanical, photocopying, recording or otherwise,
without the prior permission of Oxford University Press.

Library of Congress Cataloging-in-Publication Data
Nāgārjuna, 2nd cent.
[Madhyamakakārikā. English & Sanskrit]
The fundamental wisdom of the middle way :
Nāgārjuna's Mūlamadhyamakakārikā /
Translation and commentary by
Jay L. Garfield.
p.   cm.
ISBN13 978-0-19-509336-0 (pbk.);

ISBN13 978-0-19-510317-5 (cloth)

1. Mādhyamika (Buddhism)—Early works to 1800.
I. Garfield, Jay L., 1955—.
BQ2792.E5G37   1995   294.3'85—dc20   95-1051

23 24 25 26 27 28 29 30

Printed in the United States of America

I dedicate this work,
with profound gratitude
and respect,
to the Most Ven. Professor Samdhong Rinpoche:
scholar, educator, statesman, public servant
and shining exemplar of monastic life.

Preface

This is a translation of the Tibetan text of *Mūlamadhyamakakā-rikā*. It is perhaps an odd idea to translate a Tibetan translation of a Sanskrit text and to retranslate a text of which there are four extant English versions. My reasons for doing so are these: First, I am not satisfied with any of the other English versions. Every translation, this one included, of any text embodies an interpretation, and my interpretation differs in various respects from those of my predecessors in this endeavor. This is to be expected. As Tuck (1990) has correctly observed, Nāgārjuna, like any philosopher from a distant cultural context, is always read against an interpretive backdrop provided by the philosophical presuppositions of the interpreter, and by previous readings of Nāgārjuna. So I claim no special privileged position vis à vis Streng (1967), Inada (1970), Sprung (1979), or Kalupahana (1986)—only a different position, one that I hope will prove useful in bringing *Mūlamadhyama-kakārikā* into contemporary philosophical discourse. I, like any translator/interpreter must acknowledge that there is simply no fact of the matter about the correct rendering of any important and genuinely interesting text. Interpretations, and with them, translations, will continue to evolve as our understanding of the text evolves and as our interpretive horizon changes. Matters are even more complex and indeterminate when the translation crosses centuries, traditions and languages, and sets of philosophical assumptions that are quite distant from one another, as is the case in the present project. So each of the available versions of the text embodies a reading. Inada reads Nāgārjuna from the standpoint of the Zen tradition, and his translation reflects that reading; Kalu-pahana reads Nāgārjuna as a Theravada commentator on the *Kaccāyānagotta-sūtra*, and his translation reflects that reading, as well as his view about the affinities between James's pragmatism and Theravada Buddhism. Sprung adopts Murti's Kantian interpretation of Mādhyamika, and his translation reflects that interpretation. Streng reads the text as primarily concerned with religious phenomenology. There is no translation of this text into English, and no commentary on it, that specifically reflects an Indo-Tibetan Prāsaṅgika-Mādhyamika interpretation. Inasmuch as this is my own preferred way to read Nāgārjuna, and the reading dominant in Tibetan and highly influential in Japanese and Chinese discussions of *Mūlamadhyamakakārikā*, I believe that it is important to fill this lacuna in the English bibliography.

Having argued that all translation involves some interpretation and, hence, that there is always some distance between an original text and a translation, however good and canonical that translation may be, it follows that *Mūlamadhyamakakārikā* and *dBu-ma rtsa-ba shes-rab* differ, however close they may be and however canonically the latter is treated. Since *dBu-ma rtsa-ba shes-rab* is the text read by and commented on by generations of Tibetan philosophers, I think that it is important that an English translation of this very text be available to the Western philosophical public. This text is hence worthy in its own right of translation inasmuch as it is the proper subject of the Tibetan philosophical literature I and others find so deep and fascinating.

This is not a critical scholarly edition of the text. It is not philological in intent; nor is it a discussion of the commentarial literature on Nāgārjuna's text. There is indeed a need for such a book, but that need will have to be filled by someone else. This is rather meant to be a presentation of a philosophical text to philosophers, and not an edition of the text for Buddhologists. If philosophers and students who read my book thereby gain an entrance into Nāgārjuna's philosophy and see *Mūlamadhyamakakārikā*, as interpreted herein, as a text worthy of study and discussion, this work will have served its purpose. Since my intended audience is not Buddhologists, per se, but Western philosophers who are interested in Buddhist philosophy, I have tried to balance standard renderings of Buddhist terminology with more perspicuous contemporary philosophical language. I am not sure that I have always made the right decisions or that I have found the middle path between the extremes of Buddhological orthodoxy and Western revisionism. But that is the aim.

I am also striving for that elusive middle path between two other extremes in translation: I am trying on the one hand to avoid the unreadable literalism of translations that strive to provide a verbatim report of the words used the original, regardless of whether that results in a comprehensible English text. But there is on the other hand the extreme represented by a translation written in lucid English prose purporting to be what the original author *would* have written had he been a twentieth-century philosopher writing in English, or one that, in an attempt to convey what the text *really means* on some particular interpretation, is in fact not a translation of the original text, but a completely new book, bearing only a distant relation to the original. This hopelessly mixes the tasks of translation on the one hand and critical commentary on the other. Of course, as I have noted above, these tasks are intertwined. But there is the fault of allowing the translation to become *so* mixed with the commentary that one no longer has a grip on, for example, what is Nāgārjuna and what is Garfield. After all, although the text is interpreted in being translated, this text should still come out in translation as a text which *could* be interpreted in the ways that others have read it. Because the original *does* indeed justify competing interpretations. That is one of the things that makes it such an important philosophical work.

Amherst, Mass.   J. L. G.
November 1994

Acknowledgments

Thanks are already due to many who have helped at different stages of this project: Thanks to Bob Thurman and David Sloss for first introducing me to Buddhist philosophy and then for encouraging me to wade deeper. Thanks to David Kalupahana, Steve Odin, Kenneth Inada, and Guy Newland, as well as to David Karnos, Joel Aubel, Dick Garner, and William Herbrechtsmeier for many hours of valuable and enjoyable discussion of this text at the National Endowment for the Humanities Summer institute on Nāgārjuna in Hawaii. And thanks to the NEH for the grant support that enabled my participation in that institute. I am especially grateful to Guy Newland for many subsequent conversations, useful suggestions, encouragement, and a critical reading of my work. Thanks to Janet Gyatso for countless hours of profitable and enjoyable philosophical conversation and for many useful and detailed criticisms and suggestions on this and other related work. Thanks to the Ven. Geshe Lobzang Tsetan for starting me in Tibetan, for much useful philosophical interchange, for teaching me an immense amount about Mādhyamika, and for his close criticism of this text; to Georges Dreyfus (Geshe Sengye Samdup) for much useful advice and discussion; and to Joshua and Dianne Cutler and the Tibetan Buddhist Learning Center of North America for hospitality. I also thank John Dunne for detailed comments on several chapters of an earlier draft of this translation.

I am grateful to the Indo-American Foundation, the Council for the International Exchange of Scholars, and the Smithsonian Institution for an Indo-American Fellowship in 1990–91. During that

time, as a Visiting Senior Research Scholar at the Central Institute
of Higher Tibetan Studies, I began work on this project. I owe an
enormous debt of gratitude to The Most Ven. Prof. Samdhong
Rinpoche and his staff for hosting me and my family at the Central
Institute of Higher Tibetan Studies and to Rinpoche himself for his
generous personal help. I thank the Ven. Geshe Ngawang Sherab
for all of his kind logistical help at Santarakshita Library and for
friendship and philosophical interchange. Thanks also to the Ven.
Lobzang Norbu Shastri and the Ven. Acarya Ngawang Samten for
extensive conversations from which I learned much and for useful
comments on this work and to Karma for Tibetan lessons.

I am deeply grateful to the Ven. Prof. Geshe Yeshes Thap-Khas
for reading *dBu-ma rtsa-ba shes-rab* and related texts with me and
for giving me his invaluable oral commentary on these texts during
that year and on many subsequent occasions. Nobody has taught me
more about Mādhyamika philosophy, and it is hard to imagine a
more patient, generous, and incisive scholar and teacher. Without
his lucid teachings, and without Geshe-la's enormous patience, I
could never have approached this text with any degree of success.
While he would not agree with everything I say, my own reading of
this text is enormously influenced by his. Special thanks to Sri Yeshi
Tashi Shastri for his translation and transcription assistance during
many of these sessions and for an enormous amount of cheerful and
generous general research assistance, including a great deal of careful proofreading and detailed comments on this translation.

During that year and in subsequent years I also benefited greatly
from my visits to the Institute of Buddhist Dialectics. I am deeply
grateful to the Ven. Prof. Geshe Lobzang Gyatso for his hospitality
and for his teaching. In our many conversations and from his writ-
ings I have learned a great deal, and this project certainly reflects
his influence. Without his patient advice on interpretative and
expository details and without his vigorous critique of many of my
ideas it would have been impossible to produce this commentary. I
thank the Ven. Sherab Gyatso for his tireless and invaluable translation and assistance during that time. The Ven. Sherab Gyasto,
The Ven. Graham Woodhouse, the Ven. Tenzin Dechen, and the
Ven. Huen have given much to me in many hours of philosophical
interchange through translation help and through their hospitality

and friendship. Mr. Phillipe Goldin has also offered many helpful suggestions on the translation and commentary. I also thank the Ven. Khamtrul Rinpoche, the Ven. Geshe Yeshe Topden (Gen Drup-Thop) and Gen Lam-Rim-pa for their teachings and Acarya Nyima Tshering for his introduction and translation on those occasions. Special thanks to Nyima Penthog for improving my Tibetan.

I thank His Holiness the Dalai Lama for his encouragement and for valuable discussion of some difficult interpretative issues.

I am also very grateful to friends and colleagues at Drepung Loseling Monastic College. My visit there was extremely enjoyable and also philosophically fruitful. Thanks to the Ven. Geshe Dak-pa Toepgyal and the Ven. Thupten Dorjee for arranging everything and for talking with me about this and other work. I am very grateful to the Ven. Geshe Namgyal Wangchen for detailed comments and encouragement on this work and for useful discussions about Mādhyamika, translation, the task of presenting Buddhist philosophical texts to the West, and other topics.

My acknowledgment of help in India would not be complete without acknowledging the gracious hospitality and assistance in living of Sri N. N. Rai, Sri Arun Kumar Rai, Sri A. R. Singh, and their families in Sarnath; the hospitality of Kunzom Topden Martam and his family in Sikkim—it was the Martam house in which the writing actually got started; and Dr. L. S. Suri of the American Institute of Indian Studies in New Delhi, whose administrative efficiency kept everything moving smoothly.

I am deeply grateful to four friends who read a complete draft of this work and provided honest, searching, sometimes scathing criticism. What more could one ask from colleagues and friends? Many of their suggestions are incorporated in the book as it now stands, and much of whatever is good in it is due to their enormous contributions. Sometimes I have disagreed with each of them. And whatever errors remain are certainly my own. So thanks especially to the Ven. Gareth Sparham, the Ven. Sherab Gyatso, Guy Newland, and Jane Braaten for copious corrections and criticism and for extensive productive discussion. Thanks also to Prof. Alan Sponberg for useful comments on an earlier draft and to Janet Gyatso, Graham Parkes, and Georges Dreyfus for reading and commenting on the penultimate draft.

Another group of colleagues to whom I owe thanks are those who kept faith. This may require some explanation. I discovered when I—a Western, analytically trained philosopher of mind—began to work on Buddhist philosophy that many in philosophy and cognitive science took this as evidence of some kind of insanity, or at least as an abandonment of philosophy, per se. This is not the place to speculate on the origins or nature of the stigma attaching in some parts of our profession to Asian philosophy. But it is a sad fact to be noted and to be rectified. In any case, I therefore owe special thanks to those who went out of their way to support this work and to let me know that they took it and me seriously. I thank especially my friend and colleague Meredith Michaels for constant support, advice, and encouragement. And I thank Murray Kiteley, John Connolly, Nalini Bhushan, Kathryn Addelson, Elizabeth Spellman, Frederique Marglin, Lee Bowie, Tom Wartenburg, Vere Chappell, Gareth Matthews, and John Robison, as well as Dan Lloyd, Steve Horst, and Joe Rouse. Thanks under this head also go to many of my nonphilosopher colleagues in the Hampshire College Cultural Studies program. I single out Mary Russo, Joan Landes, Susan Douglas, Jeffery Wallen, Norman Holland, and L. Brown Kennedy.

I also gratefully acknowledge the support of several Hewlett-Mellon faculty development grants from Hampshire College and thank the deans of the college for supporting this work so generously. I am also grateful for the support of this project and of related projects involving academic exchange between the American and Tibetan academic communities from President Greg Prince of Hampshire College. Thanks also to Ms. Ruth Hammen and Ms. Leni Bowen for regular logistical support, to Mr. Andrew Janiak for his extensive assistance and editorial suggestions in the final stages of manuscript preparation, and to Mr. Shua Garfield and Mr. Jeremy Mage for additional assistance in manuscript preparation and proofreading. Thanks as well to many groups of students in "Convention, Knowledge and Existence: European and Indo-Tibetan Perspectives" for putting up with and helping me to refine my presentation of this text and for my students in Buddhist Philosophy at Mount Holyoke College for working through an earlier draft of this text.

Portions of the translations of and commentaries on Chapters I, II, XIII, and XXIV appeared in *Philosophy East and West* in Garfield (1990) and (1994). I thank the editors for permission to use that material here. The Tibetan edition of the text is from dGe 'dun grub, *dBu ma rtsa shes rtsa 'grel bzhugs* (Commentary on *Mūlamadhyamakakārikā*), Ge Lugs Pa Students' Welfare Publishing, Central Institute of Higher Tibetan Studies, Sarnath, 1987.

I am more grateful than I could ever express to my family for accompanying me to India for one year, for enduring my absence when I have been in India alone, and for enduring my preoccupation with this and related philosophical projects. I am especially grateful to Blaine Garson, who has shouldered far more than her fair share of parenting and other household responsibilities. Every stage of this project is dependent upon her help, sacrifice, and support.

I hope that I haven't forgotten anybody.

Contents

Part One
The Text of *Mūlamadhyamakakārikā*

**Part Two
The Text and Commentary**

PART ONE

The Text of
Mūlamadhyamakakārikā

Dedicatory Verses

I prostrate to the Perfect Buddha,
The best of teachers, who taught that
Whatever is dependently arisen is
Unceasing, unborn,
Unannihilated, not permanent,
Not coming, not going,
Without distinction, without identity,
And free from conceptual construction.

Chapter I

Examination of Conditions

1. Neither from itself nor from another,
    Nor from both,
    Nor without a cause,
    Does anything whatever, anywhere arise.

2. There are four conditions: efficient condition;
    Percept-object condition; immediate condition;
    Dominant condition, just so.
    There is no fifth condition.

3. The essence of entities
    Is not present in the conditions, etc . . . .
    If there is no essence,
    There can be no otherness-essence.

4. Power to act does not have conditions.
    There is no power to act without conditions.
    There are no conditions without power to act.
    Nor do any have the power to act.

5. These give rise to those,
    So these are called conditions.
    As long as those do not come from these,
    Why are these not non-conditions?

6.   For neither an existent nor a non-existent thing
       Is a condition appropriate.
       If a thing is non-existent, how could it have a
           condition?
       If a thing is already existent, what would a condition
           do?

7.   When neither existents nor
       Non-existents nor existent non-existents are
           established,
       How could one propose a "productive cause?"
       If there were one, it would be pointless.

8.   An existent entity (mental episode)
       Has no object.
       Since a mental episode is without an object,
       How could there be any percept-condition?

9.   Since things are not arisen,
       Cessation is not acceptable.
       Therefore, an immediate condition is not reasonable.
       If something has ceased, how could it be a condition?

10.   If things did not exist
       Without essence,
       The phrase, "When this exists so this will be,"
       Would not be acceptable.

11.   In the several or united conditions
       The effect cannot be found.
       How could something not in the conditions
       Come from the conditions?

12.   However, if a nonexistent effect
       Arises from these conditions,
       Why does it not arise
       From non-conditions?

13.   If the effect's essence is the conditions,
        But the conditions don't have their own essence,
        How could an effect whose essence is the conditions
        Come from something that is essenceless?

14.   Therefore, neither with conditions as their essence,
        Nor with non-conditions as their essence are there any
            effects.
        If there are no such effects,
        How could conditions or non-conditions be evident?

Chapter II

Examination of Motion

1.   What has been moved is not moving.
        What has not been moved is not moving.
        Apart from what has been moved and what has not
            been moved,
        Movement cannot be conceived.

2.   Where there is change, there is motion.
        Since there is change in the moving,
        And not in the moved or not-moved,
        Motion is in that which is moving.

3.   How would it be acceptable
        For motion to be in the mover?
        When it is not moving, it is not acceptable
        To call it a mover.

4.   For whomever there is motion in the mover,
        There could be non-motion
        Evident in the mover.
        But having motion follows from being a mover.

5.   If motion is in the mover,
        There would have to be a twofold motion:

One in virtue of which it is a mover,
And one in virtue of which it moves.

6.   If there were a twofold motion,
The subject of that motion would be twofold.
For without a subject of motion,
There cannot be motion.

7.   If without a mover
It would not be correct to say that there is motion,
Then if there were no motion,
How could there be a mover?

8.   Inasmuch as a real mover does not move,
And a non-mover does not move,
Apart from a mover and a non-mover,
What third thing could move?

9.   When without motion,
It is unacceptable to call something a mover,
How will it be acceptable
To say that a mover moves?

10.   For him from whose perspective a mover moves,
There would be the consequence that
Without motion there could be a mover.
Because a mover moves.

11.   If a mover were to move,
There would be a twofold motion:
One in virtue of which he is a mover,
And one in virtue of which the mover moves.

12.   Motion does not begin in what has moved,
Nor does it begin in what has not moved,
Nor does it begin in what is moving.
In what, then, does motion begin?

13.   Prior to the beginning of motion,
       There is no beginning of motion in
       The going or in the gone.
       How could there be motion in the not-gone?

14.   Since the beginning of motion
       Cannot be conceived in any way,
       What gone thing, what going thing,
       And what non-going thing can be posited?

15.   Just as a moving thing is not stationary,
       A non-moving thing is not stationary.
       Apart from the moving and the non-moving,
       What third thing is stationary?

16.   If without motion
       It is not appropriate to posit a mover,
       How could it be appropriate to say
       That a moving thing is stationary?

17.   One does not halt from moving,
       Nor from having moved or not having moved.
       Motion and coming to rest
       And starting to move are similar.

18.   That motion just is the mover itself
       Is not correct.
       Nor is it correct that
       They are completely different.

19.   It would follow from
       The identity of mover and motion
       That agent and action
       Are identical.

20.   It would follow from
       A real distinction between motion and mover
       That there could be a mover without motion
       And motion without a mover.

21.   When neither in identity
        Nor in difference
        Can they be established,
        How can these two be established at all?

22.   The motion by means of which a mover is manifest
        Cannot be the motion by means of which he moves.
        He does not exist before that motion,
        So what and where is the thing that moves?

23.   A mover does not carry out a different motion
        From that by means of which he is manifest as a mover.
        Moreover, in one mover
        A twofold motion is unacceptable.

24.   A really existent mover
        Doesn't move in any of the three ways.
        A non-existent mover
        Doesn't move in any of the three ways.

25.   Neither an entity nor a non-entity
        Moves in any of the three ways.
        So motion, mover and
        And route are non-existent.

Chapter III

Examination of the Senses

1.   Seeing, hearing, smelling,
      Tasting, touching, and mind
      Are the six sense faculties.
      Their spheres are the visible objects, etc. . . .

2.   That very seeing does not see
      Itself at all.
      How can something that cannot see itself
      See another?

3.   The example of fire
      Cannot elucidate seeing.
      Along with the moved and not-moved and motion
      That has been answered.

4.   When there is not even the slightest
      Nonseeing seer,
      How could it makes sense to say
      That seeing sees?

5.   Seeing itself does not see.
      Nonseeing itself does not see.
      Through seeing itself
      The clear analysis of the seer is understood.

6. Without detachment from vision there is no seer.
   Nor is there a seer detached from it.
   If there is no seer
   How can there be seeing or the seen?

7. Just as the birth of a son is said to occur
   In dependence on the mother and father,
   So consciousness is said to arise
   In dependence on the eye and material form.

8. From the nonexistence of seeing and the seen it follows
   that
   The other four faculties of knowledge do not exist.
   And all the aggregates, etc.,
   Are the same way.

9. Like the seen, the heard, the smelled,
   The tasted, and the touched,
   The hearer, sound, etc.,
   And consciousness should be understood.

Chapter IV

Examination of the Aggregates

1.   Apart from the cause of form,
     Form cannot be conceived.
     Apart from form,
     The cause of form is not seen.

2.   If apart from the cause of form, there were form,
     Form would be without cause.
     But nowhere is there an effect
     Without a cause.

3.   If apart from form
     There were a cause of form,
     It would be a cause without an effect.
     But there are no causes without effects.

4.   When form exists,
     A cause of the arising of form is not tenable.
     When form is non-existent,
     A cause of the arising of form is not tenable.

5.   Form itself without a cause
     Is not possible or tenable.
     Therefore, think about form, but
     Do not construct theories about form.

6. The assertion that the effect and cause are similar
    Is not acceptable.
    The assertion that they are not similar
    Is also not acceptable.

7. Feelings, discriminations, and dispositions
    And consciousness and all such things
    Should be thought of
    In the same way as material form.

8. When an analysis is made through emptiness,
    If someone were to offer a reply,
    That reply will fail, since it will presuppose
    Exactly what is to be proven.

9. When an explanation is made through emptiness,
    Whoever would find fault with it
    Will find no fault, since the criticism will presuppose
    Exactly what is to be proven.

Chapter V

Examination of Elements

1.   Prior to a characteristic of space
There is not the slightest space.
If it arose prior to the characteristic
Then it would, absurdly, arise without a characteristic.

2.   A thing without a characteristic
Has never existed.
If nothing lacks a characteristic,
Where do characteristics come to be?

3.   Neither in the uncharacterized nor in the characterized
Does a characteristic arise.
Nor does it arise
In something different from these two.

4.   If characteristics do not appear,
Then it is not tenable to posit the characterized object.
If the characterized object is not posited,
There will be no characteristic either.

5.   From this it follows that there is no characterized
And no existing characteristic.
Nor is there any entity
Other than the characterized and the characteristic.

6.	If there is no existent thing,
	Of what will there be nonexistence?
	Apart from existent and nonexistent things
	Who knows existence and nonexistence?

7.	Therefore, space is not an entity.
	It is not a nonentity.
	Not characterized, not without character.
	The same is true of the other five elements.

8.	Fools and reificationists who perceive
	The existence and nonexistence
	Of objects
	Do not see the pacification of objectification.

Chapter VI

Examination of Desire and the Desirous

1. If prior to desire
    And without desire there were a desirous one,
    Desire would depend on him.
    Desire would exist when there is a desirous one.

2. Were there no desirous one, moreover,
    Where would desire occur?
    Whether or not desire or the desirous one exist,
    The analysis would be the same.

3. Desire and the desirous one
    Cannot arise together.
    In that case, desire and the desirous one
    Would not be mutually contingent.

4. In identity there is no simultaneity.
    A thing is not simultaneous with itself.
    But if there is difference,
    Then how would there be simultaneity?

5.   If in identity there were simultaneity,
      Then it could occur without association.
      If in difference there were simultaneity,
      It could occur without association.

6.   If in difference there were simultaneity,
      How could desire and the desirous one,
      Being different, be established?
      If they were, they would be simultaneous.

7.   If desire and the desirous one
      Are established as different,
      Then why would you think
      That they are simultaneous?

8.   Since difference is not established,
      If you assert that they are simultaneous,
      Since they are established as simultaneous,
      Do you also assert that they are different?

9.   Since nothing different has been established,
      If one is asserting simultaneity,
      Which different thing
      Do you want to say is simultaneous?

10.   Thus desire and the desirous one
      Cannot be established as simultaneous or not
          simultaneous.
      So, like desire, nothing whatever
      Can be established either as simultaneous or as
          nonsimultaneous.

Chapter VII

Examination of the Conditioned

1.   If arising were produced,
        Then it would also have the three characteristics.
        If arising is not produced,
        How could the characteristics of the produced exist?

2.   If the three, arising, etc., are separate,
        They cannot function as the characteristics of the
              produced.
        But how could they be joined
        In one thing simultaneously?

3.   If arising, abiding, and ceasing
        Have characteristics other than those of the produced,
        There would be an infinite regress.
        If they don't, they would not be produced.

4.   The arising of arising only gives rise
        To the basic arising.
        The arising of the basic arising
        Gives rise to arising.

5.   If, as you say, the arising of arising
        Gives rise to the basic arising,

How, according to you, does this,
Not arisen from the basic arising, give rise to that?

6.   If, as you say, that which is arisen from basic arising
Gives rise to the basis,
How does that nonarisen basis
Give rise to it?

7.   If this nonarisen
Could give rise to that,
Then, as you wish,
It will give rise to that which is arising.

8.   Just as a butterlamp
Illuminates itself as well as others,
So arising gives rise to itself
And to other arisen things.

9.   In the butterlamp and its place,
There is no darkness.
What then does the butterlamp illuminate?
For illumination is the clearing of darkness.

10.   If the arising butterlamp
Does not reach darkness,
How could that arising butterlamp
Have cleared the darkness?

11.   If the illumination of darkness occurs
Without the butterlamp reaching darkness,
All of the darkness in the world
Should be illuminated.

12.   If, when it is illuminated,
The butterlamp illuminates itself and others,
Darkness should, without a doubt,
Conceal itself and others.

13.   How could this arising, being nonarisen,
             Give rise to itself?
             And if it is arisen from another,
             Having arisen, what is the need for another arising?

14.   The arisen, the nonarisen, and that which is arising
             Do not arise in any way at all.
             Thus they should be understood
             Just like the gone, the not-gone, and the going.

15.   When there is arising but not yet
             That which is arising,
             How can we say that that which is arising
             Depends on this arising?

16.   Whatever is dependently arisen,
             Such a thing is essentially peaceful.
             Therefore that which is arising and arising itself
             Are themselves peaceful.

17.   If a nonarisen entity
             Anywhere exists,
             That entity would have to arise.
             But if it were nonexistent, what could arise?

18.   If this arising
             Gave rise to that which is arising,
             By means of what arising
             Does that arising arise?

19.   If another arising gives rise to this one,
             There would be an infinite regress.
             If something nonarisen is arisen,
             Then all things could arise in this way.

20.   Neither an existent nor a nonexistent
             Can be properly said to arise.

As it is taught before with
"For neither an existent nor a nonexistent."

21.   The arising of a ceasing thing
        Is not tenable.
        But to say that it is not ceasing
        Is not tenable for anything.

22.   A static existent does not endure.
        A nonstatic existent does not endure.
        Stasis does not endure.
        What nonarisen can endure?

23.   The endurance of a ceasing entity
        Is not tenable.
        But to say that it is not ceasing
        Is not tenable for anything.

24.   Inasmuch as the nature of all things
        Is aging and death,
        Without aging and death,
        What existents can endure?

25.   Stasis cannot endure through itself
        Or through another stasis.
        Just as arising cannot arise from itself
        Or from another arising.

26.   The ceasing of what has ceased does not happen.
        What has not yet ceased does not cease.
        Nor does that which is ceasing.
        What nonarisen can cease?

27.   The cessation of what is static
        Is not tenable.
        Nor is the cessation of
        Something not static tenable.

28. Being static does not cease
Through being static itself.
Nor does being static cease
Through another instance of being static.

29. When the arising of any entity
Is not tenable,
Then the cessation of any entity
Is not tenable.

30. For an existent thing
Cessation is not tenable.
A single thing being an entity and
A nonentity is not tenable.

31. Moreover, for a nonentity,
Cessation would be untenable.
Just as a second beheading
Cannot be performed.

32. Cessation does not cease by means of itself.
Nor does it cease by means of another.
Just as arising cannot arise from itself
Or from another arising.

33. Since arising, ceasing, and abiding
Are not established, there are no compounded things.
If all compounded things are unestablished,
,   How could the uncompounded be established?

34. Like a dream, like an illusion,
Like a city of Gandharvas,
So have arising, abiding,
And ceasing been explained.

Chapter VIII

Examination of the Agent and Action

1. This existent agent
    Does not perform an existent action.
    Nor does some nonexistent agent
    Perform some nonexistent action.

2. An existent entity has no activity.
    There would also be action without an agent.
    An existent entity has no activity.
    There would also be agent without action.

3. If a nonexistent agent
    Were to perform a nonexistent action,
    Then the action would be without a cause
    And the agent would be without a cause.

4. Without a cause, the effect and
    Its cause will not occur.
    Without this, activity and
    Agent and action are not possible.

5.   If activity, etc., are not possible,
      Entities and nonentities are not possible.
      If there are neither entities nor nonentities,
      Effects cannot arise from them.

6.   If there are no effects, liberation and
      Paths to higher realms will not exist.
      So all of activity
      Would be without purpose.

7.   An existent and nonexistent agent
      Does not perform an existent and nonexistent action.
      Existence and nonexistence cannot pertain to the same
          thing.
      For how could they exist together?

8.   An actual agent
      Does not perform a nonactual action.
      Nor by a nonactual one is an actual one performed.
      From this, all of those errors would follow.

9.   An existent agent
      Does not perform an action that
      Is unreal or both real and unreal
      As we have already agreed.

10.   A nonexistent agent
      Does not perform an action that
      Is unreal or both real and unreal
      As we have already agreed.

11.   An existent and nonexistent agent
      does not perform an action that
      Is unreal or both real and unreal
      As we have agreed.

12.   Action depends upon the agent.
        The agent itself depends on action.
        One cannot see any way
        To establish them differently.

13.   From this elimination of agent and action,
        One should elucidate appropriation in the same way.
        Through action and agent
        All remaining things should be understood.

Chapter IX

Examination of the Prior Entity

1. Since sight and hearing, etc., and
    Feeling, etc., exist,
    He who has and uses them
    Must exist prior to those, some say.

2. If there were no existent thing,
    How could seeing, etc., arise?
    It follows from this that prior to this,
    there is an existent thing.

3. How is an entity existing prior to
    Seeing, hearing, etc., and
    The felt, etc.,
    Itself known?

4. If it can abide
    Without the seen, etc.,
    Then, without a doubt,
    They can abide without it.

5. Someone is disclosed by something.
    Something is disclosed by someone.
    Without something how can someone exist?
    Without someone how can something exist?

6.　While prior to all of seeing, etc.,
　　That prior entity doesn't exist,
　　Through seeing, etc., by another one,
　　That other one becomes disclosed.

7.　If prior to all of seeing, etc.,
　　No prior entity exists,
　　How could an entity prior
　　To each seeing exist?

8.　If the seer itself is the hearer itself,
　　And the feeler itself, at different times,
　　Prior to each of these he would have to arise.
　　But this makes no sense.

9.　If the seer itself is distinct,
　　The hearer is distinct and the feeler is distinct,
　　Then when there is a seer there would also be a hearer,
　　And there would have to be many selves.

10.　Seeing and hearing, etc.,
　　And feeling, etc.,
　　And that from which these are arisen:
　　There is no existent there.

11.　Seeing and hearing, etc.,
　　And feeling, etc.,
　　If that to which they belong does not exist,
　　they themselves do not exist.

12.　For whomever prior to,
　　Simultaneous with, or after seeing, etc., there is
　　　　nothing,
　　For such a one, assertions like "it exists" or "it does not
　　　　exist"—
　　Such conceptions will cease.

Chapter X

Examination of Fire and Fuel

1. If fuel were fire
    Then agent and action would be one.
    If fire were different from fuel,
    Then it could arise without fuel.

2. It would be forever aflame;
    Flames could be ignited without a cause.
    Its beginning would be meaningless.
    In that case, it would be without any action.

3. Since it would not depend on another
    Ignition would be without a cause.
    If it were eternally in flames,
    Starting it would be meaningless.

4. So, if one thinks that
    That which is burning is the fuel,
    If it is just this,
    How is this fuel being burned?

5. If they are different, and if one not yet connected isn't
        connected,
    The not yet burned will not be burned.

They will not cease. If they do not cease
Then it will persist with its own characteristic.

6.   Just as a man and a woman
       Connect to one another as man and woman,
       So if fire were different from fuel,
       Fire and fuel would have to be fit for connection.

7.   And, if fire and fuel
       Preclude each other,
       Then fire being different from fuel,
       It must still be asserted that they connect.

8.   If fire depends on fuel,
       And fuel depends on fire,
       On what are fire and fuel established as dependent?
       Which one is established first?

9.   If fire depends on fuel,
       It would be the establishment of an established fire.
       And the fuel could be fuel
       Without any fire.

10.   If that on which an entity depends
       Is established on the basis
       Of the entity depending on it,
       What is established in dependence on what?

11.   What entity is established through dependence?
       If it is not established, then how could it depend?
       However, if it is established merely through
             dependence,
       That dependence makes no sense.

12.   Fire is not dependent upon fuel.
       Fire is not independent of fuel.
       Fuel is not dependent upon fire.
       Fuel is not independent of fire.

13.   Fire does not come from something else,
Nor is fire in fuel itself.
Moreover, fire and the rest are just like
The moved, the not-moved, and the goer.

14.   Fuel is not fire.
Fire does not arise from anything different from fuel.
Fire does not possess fuel.
Fuel is not in fire, nor vice versa.

15.   Through discussion of fire and fuel,
The self and the aggregates, the pot and cloth
All together,
Without remainder have been explained.

16.   I do not think that
Those who teach that the self
Is the same as or different from the entities
Understand the meaning of the doctrine.

Chapter XI

Examination of the Initial and Final Limits

1. When asked about the beginning,
    The Great Sage said that nothing is known of it.
    Cyclic existence is without end and beginning.
    So there is no beginning or end.

2. Where there is no beginning or end,
    How could there be a middle?
    It follows that thinking about this in terms of
    Prior, posterior, and simultaneous is not appropriate.

3. If birth came first,
    And then old age and death,
    Then birth would be ageless and deathless,
    And a deathless one would be born.

4. If birth were to come after,
    And old age and death first,
    How could there be a causeless aging and death
    Of one not born?

5.   Birth and age and death
        Cannot occur at one time.
        Then what is being born would be dying
        And both would occur without cause.

6.   When the series of the prior, simultaneous, and
                posterior
        Is not possible,
        Why are you led to posit
        This birth, aging, and death?

7.   Not only is cyclic existence itself without beginning,
        No existent has a beginning:
        Neither cause and effect;
        Nor character and characterized . . .

8.   Nor feeling and the feeler;
        Whatever there is:
        All entities
        Are without beginning.

Chapter XII

Examination of Suffering

1. Some say suffering is self-produced,
    Or produced from another or from both.
    Or that it arises without a cause.
    It is not the kind of thing to be produced.

2. If suffering came from itself,
    Then it would not arise dependently.
    For those aggregates
    Arise in dependence on these aggregates.

3. If those were different from these,
    Or if these were different from those,
    Suffering could arise from another.
    These would arise from those others.

4. If suffering were caused by a person himself,
    Then who is that person—
    By whom suffering is caused—
    Who exists distinct from suffering?

5. If suffering comes from another person,
    Then who is that person—
    When suffering is given by another—
    Who exists distinct from suffering?

6.   If another person causes suffering,
       Who is that other one
       Who bestowed that suffering,
       Distinct from suffering?

7.   When self-caused is not established,
       How could suffering be caused by another?
       Whoever caused the suffering of another
       Must have caused his own suffering.

8.   No suffering is self-caused.
       Nothing causes itself.
       If another is not self-made,
       How could suffering be caused by another?

9.   If suffering were caused by each,
       Suffering could be caused by both.
       Not caused by self or by other,
       How could suffering be uncaused?

10.   Not only does suffering not exist
       In any of the fourfold ways:
       No external entity exists
       In any of the fourfold ways.

Chapter XIII

Examination of Compounded Phenomena

1.   The Victorious Conqueror has said that whatever
     Is deceptive is false.
     Compounded phenomena are all deceptive.
     Therefore they are all false.

2.   If whatever is deceptive is false,
     What deceives?
     The Victorious Conqueror has said about this
     That emptiness is completely true.

3.   All things lack entitihood,
     Since change is perceived.
     There is nothing without entity
     Because all things have emptiness.

4.   If there is no entitihood,
     What changes?
     If there were entity,
     How could it be correct that something changes?

5.   A thing itself does not change.
      Something different does not change.
      Because a young man doesn't grow old,
      And because and an old man doesn't grow old either.

6.   If a thing itself changed,
      Milk itself would be curd.
      Or curd would have come to be
      An entity different from milk.

7.   If there were even a trifle nonempty,
      Emptiness itself would be but a trifle.
      But not even a trifle is nonempty.
      How could emptiness be an entity?

8.   The victorious ones have said
      That emptiness is the relinquishing of all views.
      For whomever emptiness is a view,
      That one will accomplish nothing.

Chapter XIV

Examination of Connection

1. The seen, seeing, and the seer:
    These three—pairwise or
    All together—
    Do not connect to one another.

2. Similarly desire, the desirous one, the object of desire,
    And the remaining afflictions
    And the remaining sources of perception
    Are understood in this threefold way.

3. Since different things connect to one another,
    But in seeing, etc.,
    There is no difference,
    They cannot connect.

4. Not only in seeing, etc.,
    Is there no such difference:
    When one thing and another are simultaneous,
    It is also not tenable that there is difference.

5. A different thing depends on a different thing for its
        difference.
    Without a different thing, a different thing wouldn't be
        different.

It is not tenable for that which depends on something
  else
To be different from it.

6.   If a different thing were different from a different
          thing,
        Without a different thing, a different thing could exist.
        But without that different thing, that different thing
          does not exist.
        It follows that it doesn't exist.

7.   Difference is not in a different thing.
        Nor is it in a nondifferent thing.
        If difference does not exist,
        Neither different nor identical things exist.

8.   That does not connect to itself.
        Nor do different things connect to one another.
        Neither connection nor
        Connected nor connector exist.

Chapter XV

Examination of Essence

1. Essence arising from
   Causes and conditions makes no sense.
   If essence came from causes and conditions,
   Then it would be fabricated.

2. How could it be appropriate
   For fabricated essence to come to be?
   Essence itself is not artificial
   And does not depend on another.

3. If there is no essence,
   How can there be difference in entities?
   The essence of difference in entities
   Is what is called the entity of difference.

4. Without having essence or otherness-essence,
   How can there be entities?
   If there are essences and entities
   Entities are established.

5. If the entity is not established,
   A nonentity is not established.
   An entity that has become different
   Is a nonentity, people say.

6.   Those who see essence and essential difference
      And entities and nonentities,
      They do not see
      The truth taught by the Buddha.

7.   The Victorious One, through knowledge
      Of reality and unreality,
      In the *Discourse to Katyāyāna,*
      Refuted both "it is" and "it is not."

8.   If existence were through essence,
      Then there would be no nonexistence.
      A change in essence
      Could never be tenable.

9.   If there is no essence,
      What could become other?
      If there is essence,
      What could become other?

10.   To say "it is" is to grasp for permanence.
      To say "it is not" is to adopt the view of nihilism.
      Therefore a wise person
      Does not say "exists" or "does not exist."

11.   "Whatever exists through its essence
      Cannot be nonexistent" is eternalism.
      "It existed before but doesn't now"
      Entails the error of nihilism.

Chapter XVI

Examination of Bondage

1. If compounded phenomena transmigrate,
   They do not transmigrate as permanent.
   If they are impermanent they do not transmigrate.
   The same approach applies to sentient beings.

2. If someone transmigrates,
   Then if, when sought in the fivefold way
   In the aggregates and in the sense spheres and in the
      elements,
   He is not there, what transmigrates?

3. If one transmigrates from grasping to grasping, then
   One would be nonexistent.
   Neither existent nor grasping,
   Who could this transmigrator be?

4. How could compounded phenomena pass into nirvāṇa?
   That would not be tenable.
   How could a sentient being pass into nirvāṇa?
   That would not be tenable.

5. All compounded phenomena, as arising and ceasing
      things,
   Are not bound and not released.

For this reason a sentient being
Is not bound, not released.

6.   If grasping were bondage,
Then the one who is grasping would not be bound.
But one who is not grasping is not bound.
In what circumstances will one be bound?

7.   If prior to binding
There is a bound one,
There would be bondage, but there isn't.
The rest has been explained by the gone, the not-gone,
and the goer.

8.   Whoever is bound is not released.
Whoever is not bound does not get released.
If a bound one were being released,
Bondage and release would occur simultaneously.

9.   "I, without grasping, will pass beyond sorrow,
And I will attain nirvāṇa," one says.
Whoever grasps like this
Has a great grasping.

10.   When you can't bring about nirvāṇa,
Nor the purification of cyclic existence,
What is cyclic existence,
And what is the nirvāṇa you examine?

Chapter XVII

Examination of Actions and Their Fruits

1. Self-restraint and benefiting others
   With a compassionate mind is the Dharma.
   This is the seed for
   Fruits in this and future lives.

2. The Unsurpassed Sage has said
   That actions are either intention or intentional.
   The varieties of these actions
   Have been announced in many ways.

3. Of these, what is called "intention"
   Is mental desire.
   What is called "intentional"
   Comprises the physical and verbal.

4. Speech and action and all
   Kinds of unabandoned and abandoned actions,
   And resolve
   As well as . . .

5.   Virtuous and nonvirtuous actions
        Derived from pleasure,
        As well as intention and morality:
        These seven are the kinds of action.

6.   If until the time of ripening
        Action had to remain in place, it would have to be
                permanent.
        If it has ceased, then having ceased,
        How will a fruit arise?

7.   As for a continuum, such as the sprout,
        It comes from a seed.
        From that arises the fruit. Without a seed,
        It would not come into being.

8.   Since from the seed comes the continuum,
        and from the continuum comes the fruit,
        The seed precedes the fruit.
        Therefore there is neither nonexistence nor
                permanence.

9.   So, in a mental continuum,
        From a preceding intention
        A consequent mental state arises.
        Without this, it would not arise.

10.   Since from the intention comes the continuum,
        And from the continuum the fruit arises,
        Action precedes the fruit.
        Therefore there is neither nonexistence nor
                permanence.

11.   The ten pure paths of action
        Are the method of realizing the Dharma.
        These fruits of the Dharma in this and other lives
        Are the five pleasures.

12. If such an analysis were advanced,
     There would be many great errors.
     Therefore, this analysis
     Is not tenable here.

13. I will then explain what is tenable here:
     The analysis propounded by all
     Buddhas, self-conquerors
     And disciples according to which . . .

14. Action is like an uncancelled promissory note
     And like a debt.
     Of the realms it is fourfold.
     Moreover, its nature is neutral.

15. By abandoning, that is not abandoned.
     Abandonment occurs through meditation.
     Therefore, through the nonexpired,
     The fruit of action arises.

16. If abandonment occurred through abandoning, and
     If action were destroyed through transformation,
     The destruction of action, etc.,
     And other errors would arise.

17. From all these actions in a realm,
     Whether similar or dissimilar,
     At the moment of birth
     Only one will arise.

18. In this visible world,
     All actions of the two kinds,
     Each comprising action and the unexpired separately,
     Will remain while ripening.

19. That fruit, if extinction or death
     Occurs, ceases.

Regarding this, a distinction between the stainless
And the stained is drawn.

20. Emptiness and nonannihilation;
    Cyclic existence and nonpermanence:
    That action is nonexpiring
    Is taught by the Buddha.

21. Because action does not arise,
    It is seen to be without essence.
    Because it is not arisen,
    It follows that it is nonexpiring.

22. If action had an essence,
    It would, without doubt, be eternal.
    Action would be uncreated.
    Because there can be no creation of what is eternal.

23. If an action were uncreated,
    Fear would arise of encountering something not done.
    And the error of not preserving
    One's vows would arise.

24. All conventions would then
    Be contradicted, without doubt.
    It would be impossible to draw a distinction
    Between virtue and evil.

25. Whatever is mature would mature
    Time and time again.
    If there were essence, this would follow,
    Because action would remain in place.

26. While this action has affliction as its nature
    This affliction is not real in itself.
    If affliction is not in itself,
    How can action be real in itself?

27.   Action and affliction
        Are taught to be the conditions that produce bodies.
        If action and affliction
        Are empty, what would one say about bodies?

28.   Obstructed by ignorance,
        And consumed by passion, the experiencer
        Is neither different from the agent
        Nor identical with it.

29.   Since this action
        Is not arisen from a condition,
        Nor arisen causelessly,
        It follows that there is no agent.

30.   If there is no action and agent,
        Where could the fruit of action be?
        Without a fruit,
        Where is there an experiencer?

31.   Just as the teacher, by magic,
        Makes a magical illusion, and
        By that illusion
        Another illusion is created,

32.   In that way are an agent and his action:
        The agent is like the illusion.
        The action
        Is like the illusion's illusion.

33.   Afflictions, actions, bodies,
        Agents and fruits are
        Like a city of Gandharvas and
        Like a mirage or a dream.

Chapter XVIII

Examination of Self and Entities

1.   If the self were the aggregates,
   It would have arising and ceasing (as properties).
   If it were different from the aggregates,
   It would not have the characteristics of the aggregates.

2.   If there were no self,
   Where would the self's (properties) be?
   From the pacification of the self and what belongs to it,
   One abstains from grasping onto "I" and "mine."

3.   One who does not grasp onto "I" and "mine,"
   That one does not exist.
   One who does not grasp onto "I" and "mine,"
   He does not perceive.

4.   When views of "I" and "mine" are extinguished,
   Whether with respect to the internal or external,
   The appropriator ceases.
   This having ceased, birth ceases.

5.   Action and misery having ceased, there is nirvāṇa.
   Action and misery come from conceptual thought.
   This comes from mental fabrication.
   Fabrication ceases through emptiness.

6.   That there is a self has been taught,
     And the doctrine of no-self,
     By the buddhas, as well as the
     Doctrine of neither self nor nonself.

7.   What language expresses is nonexistent.
     The sphere of thought is nonexistent.
     Unarisen and unceased, like nirvāṇa
     Is the nature of things.

8.   Everything is real and is not real,
     Both real and not real,
     Neither real nor not real. ·
     This is Lord Buddha's teaching.

9.   Not dependent on another, peaceful and
     Not fabricated by mental fabrication,
     Not thought, without distinctions,
     That is the character of real*ity* (that-ness).

10. Whatever comes into being dependent on another
     Is not identical to that thing.
     Nor is it different from it.
     Therefore it is neither nonexistent in time nor
          permanent.

11. By the buddhas, patrons of the world,
     This immortal truth is taught:
     Without identity, without distinction;
     Not nonexistent in time, not permanent.

12. When the fully enlightened ones do not appear,
     And when the disciples have disappeared,
     The wisdom of the self-enlightened ones
     Will arise completely without a teacher.

Chapter XIX

Examination of Time

1. If the present and the future
    Depend on the past,
    Then the present and the future
    Would have existed in the past.

2. If the present and the future
    Did not exist there,
    How could the present and the future
    Be dependent upon it?

3. If they are not dependent upon the past,
    Neither of the two would be established.
    Therefore neither the present
    Nor the future would exist.

4. By the same method,
    The other two divisions—past and future,
    Upper, lower, middle, etc.,
    Unity, etc., should be understood.

5. A nonstatic time is not grasped.
    Nothing one could grasp as
    Stationary time exists.
    If time is not grasped, how is it known?

6.   If time depends on an entity,
      Then without an entity how could time exist?
      There is no existent entity.
      So how can time exist?

Chapter XX

Examination of Combination

1.   If, arising from the combination of
Causes and conditions,
The effect is in the combination,
How could it arise from the combination?

2.   If, arising from the combination of
Causes and conditions,
The effect is not in the combination,
How could it arise from the combination?

3.   If the effect is in the combination
Of causes and conditions,
Then it should be grasped in the combination.
But it is not grasped in the combination.

4.   If the effect is not in the combination
Of causes and conditions,
Then actual causes and conditions
Would be like noncauses and nonconditions.

5.   If the cause, in having its effect,
Ceased to have its causal status,

There would be two kinds of cause:
With and without causal status.

6. If the cause, not yet having
Produced its effect, ceased,
Then having arisen from a ceased cause,
The effect would be without a cause.

7. If the effect were to arise
Simultaneously with the collection,
Then the produced and the producer
Would arise simultaneously.

8. If the effect were to arise
Prior to the combination,
Then, without causes and conditions,
The effect would arise causelessly.

9. If, the cause having ceased, the effect
Were a complete transformation of the cause,
Then a previously arisen cause
Would arise again.

10. How can a cause, having ceased and dissolved,
Give rise to a produced effect?
How can a cause joined with its effect produce it
If they persist together?

11. Moreover, if not joined with its cause,
What effect can be made to arise?
Neither seen nor unseen by causes
Are effects produced.

12. There is never a simultaneous connection
Of a past effect
With a past, a nonarisen,
Or an arisen cause.

13.   There is never a simultaneous connection
       Of an arisen effect
       With a past, a nonarisen,
       Or an arisen cause.

14.   There is never a simultaneous connection
       Of a nonarisen effect
       With a past, a nonarisen,
       Or an arisen cause.

15.   Without connecting,
       How can a cause produce an effect?
       Where there is connection,
       How can a cause produce an effect?

16.   If the cause is empty of an effect,
       How can it produce an effect?
       If the cause is not empty of an effect,
       How can it produce an effect?

17.   A nonempty effect does not arise.
       The nonempty would not cease.
       This nonempty would be
       The nonceased and the nonarisen.

18.   How can the empty arise?
       How can the empty cease?
       The empty will hence also
       Be the nonceased and nonarisen.

19.   For cause and effect to be identical
       Is not tenable.
       For cause and effect to be different
       Is not tenable.

20.   If cause and effect were identical,
       Produced and producer would be identical.

If cause and effect were different,
Cause and non-cause would be alike.

21.　　If an effect had entitihood,
What could have caused it to arise?
If an effect had no entitihood,
What could have caused it to arise?

22.　　If something is not producing an effect,
It is not tenable to attribute causality.
If it is not tenable to attribute causality,
Then of what will the effect be?

23.　　If the combination
Of causes and conditions
Is not self-produced,
How does it produce an effect?

24.　　Therefore, not made by combination,
And not without a combination can the effect arise.
If there is no effect,
Where can there be a combination of conditions?

Chapter XXI

Examination of Becoming and Destruction

1. Destruction does not occur without becoming.
    It does not occur together with it.
    Becoming does not occur without destruction.
    It does not occur together with it.

2. How could there be destruction
    Without becoming?
    How could there be death without birth?
    There is no destruction without becoming.

3. How could destruction and becoming
    Occur simultaneously?
    Death and birth
    Do not occur simultaneously.

4. How could there be becoming
    Without destruction?
    For impermanence
    Is never absent from entities.

5. How could destruction
    And becoming occur simultaneously?
    Just as birth and death
    Do not occur simultaneously.

6. How, when things cannot
    Be established as existing,
    With, or apart from one another,
    Can they be established at all?

7. There is no becoming of the disappeared.
    There is no becoming of the nondisappeared.
    There is no destruction of the disappeared.
    There is no destruction of the nondisappeared.

8. When no entities exist,
    There is no becoming or destruction.
    Without becoming and destruction,
    There are no existent entities.

9. It is not tenable for the empty
    To become or to be destroyed.
    It is not tenable for the nonempty
    To become or to be destroyed.

10. It is not tenable
    That destruction and becoming are identical.
    It is not tenable
    That destruction and becoming are different.

11. If you think you see both
    Destruction and becoming,
    Then you see destruction and becoming
    Through impaired vision.

12. An entity does not arise from an entity.
    An entity does not arise from a nonentity.
    A nonentity does not arise from a nonentity.
    A nonentity does not arise from an entity.

13.   An entity does not arise from itself.
        It is not arisen from another.
        It is not arisen from itself and another.
        How can it be arisen?

14.   If one accepts the existence of entities,
        Permanence and the view of complete nonexistence
            follow.
        For these entities
        Must be both permanent and impermanent.

15.   If one accepts the existence of entities
        Nonexistence and permanence will not follow.
        Cyclic existence is the continuous
        Becoming and destruction of causes and effects.

16.   If cyclic existence is the continuous
        Becoming and destruction of causes and effects,
        Then from the nonarising of the destroyed
        Follows the nonexistence of cause.

17.   If entities exist with entitihood,
        Then their nonexistence would make no sense.
        But at the time of nirvāṇa,
        Cyclic existence ceases completely, having been
            pacified.

18.   If the final one has ceased,
        The existence of a first one makes no sense.
        If the final one has not ceased,
        The existence of a first one makes no sense.

19.   If when the final one was ceasing,
        Then the first was arising,
        The one ceasing would be one.
        The one arising would be another.

20.   If, absurdly, the one arising
        And the one ceasing were the same,
        Then whoever is dying with the aggregates
        Is also arising.

21.   Since the series of cyclic existence is not evident
        In the three times,
        If it is not in the three times,
        How could there be a series of cyclic existence?

Chapter XXII

Examination of the Tathāgata

1. Neither the aggregates, nor different from the
    aggregates,
    The aggregates are not in him, nor is he in the
    aggregates.
    The Tathāgata does not possess the aggregates.
    What is the Tathāgata?

2. If the Buddha depended on the aggregates,
    He would not exist through an essence.
    Not existing through an essence,
    How could he exist through otherness-essence?

3. Whatever is dependent on another entity,
    Its selfhood is not appropriate.
    It is not tenable that what lacks a self
    Could be a Tathāgata.

4. If there is no essence,
    How could there be otherness-essence?
    Without possessing essence or otherness-essence,
    What is the Tathāgata?

5.   If without depending on the aggregates
      There were a Tathāgata,
      Then now he would be depending on them.
      Therefore he would exist through dependence.

6.   Inasmuch as there is no Tathāgata
      Dependent upon the aggregates,
      How could something that is not dependent
      Come to be so?

7.   There is no appropriation.
      There is no appropriator.
      Without appropriation
      How can there be a Tathāgata?

8.   Having been sought in the fivefold way,
      What, being neither identical nor different,
      Can be thought to be the Tathāgata
      Through grasping?

9.   Whatever grasping there is
      Does not exist through essence.
      And when something does not exist through itself,
      It can never exist through otherness-essence.

10.   Thus grasping and grasper
      Together are empty in every respect.
      How can an empty Tathāgata
      Be known through the empty?

11.   "Empty" should not be asserted.
      "Nonempty" should not be asserted.
      Neither both nor neither should be asserted.
      They are only used nominally.

12.   How can the tetralemma of permanent and
            impermanent, etc.,
      Be true of the peaceful?

How can the tetralemma of finite, infinite, etc.,
Be true of the peaceful?

13. One who grasps the view that the Tathāgata exists,
Having seized the Buddha,
Constructs conceptual fabrications
About one who has achieved nirvāṇa.

14. Since he is by nature empty,
The thought that the Buddha
Exists or does not exist
After nirvāṇa is not appropriate.

15. Those who develop mental fabrications with regard to
the Buddha,
Who has gone beyond all fabrications,
As a consequence of those cognitive fabrications,
Fail to see the Tathāgata.

16. Whatever is the essence of the Tathāgata,
That is the essence of the world.
The Tathāgata has no essence.
The world is without essence.

Chapter XXIII

Examination of Errors

1. Desire, hatred and confusion all
    Arise from thought, it is said.
    They all depend on
    The pleasant, the unpleasant, and errors.

2. Since whatever depends on the pleasant and the
        unpleasant
    Does not exist through an essence,
    The defilements
    Do not really exist.

3. The self's existence or nonexistence
    Has in no way been established.
    Without that, how could the defilements'
    Existence or nonexistence be established?

4. The defilements are somebody's.
    But that one has not been established.
    Without that possessor,
    The defilements are nobody's.

5. View the defilements as you view your self:
    They are not in the defiled in the fivefold way.

View the defiled as you view your self:
It is not in the defilements in the fivefold way.

6.   The pleasant, the unpleasant, and the errors
Do not exist through essence.
Which pleasant, unpleasant, and errors
could the defilements depend upon?

7.   Form, sound, taste, touch,
Smell, and concepts of things: These six
Are thought of as the foundation of
Desire, hatred, and confusion.

8.   Form, sound, taste, touch,
Smell, and concepts of things: These six
Should be seen as only like a city of the Gandharvas
  and
Like a mirage or a dream.

9.   How could the
Pleasant and unpleasant arise
In those that are like an illusory person
And like a reflection?

10.   We say that the unpleasant
Is dependent upon the pleasant,
Since without depending on the pleasant there is none.
It follows that the pleasant is not tenable.

11.   We say that the pleasant
Is dependent upon the unpleasant.
Without the unpleasant there wouldn't be any.
It follows that the unpleasant is not tenable.

12.   Where there is no pleasant,
How can there be desire?
Where there is no unpleasant,
How can there be anger?

13. If to grasp onto the view
    "The impermanent is permanent" were an error,
    Since in emptiness there is nothing impermanent,
    How could that grasping be an error?

14. If to grasp onto the view
    "The impermanent is permanent" were an error,
    Why isn't grasping onto the view
    "In emptiness there is nothing impermanent" an error?

15. That by means of which there is grasping, and the
        grasping,
    And the grasper, and all that is grasped:
    All are being relieved.
    It follows that there is no grasping.

16. If there is no grasping,
    Whether erroneous or otherwise,
    Who will come to be in error?
    Who will have no error?

17. Error does not develop
    In one who is in error.
    Error does not develop
    In one who is not in error.

18. Error does not develop
    In one in whom error is arising.
    In whom does error develop?
    Examine this on your own!

19. If error is not arisen,
    How could it come to exist?
    If error has not arisen,
    How could one be in error?

20. Since an entity does not arise from itself,
    Nor from another,

Nor from another and from itself,
How could one be in error?

21.   If the self and the pure,
The permanent and the blissful existed,
The self, the pure, the permanent,
And the blissful would not be deceptive.

22.   If the self and the pure,
The permanent and the blissful did not exist,
The nonself, the impure, the permanent,
And suffering would not exist.

23.   Thus, through the cessation of error
Ignorance ceases.
When ignorance ceases
The compounded phenomena, etc., cease.

24.   If someone's defilements
Existed through his essence,
How could they be relinquished?
Who could relinquish the existent?

25.   If someone's defilements
Did not exist through his essence,
How could they be relinquished?
Who could relinquish the nonexistent?

Chapter XXIV

Examination of the Four Noble Truths

1. If all of this is empty,
    Neither arising nor ceasing,
    Then for you, it follows that
    The Four Noble Truths do not exist.

2. If the Four Noble Truths do not exist,
    Then knowledge, abandonment,
    Meditation and manifestation
    Will be completely impossible.

3. If these things do not exist,
    The four fruits will not arise.
    Without the four fruits, there will be no attainers of the
        fruits.
    Nor will there be the faithful.

4. If so, the spiritual community will not exist.
    Nor will the eight kinds of person.
    If the Four Noble Truths do not exist,
    There will be no true Dharma.

5.   If there is no doctrine and spiritual community,
       How can there be a Buddha?
       If emptiness is conceived in this way,
       The three jewels are contradicted.

6.   Hence you assert that there are no real fruits.
       And no Dharma. The Dharma itself
       And the conventional truth
       Will be contradicted.

7.   We say that this understanding of yours
       Of emptiness and the purpose of emptiness
       And of the significance of emptiness is incorrect.
       As a consequence you are harmed by it.

8.   The Buddha's teaching of the Dharma
       Is based on two truths:
       A truth of worldly convention
       And an ultimate truth.

9.   Those who do not understand
       The distinction drawn between these two truths
       Do not understand
       The Buddha's profound truth.

10.   Without a foundation in the conventional truth,
       The significance of the ultimate cannot be taught.
       Without understanding the significance of the ultimate,
       Liberation is not achieved.

11.   By a misperception of emptiness
       A person of little intelligence is destroyed.
       Like a snake incorrectly seized
       Or like a spell incorrectly cast.

12.   For that reason—that the Dharma is
       Deep and difficult to understand and to learn—
       The Buddha's mind despaired of
       Being able to teach it.

13.   You have presented fallacious refutations
      That are not relevant to emptiness.
      Your confusion about emptiness
      Does not belong to me.

14.   For him to whom emptiness is clear,
      Everything becomes clear.
      For him to whom emptiness is not clear,
      Nothing becomes clear.

15.   When you foist on us
      All of your errors
      You are like a man who has mounted his horse
      And has forgotten that very horse.

16.   If you perceive the existence of all things
      In terms of their essence,
      Then this perception of all things
      Will be without the perception of causes and
          conditions.

17.   Effects and causes
      And agent and action
      And conditions and arising and ceasing
      And effects will be rendered impossible.

18.   Whatever is dependently co-arisen
      That is explained to be emptiness.
      That, being a dependent designation,
      Is itself the middle way.

19.   Something that is not dependently arisen,
      Such a thing does not exist.
      Therefore a nonempty thing
      Does not exist.

20.   If all this were nonempty, as in your view,
         There would be no arising and ceasing.
         Then the Four Noble Truths
         Would become nonexistent.

21.   If it is not dependently arisen,
         How could suffering come to be?
         Suffering has been taught to be impermanent,
         And so cannot come from its own essence.

22.   If something comes from its own essence,
         How could it ever be arisen?
         It follows that if one denies emptiness
         There can be no arising (of suffering).

23.   If suffering had an essence,
         Its cessation would not exist.
         So if an essence is posited,
         One denies cessation.

24.   If the path had an essence,
         Cultivation would not be appropriate.
         If this path is indeed cultivated,
         It cannot have an essence.

25.   If suffering, arising, and
         Ceasing are nonexistent,
         By what path could one seek
         To obtain the cessation of suffering?

26.   If nonunderstanding comes to be
         Through its essence,
         How will understanding arise?
         Isn't essence stable?

27.   In the same way, the activities of
         Relinquishing, realizing, and meditating

And the four fruits
Would not be possible.

28.   For an essentialist,
Since the fruits through their essence
Are already unrealized,
In what way could one attain them?

29.   Without the fruits, there are no attainers of the fruits,
Or enterers. From this it follows that
The eight kinds of persons do not exist.
If these don't exist, there is no spiritual community.

30.   From the nonexistence of the Noble Truths
Would follow the nonexistence of the true doctrine.
If there is no doctrine and no spiritual community,
How could a Buddha arise?

31.   For you, it would follow that a Buddha
Arises independent of enlightenment.
And for you, enlightenment would arise
Independent of a Buddha.

32.   For you, one who through his essence
Was unenlightened,
Even by practicing the path to enlightenment
Could not achieve enlightenment.

33.   Moreover, one could never perform
Right or wrong actions.
If this were all nonempty what could one do?
That with an essence cannot be produced.

34.   For you, from neither right nor wrong actions
Would the fruit arise.
If the fruit arose from right or wrong actions,
According to you, it wouldn't exist.

35.   If, for you, a fruit arose
        From right or wrong actions,
        Then, having arisen from right or wrong actions,
        How could that fruit be nonempty?

36.   If dependent arising is denied,
        Emptiness itself is rejected.
        This would contradict
        All of the worldly conventions.

37.   If emptiness itself is rejected,
        No action will be appropriate.
        There would be action which did not begin,
        And there would be agent without action.

38.   If there is essence, the whole world
        Will be unarising, unceasing,
        And static. The entire phenomenal world
        Would be immutable.

39.   If it (the world) were not empty,
        Then action would be without profit.
        The act of ending suffering and
        Abandoning misery and defilement would not exist.

40.   Whoever sees dependent arising
        Also sees suffering
        And its arising
        And its cessation as well as the path.

Chapter XXV

Examination of Nirvāṇa

1. If all this is empty,
   Then there is no arising or passing away.
   By the relinquishing or ceasing of what
   Does one wish nirvāṇa to arise?

2. If all this is nonempty,
   Then there is no arising or passing away.
   By the relinquishing or ceasing of what
   Does one wish nirvāṇa to arise?

3. Unrelinquished, unattained,
   Unannihilated, not permanent,
   Unarisen, unceased:
   This is how nirvāṇa is described.

4. Nirvāṇa is not existent.
   It would then have the characteristics of age and death.
   There is no existent entity
   Without age and death.

5. If nirvāṇa were existent,
   Nirvāṇa would be compounded.
   A noncompounded existent
   Does not exist anywhere.

6.   If nirvāṇa were existent,
      How could nirvāṇa be nondependent?
      A nondependent existent
      Does not exist anywhere.

7.   If nirvāṇa were not existent,
      How could it be appropriate for it to be nonexistent?
      Where nirvāṇa is not existent,
      It cannot be a nonexistent.

8.   If nirvāṇa were not existent,
      How could nirvāṇa be nondependent?
      Whatever is nondependent
      Is not nonexistent.

9.   That which comes and goes
      Is dependent and changing.
      That, when it is not dependent and changing,
      Is taught to be nirvāṇa.

10.   The teacher has spoken of relinquishing
      Becoming and dissolution.
      Therefore, it makes sense that
      Nirvāṇa is neither existent nor nonexistent.

11.   If nirvāṇa were both
      Existent and nonexistent,
      Passing beyond would, impossibly,
      Be both existent and nonexistent.

12.   If nirvāṇa were both
      Existent and nonexistent,
      Nirvāṇa would not be nondependent.
      Since it would depend on both of these.

13.   How could nirvāṇa
      Be both existent and nonexistent?
      Nirvāṇa is uncompounded.
      Both existents and nonexistents are compounded.

14. How could nirvāṇa
Be both existent and nonexistent?
These two cannot be in the same place.
Like light and darkness.

15. Nirvāṇa is said to be
Neither existent nor nonexistent.
If the existent and the nonexistent were established,
This would be established.

16. If nirvāṇa is
Neither existent nor nonexistent,
Then by whom is it expounded
"Neither existent nor nonexistent"?

17. Having passed into nirvāṇa, the Victorious Conqueror
Is neither said to be existent
Nor said to be nonexistent.
Neither both nor neither are said.

18. So, when the victorious one abides, he
Is neither said to be existent
Nor said to be nonexistent.
Neither both nor neither are said.

19. There is not the slightest difference
Between cyclic existence and nirvāṇa.
There is not the slightest difference
Between nirvāṇa and cyclic existence.

20. Whatever is the limit of nirvāṇa,
That is the limit of cyclic existence.
There is not even the slightest difference between
them,
Or even the subtlest thing.

21. Views that after cessation there is a limit, etc.,
And that it is permanent, etc.,

Depend upon nirvāṇa, the final limit,
And the prior limit.

22.   Since all existents are empty,
What is finite or infinite?
What is finite and infinite?
What is neither finite nor infinite?

23.   What is identical and what is different?
What is permanent and what is impermanent?
What is both permanent and impermanent?
What is neither?

24.   The pacification of all objectification
And the pacification of illusion:
No Dharma was taught by the Buddha
At any time, in any place, to any person.

Chapter XXVI

Examination of the Twelve Links

1. Wrapped in the darkness of ignorance,
    One performs the three kinds of actions
    Which as dispositions impel one
    To continue to future existences.

2. Having dispositions as its conditions,
    Consciousness enters transmigration.
    Once consciousness has entered transmigration,
    Name and form come to be.

3. Once name and form come to be,
    The six sense spheres come into being.
    Depending on the six sense spheres,
    Contact comes into being.

4. That is only dependent
    On eye and form and apprehension.
    Thus, depending on name and form,
    And which produces consciousness—

5. That which is assembled from the three—
    Eye and form and consciousness,
    Is contact. From contact
    Feeling comes to be.

6.   Conditioned by feeling is craving.
        Craving arises because of feeling.
        When it appears, there is grasping,
        The four spheres of grasping.

7.   When there is grasping, the grasper
        Comes into existence.
        If he did not grasp,
        Then being freed, he would not come into existence.

8.   This existence is also the five aggregates.
        From existence comes birth,
        Old age and death and misery and
        Suffering and grief and . . .

9.   Confusion and agitation.
        All these arise as a consequence of birth.
        Thus this entire mass of suffering
        Comes into being.

10.   The root of cyclic existence is action.
        Therefore, the wise one does not act.
        Therefore, the unwise is the agent.
        The wise one is not because of his insight.

11.   With the cessation of ignorance
        Action will not arise.
        The cessation of ignorance occurs through
        Meditation and wisdom.

12.   Through the cessation of this and that
        This and that will not be manifest.
        The entire mass of suffering
        Indeed thereby completely ceases.

Chapter XXVII

Examination of Views

1. The views "in the past I was" or "I was not"
    And the view that the world is permanent, etc.,
    All of these views
    Depend on a prior limit.

2. The view "in the future I will become other" or "I will
          not do so"
    And that the world is limited, etc.,
    All of these views
    Depend on a final limit.

3. To say "I was in the past"
    Is not tenable.
    What existed in the past
    Is not identical to this one.

4. According to you, this self is that,
    But the appropriator is different.
    If it is not the appropriator,
    What is your self?

5. Having shown that there is no self
    Other than the appropriator,
    The appropriator should be the self.
    But it is not your self.

6.   Appropriating is not the self.
      It arises and ceases.
      How can one accept that
      Future appropriating is the appropriator?

7.   A self that is different
      From the appropriating is not tenable.
      If it were different, then in a nonappropriator
      There should be appropriation. But there isn't.

8.   So it is neither different from the appropriating
      Nor identical to the appropriating.
      There is no self without appropriation.
      But it is not true that it does not exist.

9.   To say "in the past I wasn't"
      Would not be tenable.
      This person is not different
      From whoever existed in previous times.

10.   If this one were different,
      Then if that one did not exist, I would still exist.
      If this were so,
      Without death, one would be born.

11.   Annihilation and the exhaustion of action would follow;
      Different agents' actions
      Would be experienced by each other.
      That and other such things would follow.

12.   Nothing comes to exist from something that did not
            exist.
      From this errors would arise.
      The self would be produced
      Or, existing, would be without a cause.

13.   So, the views "I existed," "I didn't exist,"
      Both or neither,

In the past
Are untenable.

14.   To say "in the future I will exist or
        Will not exist,"
        Such a view is like
        Those involving the past.

15.   If a human were a god,
        On such a view there would be permanence.
        The god would be unborn.
        For any permanent thing is unborn.

16.   If a human were different from a god,
        On such a view there would be impermanence.
        If the human were different from the god,
        A continuum would not be tenable.

17.   If one part were divine and
        One part were human,
        It would be both permanent and impermanent.
        That would be irrational.

18.   If it could be established that
        It is both permanent and impermanent,
        Then it could be established that
        It is neither permanent nor impermanent.

19.   If anyone had come from anyplace
        And were then to go someplace,
        It would follow that cyclic existence was beginningless.
        This is not the case.

20.   If nothing is permanent,
        What will be impermanent,
        Permanent and impermanent,
        Or neither?

21.   If the world were limited,
        How could there be another world?
        If the world were unlimited,
        How could there be another world?

22.   Since the continuum of the aggregates
        Is like the flame of a butterlamp,
        It follows that neither its finitude
        Nor its infinitude makes sense.

23.   If the previous were disintegrating
        And these aggregates, which depend
        Upon those aggregates, did not arise,
        Then the world would be finite.

24.   If the previous were not disintegrating
        And these aggregates, which depend
        Upon those aggregates, did not arise,
        Then the world would be infinite.

25.   If one part were finite and
        One part were infinite,
        Then the world would be finite and infinite.
        This would make no sense.

26.   How could one think that
        One part of the appropriator is destroyed
        And one part is not destroyed?
        This position makes no sense.

27.   How could one think that
        One part of the appropriation is destroyed
        And one part is not destroyed?
        This position makes no sense.

28.   If it could be established that
        It is both finite and infinite,

Then it could be established that
It is neither finite nor infinite.

29.   So, because all entities are empty,
       Which views of permanence, etc., would occur,
       And to whom, when, why, and about what
       Would they occur at all?

30.   I prostrate to Gautama
       Who through compassion
       Taught the true doctrine,
       Which leads to the relinquishing of all views.

PART TWO

The Text and Commentary

Introduction to the Commentary

Nāgārjuna, who lived in South India in approximately the second century C.E., is undoubtedly the most important, influential, and widely studied Mahāyāna Buddhist philosopher. He is the founder of the Mādhyamika, or Middle Path schools of Mahāyāna Buddhism. His considerable corpus includes texts addressed to lay audiences, letters of advice to kings, and the set of penetrating metaphysical and epistemological treatises that represent the foundation of the highly sceptical and dialectical analytic philosophical school known as Mādhyamika. Most important of these is his largest and best known text, *Mūlamadhyamakakārikā* (literally *Fundamental Verses on the Middle Way*). This text in turn inspires a huge commentarial literature in Sanskrit, Tibetan, Chinese, Korean and Japanese. Divergences on interpretation of *Mūlamadhyamakakārikā* often determine the splits between major philosophical schools. So, for instance, the distinction between two of the three major Mahāyāna philosophical schools, Svātantrika-Mādhyamika and Prāsaṅgika-Mādhyamika reflect, inter alia, distinct readings of this text, itself taken as fundamental by scholars within each of these schools.[1]

The treatise itself is composed in very terse, often cryptic verses, with much of the explicit argument suppressed, generating significant interpretive challenges. But the uniformity of the philosophical methodology and the clarity of the central philosophical vision

---

1. See, for instance, Nagao (1989 and 1991), Lopez (1987), and Cabezon (1992) for more detailed discussion of *Yogācāra* and *Svātantrika* readings.

expressed in the text together provide a considerable fulcrum for exegesis. Moreover, the rich commentarial literature generates a number of distinct and illuminating readings. The central topic of the text is emptiness—the Buddhist technical term for the lack of independent existence, inherent existence, or essence in things. Nāgārjuna relentlessly analyzes phenomena or processes that appear to exist independently and argues that they cannot so exist, and yet, though lacking the inherent existence imputed to them either by naive common sense or by sophisticated realistic philosophical theory,[2] these phenomena are not nonexistent—they are, he argues, conventionally real.

This dual thesis of the conventional reality of phenomena together with their lack of inherent existence depends upon the complex doctrine of the two truths or two realities—a conventional or nominal truth and an ultimate truth—and upon a subtle and surprising doctrine regarding their relation. It is, in fact, this sophisticated development of the doctrine of the two truths as a vehicle for understanding Buddhist metaphysics and epistemology that is Nāgārjuna's greatest philosophical contribution. If the analysis in terms of emptiness is the substantive heart of *Mūlamadhyamaka-kārikā*, the method of reductio ad absurdum is the methodological core. Nāgārjuna, like Western sceptics, systematically eschews the defense of positive metaphysical doctrines regarding the nature of things, arguing rather that any such positive thesis is incoherent and that, in the end, our conventions and our conceptual framework can never be justified by demonstrating their correspondence

2. It cannot be overemphasized that as far as Nāgārjuna—or any Mahāyāna Buddhist philosopher, for that matter—is concerned, the view that the things we perceive and of which we conceive, to the extent that they exist at all, do so inherently originates as an innate misapprehension and is not the product of sophisticated philosophical theory. That is, we naively and pretheoretically take things as substantial. This, as Nāgārjuna will argue, and as the Buddha himself argued, is the root delusion that lies at the basis of all human suffering. We can, to be sure, make sophisticated philosophy out of this. And much of Western and Asian metaphysics is devoted to that enterprise. But it is important to see that an intellectual rejection of that sophisticated essentialist metaphysics would not, from the standpoint of Buddhism, suffice for liberation from suffering. For the innate misapprehension— the root delusion enshrined in common sense and in much of our language—would remain. Nāgārjuna's text is aimed primarily against philosophy. But its soteriological goal is the extirpation of the very root of suffering.

to an independent reality. Rather, he suggests, what counts as real depends precisely on our conventions.[3]

For Nāgārjuna and his followers this point is connected deeply and directly with the emptiness of phenomena. That is, for instance, when a Mādhyamika philosopher says of a table that it is empty, that assertion by itself is incomplete. It invites the question, Empty of what? And the answer is, Empty of inherent existence, or self-nature, or, in more Western terms, *essence*.[4] Now, to say that the table is empty is hence simply to say that it lacks essence and importantly *not* to say that it is completely nonexistent.[5] To say that it lacks essence, the Mādhyamika philosopher will explain, is to say, as the Tibetans like to put it, that it does not exist "from its own side"—that its existence *as the object that it is—as a table*—depends not on *it*, nor on any purely nonrelational characteristics, but depends on us as well. That is, if our culture had not evolved this manner of furniture, what appears to us to be an obviously unitary object might instead be correctly described as five objects:

---

3. Though in the end, as we shall see, ultimate reality depends on our conventions in a way, it depends on our conventions in a very different way from that in which conventional reality does. Despite this difference in the structure of the relation between convention and reality in the two cases, however, it remains a distinctive feature of Nāgārjuna's system that it is impossible to speak coherently of reality independent of conventions.

4. I have generally translated the Tibetan *"rang bzhin"* (Skt: *svabhāva*) with the English philosophical term "essence," as opposed to the more traditional "self-nature" or "own-being" used by many Buddhologists. (Here I agree with Cabezon [1992].) I think that this best captures Nāgārjuna's usage, and this choice makes good etymological sense as well. But there are dangers here. *"Rang bzhin"* and *"svabhāva"* have their semantic homes in Buddhist philosophical literature, and their ordinary meanings derive from their usage in that environment. "Essence" has it semantic home in the Western philosophical tradition. So there will no doubt be resonances of the original terms that are not captured by the translation and new resonances introduced that would be foreign to the original text. But this is unavoidable in a translation. Retaining the original term is worse, as it conveys nothing to the reader not already conversant with Tibetan, Sanskrit, and Buddhist philosophy. And using one of the ugly neologisms frequently introduced conveys the misleading impression that the original introduces such an ugly neologism. In the interest of not cluttering this text with philological footnotes, I will not generally defend my choices as I do here. But I do remind the reader of this and of any translation: *Caveat lector!* A great deal of interpretation goes into any translation.

5. See also Ng (1993), esp. pp. 12–15, for a good exposition. For an exposition of the contrary view, see Wood (1994). As will be clear, I disagree with his interpretation globally and on many points of detail.

four quite useful sticks absurdly surmounted by a pointless slab of stick-wood waiting to be carved. Or we would have no reason to indicate this particular temporary arrangement of this matter as an object at all, as opposed to a brief intersection of the histories of some trees. It is also to say that the table depends for its existence on its parts, on its causes, on its material, and so forth. Apart from these, there is no table. The table, we might say, is a purely arbitrary slice of space-time chosen by us as the referent of a single name and not an entity demanding, on its own, recognition and a philosophical analysis to reveal its essence. That independent character is precisely what it lacks on this view.[6]

So from the standpoint of Mādhyamika philosophy, when we ask of a phenomenon, Does it exist?, we must always pay careful attention to the sense of the word "exist" that is at work. We might mean *exist inherently,* that is, in virtue of being a substance independent of its attributes, in virtue of having an essence, and so forth, or we might mean *exist conventionally,* that is to exist dependently, to be the conventional referent of a term, but not to have any independent existence. No phenomenon, Nāgārjuna will argue, exists in the first sense. But that does *not* entail that all phenomena are nonexistent tout court. Rather, to the degree that anything exists, it exists in the latter sense, that is, nominally, or conventionally. It will be important to keep this ambiguity in "exists" in mind throughout the text, particularly in order to see the subtle interplay between the two truths and the way in which the doctrine of the emptiness of emptiness resolves apparent paradoxes in the account.

And this analysis in terms of emptiness—an analysis refusing to characterize the nature of anything precisely because it denies that we can make sense of the idea of a thing's nature—proceeding by

6. Note that nothing in this example hinges on the fact that the table is an artifact. The same points could be made about the tree from which its wood was hewn. The boundaries of the tree, both spatial and temporal (consider the junctures between root and soil, or leaf and air; between live and dead wood; between seed, shoot, and tree); its identity over time (each year it sheds its leaves and grows new ones; some limbs break; new limbs grow); its existence as a unitary object, as opposed to a collection of cells; etc., are all conventional. Removing its properties leaves no core bearer behind. Searching for the tree that is independent of and which is the bearer of its parts, we come up empty. I thank Graham Parkes for pointing out the need to stress this point.

the relentless refutation of any attempt to provide such a positive analysis, is applied by Nāgārjuna to all phenomena, including, most radically, emptiness itself. For if Nāgārjuna merely argued that all phenomena are empty, one might justly indict him for merely replacing one analysis of things with another, that is, with arguing that emptiness is the essence of all things. But Nāgārjuna, as we shall see, argues that emptiness itself is empty. It is not a self-existent void standing behind a veil of illusion comprising conventional reality, but merely a characteristic of conventional reality. And this, as we shall see, is what provides the key to understanding the deep unity between the two truths.[7]

While Nāgārjuna is a powerfully original thinker, he is clearly and self-consciously operating squarely within the framework of Buddhist philosophy. As such, Nāgārjuna accepts and takes it as incumbent upon him to provide an account of the Four Noble Truths, nirvāṇa, buddhahood, and other fundamental Buddhist soteriological conceptions. Moreover, he takes it as a fundamental philosophical task to provide an understanding of what Buddhist philosophy refers to as *pratītyasamutpāda*—dependent co-origination. This term denotes the nexus between phenomena in virtue of which events depend on other events, composites depend on their parts, and so forth. Exactly how this dependency is spelled out, and exactly what its status is, is a matter of considerable debate within Buddhist philosophy, just as the nature of causation and explanation is a matter of great dispute within Western philosophy. Nāgārjuna is very much concerned to stake out a radical and revealing position in this debate. We will, in fact, see that this position and its connection to his understanding of emptiness and the nirvāṇa-saṃsāra relation provides the key to understanding his entire text.

Mūlamadhyamakakārikā is divided into twenty-seven chapters, which fall roughly, though by no means officially, into four sections. In the first section of the text, comprising Chapters I through VII, Nāgārjuna discusses the fundamental theoretical constructs in Buddhist ontology, such as dependent origination, change and im-

---

7. Siderits (1989) puts this point nicely: "The ultimate truth is that there is no ultimate truth" (p. 6).

permanence, perception, the aggregates that compose the self, the elements that constitute the universe, and the relation between substance and attribute. In the second major section, Chapters VIII through XIII, Nāgārjuna focuses on the nature of the self and of subjective experience. Chapters XIV through XXI are primarily concerned with the external world and the relation of the self to objects. The final section, Chapters XXII through XXVII, addresses phenomena associated with the ultimate truth, such as buddhahood, emptiness, and nirvāṇa, and the relation of the conventional to the ultimate and of saṃsāra to nirvāṇa. The chapters that form the climax of the text are found in this section. But it is important to note that in fact the dialectical structure of the text requires a reading of these chapters in order to fully grasp the import of the earlier ones. This is because the doctrine of the emptiness of emptiness does not fully emerge until this point, and it is crucial to Nāgārjuna's argument that all phenomena are empty and that their emptiness is also empty.[8]

The order of the chapters is often, though not always, important. Often a chapter will consider a phenomenon held by a proponent of another philosophical school to be inherently existent. Or an opponent may charge Nāgārjuna with denying the actuality of a phenomenon in virtue of asserting its emptiness. In his analysis, Nāgārjuna will typically argue that the phenomenon proposed as inherently existent cannot be so and indeed is empty, or that the phenomenon whose existence he is charged with denying is, in fact, on his analysis, while nonexistent from the ultimate point of view, conventionally existent. In each case, he will argue that the functions the opponent thought could only be served by an inherently existent phenomenon can, in fact, be served only by empty phenomena. But quite often these analyses will inspire natural rejoinders of the form, "Yes, x might well be empty and only conventionally existent, but we can't make sense of its conventional existence without presupposing the inherent existence of y."

8. I should note that this division of the text is not in any sense canonical. Tsong Khapa sees the structure slightly differently; Kalupahana (1986) proposes yet another structure. I see my own division, like these others, simply as a useful heuristic device for parsing the argument. (It should be noted that the division of the text even into chapters is due to Candrakīrti.)

In such cases, the next chapter will typically address that natural rejoinder. So, for instance, the first chapter argues that conditions and the relation between phenomena and that on which they depend are empty. But a natural rejoinder is that even conventional but actual conditions can only be understood in the context of change or impermanence. So Chapter II addresses change. The text hence forms a single sustained argument with only a few digressions or changes of subject, generally marked by the section divisions I have suggested above.

The first chapter addresses dependent origination. While many Western commentators assert that this chapter opens the text simply because it addresses a "fundamental doctrine of Buddhism,"[9] my analysis of the text suggests that Nāgārjuna begins with causation for deeper, more systematic reasons. In Chapters II through XXI, Nāgārjuna addresses a wide range of phenomena, including external perceptibles, psychological processes, relations, putative substances, and attributes, arguing that all are empty. In the final six chapters, Nāgārjuna generalizes the particular analyses into a broad theory concerning the nature of emptiness itself and the nature of the ultimate, of liberation, and of the relation between emptiness and dependent arising. At the close, he replies to objections. It is generally, and in my view correctly, acknowledged that Chapter XXIV, the examination of the Four Noble Truths, is the central chapter of the text and the climax of the argument, with Chapter XXV on nirvāṇa and saṃsāra sharing that spotlight. One verse of Chapter XXIV, verse 18, has received so much attention that interpretations of it alone represent the foundations of major Buddhist schools in East Asia:

18.   Whatever is dependently co-arisen
        That is explained to be emptiness.
        That, being a dependent designation
        Is itself the middle way.

Here Nāgārjuna asserts the fundamental identity of (1) emptiness, or the ultimate truth; (2) the dependently originated, that is,

9. Kalupahana (1986), p. 32.

all phenomena; and (3) verbal convention. Moreover, he asserts that understanding this relation is itself the middle-way philosophical view he articulates in *Mūlamadhyamakakārikā*. This verse and the discussion in the chapters that follow provide the fulcrum for Candrakīrti's more explicit characterization of the emptiness of emptiness as an interpretation of Nāgārjuna's philosophical system—the interpretation that is definitive of the Prāsaṅgika-Mādhyamika school.[10] In what follows I will provide an interpretation of the text inspired by the centrality of this verse and of the chapters forming its context that harmonizes with Candrakīrti's. In fact, on my reading of the text this doctrine is already found in the opening chapter—the examination of conditions. Reading the text in this way locates the doctrine of the emptiness of emptiness not only as a dramatic philosophical conclusion to be drawn at the end of twenty-four chapters of argument, but as the perspective implicit in the argument from the very beginning and only rendered explicit in XXIV. Reading the text in this way will show us exactly how XXIV:18 is to be understood and just why a proper understanding of causality is so central to Buddhist philosophy.

When a Westerner first encounters *Mūlamadhyamakakārikā* or other Mādhyamika texts, the philosophical approach can appear highly metaphysical and downright weird. The unfamiliar philosophical vocabulary, the highly negative dialectic, and the cryptic verse form are indeed forbidding. Most bizarre of all, however, at first glance is the doctrine that all phenomena, including self and its objects, are empty. For indeed Nāgārjuna and his followers do argue that the entire everyday world is, from the ultimate standpoint, nonexistent. And that does appear to stand just a bit deeper into philosophical left field than even Berkeley dares to play. But if the interpretation I will urge is adopted, the real central thrust of Mādhyamika is the demystification of this apparently mystical conclusion. While it might appear that the Mādhyamikas argue that nothing really exists except a formless void, in fact the actuality of

---

10. For a translation of much of Candrakīrti's commentary (*Prasannapadā*), see Sprung (1979). Huntington and Wangchen (1993) provide an excellent translation of Candrakīrti's principal treatise on Mādhyamika (*Mādhyamakāvatāra*).

the entire phenomenal world, persons and all, is recovered within that emptiness.[11]

Now a word about the methodology and intent of this commentary: Since the intended audience is Western philosophers and students of philosophy whose primary study has been in the Western tradition, I have tried throughout, insofar as that is possible without distortion of the meaning of the text, to explain Nāgārjuna's arguments and positions in language familiar to Western philosophers. I have occasionally used analogies to positions and arguments found in Western texts, but have avoided doing so where I thought that the comparisons might force a Procrustean analysis of Nāgārjuna's own views. And it is, of course, impossible and pointless to completely recast Nāgārjuna's positions as those with which we in the West are familiar and to replace his technical terminology with ours. For Nāgārjuna is not a Western philosopher. He is an Indian Buddhist philosopher whose work we approach through a vast Asian Buddhist commentarial literature. And while many of his concerns, problems, theses, and arguments are recognizable cousins of ours, many are not, and there are genuine differences in outlook.

This is what makes Nāgārjuna's work so exciting to read and to think about—it provides a genuinely distinctive perspective on a set of problems and projects that we share. In commenting on Nāgārjuna's text, I am constantly aware of walking a philosophical and hermeneutical tightrope. On the one hand, one could provide a perfectly traditional commentary on the text—or better, a translation of one of the major Sanskrit or Tibetan commentaries—or a transcript of oral commentary by a recognized scholar of the tradition. Such a commentary would explain in great detail the way the text is seen from the perspective of its home tradition and the background of Buddhist controversies to which the text responds. A commentary like this would undoubtedly be of great use to Buddhologists and philosophers already steeped in Buddhist phi-

---

11. For useful discussions of the recovery of the conventional within emptiness and the relation between the two truths in Mādhyamika philosophy, see Sprung (1973, 1979), esp. 1973, pp. 15–20; Newland (1992); Napper (1992); Streng (1967), esp. chap. 3.

losophy and its history. And indeed Sprung's translation of most of Candrakīrti's *Prasannapadā (Lucid Exposition)*, including the root verses from *Mūlamadhyamakakārikā*, partially fulfills this need. But many of these scholars and students already have access to the relevant texts in their original languages or to teachers situated within the Buddhist tradition.

On the other hand, one could try to comment on the text by presenting a theory of what Nāgārjuna would have said had he been a twentieth-century Western philosopher. One could then feel free to step back from the internecine debates in the classical Buddhist academy, which were so absorbing to the historical Nāgārjuna and so distant from our own context, and simply ask how his arguments would be formulated in the context of the contemporary philosophical scene. Leaving aside the question of how one would identify the possible philosopher denoted by this bizarre counterfactual, this would again be a profoundly unsatisfying enterprise. For what makes this a great text is not simply that we can extrapolate its significance to our own context, but that in reading it, to borrow Gadamer's metaphor, we are able to fuse its textual horizon with our own. It is the bringing to the present of Nāgārjuna's own concerns, insights, and arguments that is revelatory, not speculation about a related counterfactual nonentity. And for this fusion of interpretive horizons to be possible, we must, as much as possible, respect the original horizon of the text.

Having said this, one must confess the double difficulty of giving sense to the phrase "Nāgārjuna's own concerns, insights, and arguments." The recovery of authorial intent as a hermeneutic task is problematic (especially when the author is so culturotemporally remote and when his corpus is as controversial in composition and interpretation as is Nāgārjuna's). But it is equally problematic as a hermeneutic desideratum. For who is to say that Nāgārjuna was/is the best possible interpreter of *Mūlamadhyamakakārikā*? After all, he did not have the benefit of the long commentarial tradition he spawned.[12] A great text—or, as Gadamer has referred to such

---

12. The late Wilfrid Sellars was fond of saying that we understand Plato better than Plato could ever have understood himself: Plato, for instance, could never have dreamed of the consequences that would be drawn from his arguments.

texts, an "eminent text"—grows over time and merits reinterpretation and rereading as the tradition in which it participates develops and provides an ever-expanding context for its reading. Moreover, I am reading Nāgārjuna largely through the lens of the Tibetan commentarial tradition and through the Tibetan translation of his text—the text read and discussed by the scholars of this long, deep, and intellectually diverse and rich tradition, few of whom had access to Sanskrit. So the Nāgārjuna whose views I am exploring is an evolving figure, rooted in the life and writing of a first or second century Indian monk, of whom we know but little, but whose literary life and identity extends through a complex, sophisticated, and contested textual and philosophical tradition in India and Tibet and in the West.

As a consequence, in interpreting this text on the Middle Path for a Western audience, I have sought insofar as possible to find a middle path between these extremes. I have tried to explain Nāgārjuna's own arguments and their context as straightforwardly as possible without burdening the Western philosophical reader with extended discussion of the specifically ancient Indian Buddhist philosophical debates. I have indicated ways in which very specific arguments can be generalized and have commented on general structural features of arguments, chapters, and the text. I have throughout explained arguments in Western philosophical terms, while situating those arguments in their Buddhist context. There may be times when my desire to make arguments accessible has led to some distortion in Nāgārjuna's sense. There may also be times at which, by leaving arguments set firmly within the soteriological context of Buddhism, I have left those arguments looking like curios to my Western audience. Some of this may be unavoidable, but in any case I have sought specifically to minimize these difficulties.

The interpretation I offer is situated squarely within a Prāsaṅgika-Mādhyamika interpretation of Nāgārjuna (the philosophical school that reads *Mūlamadhyamakakārikā* through the commentaries of Buddhapālita and Candrakīrti). But more specifically, my reading is heavily influenced by the Tibetan Geluk-pa tradition that takes as central the commentaries of dGe-'dun-grub, mKhas-grub-rje, and especially, Je Tsong Khapa. My interpretation of the text reflects not only Candrakīrti's and Je Tsong Khapa's commentaries, but also the extended oral commentary I have received on this text from the eminent Tibetan Mādhyamika scholars, especially the Ven. Professor Geshe Yeshes Thap-Khas of the Central Institute of Higher Tibetan Studies and the Ven. Professor Gen Lobzang Gyatso of the Institute of Buddhist Dialectics (I should point out that both of these scholars—as well as others to whom I am indebted for valuable conversations, including the Most Ven. Prof. Samdhong Rinpoche and the Ven. Geshe Namgyal Wangchen—received their education at Drepung Loseling Monastic College, and so my interpretation also reflects more particularly the academic tradition of that institution).

Having characterized this as a tradition of interpretation, I must emphasize that it is not, as it is often represented, and as it often represents itself, a homogeneous tradition. Though there is a hermeneutic convention in Indo-Tibetan Buddhist literature of presenting oneself as merely expounding faithfully the views of all of the earlier commentators, this is almost never the truth. There are considerable divergences in interpretation and in philosophical position within Buddhist schools and within lineages. Indeed the Tibetan scholars I have regularly consulted, despite the fact that they shared many of the same teachers and an identical curriculum, differ widely among themselves on many issues. It would hence be impossible in any case to represent accurately *the* Prāsaṅgika-Mādhyamika interpretation, or even *the* Geluk-pa interpretation or *the* Drepung Loseling interpretation of *Mūlamadhyamakakārikā*.

I emphasize that *even if one could identify such a homogeneous interpretation,* I am *not* here presenting the interpretation or interpretations of any of these commentators or scholars, individually or collectively. There are substantial debates within these traditions regarding interpretive issues, and I do not consistently side with any particular faction (though I do think that it is true that my reading never conflicts directly with that of Candrakīrti); sometimes (as in my reading of the final chapter) I depart from the most common Geluk-pa interpretation entirely in favor of a line more closely associated with the Nyingma-pa reading of the text. Nor is the purpose of this text to compare, criticize, and resolve differences between interpretations. Instead, I here present the text as I read it, having been influenced by all of these commentators and teachers, and as I present it to my Western colleagues. And my intention in doing so is to let the text stand alone as a work of philosophy valuable in its own right to anyone interested in fundamental metaphysical, epistemological, and soteriological questions, not as a text to be studied only as part of "the history of philosophy" or "comparative philosophy."

Moreover, my exposition will be deliberately sympathetic. My goal is not to assess Nāgārjuna's philosophy, but to present and elucidate it and to do so in a way that, while making the text accessible to Western philosophers, does not disguise the fact that the text made accessible is an early Indian Mādhyamika philosophical treatise, read by a Western philosopher through an extended Indo-Tibetan commentarial and academic tradition. It is neither a contemporary treatise nor a second century text transported miraculously to us without the distortion of time and cultural distance. Buddhologists may lament the lack of critical discussion of Buddhist antecedents and commentarial sequellae, and my Tibetan colleagues may be uncomfortable with some of the tendentious extensions of arguments beyond the dialectical contexts in which they originally arose. Despite this, I hope that for Western philosophers interested in approaching Mādhyamika in particular or Buddhist philosophy in general, and for students of Nāgārjuna's philosophy in the West, this exposition will make his text more accessible.

Dedicatory Verses

I prostrate to the Perfect Buddha,
The best of teachers, who taught that
Whatever is dependently arisen is
Unceasing, unborn,
Unannihilated, not permanent,
Not coming, not going,
Without distinction, without identity,
And free from conceptual construction.

Dedicatory verses are often treated as mere performatives. But these are special and announce in a subtle but powerful way the program of the *Mūlamadhyamakakārikā*. There is a common point being made in the four pairwise denials, but also a specific insight being expressed in each. The relation between the conventional and the ultimate that will be developed in the text is also expressed poetically in the dedication. In fact, Candrakīrti, in *Prasannapadā*, argues that the dedication determines the Prāsaṅgika reading of Nāgārjuna's text.

Candrakīrti's point is this: In the four pairwise denials, Nāgārjuna is announcing that the Mādhyamika philosopher will make no positive assertions about the fundamental nature of things. But this claim must be qualified in several ways. For one thing, we must take the phrase "the nature of things" very seriously. That is, Nāgārjuna will be refusing to say anything about the essence of anything exactly because he will deny the coherence and utility of the concept of an essence. For another, it is important to see that the predications that are rejected are intended to be understood as made from the ultimate standpoint. That is, the assertions that are being denied are assertions about the final nature of phenomena that emerge from philosophical analysis. They are not meant to be ordinary assertions dependent upon conventions. Nāgārjuna will deny that it is possible to assert anything from the ultimate standpoint. He will urge that all truth is relative and conventional. In fact, as we shall see, these qualifications turn out to be mutually entailing.

But each pair is significant in its own right. To say that "whatever is dependently arisen is unceasing and unborn" is to emphasize that dependent arising amounts to emptiness, and emptiness amounts to nonexistence in the ultimate sense. While, as we shall see, Nāgārjuna defends the conventional existence of phenomena, he will urge that none of them ultimately exist—that none of them exist independently of convention with identities and natures that they possess in themselves. Therefore, he will argue, nothing ultimately is born, and from the ultimate standpoint there is nothing to cease. This is a deep point, which only emerges completely through a reading of the whole text. But we can say at this point that this insight contains within it the seeds of the eventual equation of the phenomenal world with emptiness, of saṃsāra with nirvāṇa, and of the conventional and the ultimate that are the hallmarks of the Prāsaṅgika-Mādhyamika view.

When Nāgārjuna claims that "whatever is dependently arisen is . . . unanihilated and not permanent" he indicates that the dependently arisen world and all of its contents are, in virtue of being dependently arisen and dependent upon conditions, impermanent. Phenomena come into existence when the conditions upon which they depend obtain, and they cease to exist when the conditions for their continued existence no longer obtain. This impermanence, he will argue, entails their nonexistence from the ultimate standpoint. For there will be no principled way to assert criteria for identity for phenomena that distinguish them in any principled way from their conditions. Nor can we find any essence they themselves have that determines their identity. The criteria for identity we posit will end up being purely conventional. Hence the same is true for any claims of substantial difference between things. But this impermanence and lack of intrinsic identity, while it amounts to the impossibility of ultimate existence, is not equivalent to annihilation. The empirical reality of things, on Nāgārjuna's analysis, is not denied by asserting their emptiness.

Finally, to assert that things are "not coming, not going" is to assert that the phenomenal world does not contain intrinsically identifiable entities that persist independently with those identities over time. As a consequence, there can be no sense in saying that any entity, independent of conventional imputation, comes into existence, remains in existence, or goes out of existence.[13]

The final remark—that the phenomenal world is free from conceptual imputation—raises a tension that is central to Mādhyamika philosophy and that animates the whole of the text: The tension between the desire to characterize the ultimate nature of things and the recognition that all characterization is conventional. For Nāgārjuna will urge that all conventional phenomena are conceptually designated, depending for whatever identity and existence they have on such designation, and that this merely imputed status is their ultimate nature. Despite this, however, he will urge that seeing this fact is at the same time to see that the nature naively imputed to things and the nature they appear to us to have—inherent existence—is wholly false. In themselves, from their side, things are free of that imputation, even though there is really nothing at all that can be said from their side. This dynamic philosophical tension—a tension between the Mādhyamika account of the limits of what can be coherently said and its analytical ostension of what can't be said without paradox but must be understood—must constantly be borne in mind in reading the text. It is not an incoherent mysticism, but it is a logical tightrope act at the very limits of language and metaphysics.

---

13. As Georges Dreyfus points out (personal communication), many Tibetan scholars read this line also as a comment on the selflessness of sentient beings—as indicating that there is no self that comes from previous lives and goes on to future lives.

Chapter I

Examination of Conditions

Central to this first chapter is the distinction between causes and conditions (Skt: *hetu* and *pratyaya*, Tib: *rgyu* and *rkyen*). This distinction is variously drawn and is controversial,[14] and it is arguably differently understood in Sanskrit and Tibetan. The way I will understand it here, I argue, makes good, coherent sense not only of this chapter, but of *Mūlamadhyamakakārikā* as a whole. Briefly, we will understand this distinction as follows: When Nāgārjuna uses the word "cause" (*hetu, rgyu*), he has in mind an event or state that has in it a *power* (*kriyā, bya-ba*)[15] to bring about its effect and has that power as part of its essence or nature *(svabhāva, rang bzhin)*. When he uses the term "condition" on the other hand

---

14. Some scholars with whom I have discussed this interpretation argue that there is no real difference between causes and conditions, some that a cause is one kind of condition, some that efficient causes are causes and all other causal factors contributing to an event are conditions. Some like my reading. I have found no unanimity on this interpretive question, either among Western Buddhologists or among Tibetan scholars. The canonical texts are equivocal as well. I do not argue that the distinction I here attribute to Nāgārjuna, which I defend on hermeneutical grounds, is necessarily drawn in the same way throughout the Buddhist philosophical world or even throughout the Prāsaṅgika-Mādhyamika literature. But it is the one Nāgārjuna draws.

15. Some might quarrel with this translation, preferring to reserve "power" to translate *"stob"* (Skt: *bāla* or *shakti*) and to translate *"bya-ba"* or *"kriyā"* as "activity" or "action." But in this context "power," interpreted as causal power, is just right.

(*pratyaya, rkyen*), he has in mind an event, state, or process that can be appealed to in explaining another event, state, or process without any metaphysical commitment to any occult connection between explanandum and explanans. In Chapter I, Nāgārjuna, we shall see, argues against the existence of causes and for the existence of a variety of kinds of conditions.[16] Things are not, however, quite this simple. For in the philosophical context in which Nāgārjuna is writing, there are those—indeed including most Buddhist philosophical schools—who would accept his classification of conditions, but who would then assert that in order for conditions to function as explanatory, they must themselves have an independent inherent existence. Some—such as the Sarvastivadas or Sautāntrika-Svātantrikas (despite other differences between these schools regarding causation)—would argue that the conditions must exist as substantially distinct from the conditioned; others, such as the Cittamātra, would argue that they

16. There are two kinds of cases to be made for attributing this distinction to Nāgārjuna in this chapter: Most generally, there is the hermeneutical argument that this makes the best philosophical sense of the text. It gets Nāgārjuna drawing a distinction that is clearly suggested by his philosophical outlook and that lines up nicely with the technical terms he deploys. But we can get more textually fine grained as well; in the first verse, Nāgārjuna explicitly rejects the existence of efficacy and pointedly uses the word "cause." He denies that there are such things. Nowhere in Chapter I is there a parallel denial of the existence of conditions. On the contrary, in I: 2 he positively asserts that there are four kinds of them. To be sure, this could be read as a mere partitioning of the class of effects that are described in Buddhist literature. But there are two reasons not to read it thus: First, Nāgārjuna does not couch the assertion in one of his "it might be said" locutions. Second, he never takes it back. The positive tone the text takes regarding conditions is continued in I: 4–5, where Nāgārjuna asserts that conditions are conceived without efficacy in contrast with the causes rejected in Chapter I and where he endorses a regularist view of conditions. So it seems that Nāgārjuna does use the "cause"/"condition" distinction to mark a distinction between the kind of association he endorses as an analysis of dependent arising and one he rejects. Inada (1970) among Western commentators agrees with this interpretation. Kalupahana (1986) seems to as well (see pp. 34–35). But see Streng (1973) and Wood (1994) for a contrasting interpretation, according to which Nāgārjuna is out to reject causes and conditions in the same sense, and according to which the distinction between the four conditions provides a platform for an exhaustive refutation of production with no positive account of interdependence implicated. This latter interpretation is adopted by Tsong Khapa (Sarnath ed., pp. 12ff.) and his followers as well. They attribute a like view to Candrakīrti. But I would disagree at that point with their reading of Candrakīrti's text.

can be of the same nature.[17] Nāgārjuna will evade these particular debates, however, by emphasizing that the conditions he has in mind must be thought of as empty of inherent existence and connected to the phenomena they condition neither through absolute difference nor through identity.

The argument against causation is tightly intertwined with the positive account of dependent arising and of the nature of the relation between conditions and the conditioned. Nāgārjuna begins by stating the conclusion (I: 1): Entities are neither self-caused nor do they come to be through the power of other entities. That is, there is no causation when causation is thought of as involving causal activity:[18]

1. Neither from itself nor from another,
    Nor from both,
    Nor without a cause,
    Does anything whatever, anywhere arise.

The fourfold classification of positions with regard to the relation between an active cause and its effect is meant to be exhaustive. But it is important to keep in mind that Nāgārjuna was aware of philosophical schools espousing each of these four positions. And each of them has something to say for itself if we begin by supposing a model of causation involving powers as essential properties of substantially real causes. The first view—held prominently by Samkhya philosophers[19]—is that all causation is really self-causation. A proponent of this view would argue that for a cause to be genuinely the cause of an effect, that effect must exist potentially in that cause. If it does not, then the cause might exist without the effect, in which case the cause would fail to necessitate the effect, in which case it would not be a genuine cause. This is

17. This account of the relevant contrastive views derives from the oral commentary of the Ven. Geshe Yeshes Thap-Khas and the Ven. Gen Lobzang Gyatso.
18. The Ven. Lobzang Norbu Shastri has pointed out to me that this verse may not in fact be original with Nāgārjuna, but is a quotation from sūtra. It appears in the *Kamajīka-prajñapāramitāsūtra* as well as in the *Mādhyamika-Salistambasūtra*. But the chronological relation of these sūtras to Nāgārjuna's text is not clear.
19. At least according to Tsong Khapa's commentary on this verse.

not to say that effects exist in full actuality in their causes, but that they have a genuine potential existence when their causes exist. In this case, since the effect is present in the cause, it already has a kind of existence prior to its appearance. And it is the fact of this prior potential existence that accounts for the causal character of the cause. So we can say, on this view, that a thing's prior potential existence is what gives rise to its later actual existence. So effects are in this sense self-caused. The typical kind of example appealed to in order to defend this model of causation is the seed and sprout relation. The sprout, although only actual after germination, is potential in the seed. Its potentiality is what makes the seed a seed of that sprout. Moreover, on this view, the seed and sprout cannot be distinguished as substantially different. Intuitively it makes sense to say that they are two stages of the same entity. But the seed is the cause of the sprout. Hence, the proponent of this view concludes, the sprout is self-caused.

Causation from another is a more familiar way of thinking of causation and was the dominant doctrine of causation in the Buddhist philosophical milieu in which Nāgārjuna was working. On this view, causes and their effects are genuinely distinct phenomena.[20] They can be characterized and can in principle exist independently of one another. But they are related by the fact that one has the power to bring the other about. The relations between parents and children is an example often appealed to in illustrating this doctrine. Parents bring their children into existence. But they are not identical entities.

The doctrine of causation by both self and other emerges through a juxtaposition of the doctrine of causation-from-another and the doctrine of self-causation. Let us return to the example of the seed. A proponent of other-causation might point out that seeds that are not planted, watered, and so forth, do not sprout. If the sprout were present in the seed, these other conditions, which are manifestly other than the sprout, would be otiose. On the

20. I will use the term "phenomena" throughout in the commentary as an ontologically neutral expression to cover events, states, processes, objects, properties, etc. Usually phenomena of several of these categories are at play at once. Sometimes not. Where more precision is called for, I will be more specific, unless the context makes it clear which category is relevant.

other hand, the proponent of self-causation might reply: No matter how much you water, nourish, and exhort an infertile seed—one without the potentially existent sprout—nothing happens. So all of the distinct conditions in the world will not suffice absent the potential existence of the effect. The happy compromise doctrine that emerges is the doctrine of causation-by-both: Effects are the result of the joint operation of the effect itself in potentio and the external conditions necessary to raise the effect's mode of existence from potentiality to actuality.

The fourth alternative view of causation is that things simply spontaneously arise from no particular causes—that there are no links at all between events. What might motivate such a view? Well, as we shall see (and as any reader of Sextus Empiricus, Hume, or Wittgenstein will recall), there are powerful reasons for believing that none of the three alternatives just rehearsed can be made coherent. And if one believed that only if there were either some identity or difference between causes and effects could there be a relation of dependency between phenomena, one would be forced to the nihilistic conclusion that things simply arise causelessly.

Nonetheless, Nāgārjuna notes, there are conditions—in fact four distinct kinds—that can be appealed to in the explanation and prediction of phenomena:

2.   There are four conditions: efficient condition;
Percept-object condition; immediate condition;
Dominant condition, just so.
There is no fifth condition.

The general classification of conditions Nāgārjuna employs is pretty standard in Indian and especially in Buddhist accounts of explanation. But there are two specific features of Nāgārjuna's presentation that should be noted: First, since he is writing with specifically soteriological goals in mind, which require the practicioner to develop a deep insight into the nature of his/her own mind, there is a specifically psychological emphasis in the presentation. We must be aware both of this emphasis and of the natural generalization away from that particular domain that the account supports. Second, it will be of paramount importance to Nāgārjuna that the analysis of the relation of conditions to the conditioned involves ascribing neither inherent existence nor causal power to the conditions.

Efficient conditions are those salient events that explain the occurrence of subsequent events: Striking a match is the efficient condition for its lighting. My fingers depressing the keys of this computer is the efficient condition for the creation of this text.

The percept-object condition is in its primary sense the object in the environment that is the condition for a mind's perception of it. So when you see a tree, the physical tree in the environment is the percept-object condition of your perceptual state. Now things get vexed here in a number of ways. First, there is no unanimity in the world, or even in Buddhist philosophy, regarding the analysis of perception and, hence, no consensus on the view just adumbrated— that external objects are the percept-object conditions of perceptual awareness. Idealists, for instance, argue that the percept-object conditions are to be located in the subject. Second, many fans of percept-object conditions, on both sides of the idealist/realist divide, argue that the substantial existence of such a condition, and the appropriate exercise of its power to produce perception, is a necessary condition of perception. Nāgārjuna will be concerned to reject any such analysis—whether idealist or realist—in virtue of his attack on the notions of substantial existence, substantial difference, and causal power. Third, within the psychological domain, the account generalizes beyond perception. Conceptual states, imaginings, reasoning—all can have percept-object conditions. To Western philosophical ears this seems odd. But from the standpoint of Buddhist epistemology and psychology, intentional[21] activity generally is the natural kind comprised by "perception." So the point is that the intentional existence of the golden mountain is a percept-object condition of my being able to doubt that there is such a thing. Finally, the analysis bears generalization well beyond the psychological. For at the most abstract level, what is distinct about a percept-object condition is its existence simultaneously with and as a support for what it conditions. So Nāgārjuna's attack on a substantialist

---

21. "Intentional" is here being used in the sense of Brentano and of recent Western philosophy of mind—to mean contentful or directed upon an object. I do not use the term to mean purposeful.

understanding of this kind of explanans will apply, mutatis mutandis, to the case of a table supporting a book.

The dominant condition is the purpose or end for which an action is undertaken. My hoped for understanding of Mādhyamika might be the dominant condition for my reading Nāgārjuna's text, its presence before my eyes the percept-object condition, and the reflected light striking my eyes the efficient condition. The immediate conditions are the countless intermediary phenomena that emerge upon the analysis of a causal chain, in this case, the photons striking my retina, the excitation of photoreceptor cells, and so forth.[22]

A nonpsychological example might be useful to illustrate the difference between the four kinds of condition and the picture Nāgārjuna suggests of explanation in the most general sense: Suppose that you ask, "Why are the lights on?" I might reply as follows: (1) "Because I flicked the switch." I have appealed to an efficient condition. Or, (2) "Because the wires are in good working order, the bulbs haven't burned out, and the electricity is flowing." These are supporting conditions. Or, (3) "The light is the emission of photons each of which is emitted in response to the bombardment of an atom by an electron, and so forth." I have appealed to a chain of immediate conditions. Or, (4) "So that we can see." This is the dominant condition. Any of these would be a perfectly good answer to the "Why?" question. But note that none of them makes reference to any causal powers or necessitation.[23]

22. Georges Dreyfus (personal communication) notes that the understanding of the nature of percept-object conditions and dominant conditions in Māhāyana Buddhist philosophy undergoes a significant transformation a few centuries later at the hands of Dignaga and Dharmakīrti and that Nāgārjuna is here making use of older Sarvastivādan understandings of these terms to demonstrate the emptiness of conditions so understood.
23. Wood (1994) argues (see esp. pp. 48–53, pp. 63–64) that Nāgārjuna here argues that nothing arises at all. He claims that the argument begins by providing an exhaustive enumeration of the ways in which a thing could arise and then proceeds to eliminate each of these. This analysis, however, is problematic on two counts: First, it ignores the distinction between conventional, dependently arisen phenomena and inherently existent phenomena. To say that inherently existent phenomena cannot arise in any way, or that there can be no inherently existent production, is not thereby to say that there is no conventional dependency, or that there are no dependently arisen phenomena. Second, Wood ignores the positive account of

The next three verses are crucial to Nāgārjuna's understanding of the nature of conditions and their role in explanation. Nāgārjuna first notes (I: 3) that in examining a phenomenon and its relations to its conditions, we don't find that phenomenon somehow contained potentially in those conditions:

3.   The essence of entities
       Is not present in the conditions, etc. . . .
       If there is no essence,
       There can be no otherness-essence.

The point being made in the first two lines of the verse is fairly straightforward. When we examine the set of conditions that give rise to an entity—for example, the set of conditions we detailed above for the shining of a lamp, or the conditions for seeing a tree we discussed previously—no analysis of those conditions yields the consequent effect. Dissecting light switches, wires, brains, and so forth, does not reveal any hidden light. Nor is there a tree perception to be found already in the existence of the tree, the eye, and so forth. Rather these phenomena arise as consequences of the collocation of those conditions. To borrow a Kantian turn of phrase, phenomena are not analytically contained in their condi-

---

dependence on conditions presented in this chapter. His interpretations of the various commentaries that he cites in defense of this nihilistic reading are similarly marked by inattention to this set of distinctions, which I (and many others, including both canonical and modern interpreters) argue are crucial to understanding this text. Wood says, "If Nāgārjuna wished to avoid the nihilistic conclusion that things do not originate *period*, he would never have said in 1.1a that things do not arise. Furthermore, he would either have had to specify the way that things *do* arise, but in some *miraculous* or *inexplicable* way" (p. 63 [emphasis in original]). But on my reading at I: 1, Nāgārjuna does not say that things do not arise period. He simply says that they do not arise by means of an inherently existent causal process. And he does both here and in subsequent chapters explain how things arise in a decidedly nonmiraculous way.

But see Nagao (1989) for an interpretation in accord with my own:

"Dependent co-arising refers to a causal relationship wherein no essence is present at any time in either cause or result. Thus the sentence 'Nothing arises from itself; nothing arises from another,' is not intended to refute arising. It is a negation of others that might be explained as 'from themselves' or 'from others.' " (p. 7)

tions; rather, a synthesis is required out of which a phenomenon not antecedently existent comes to be.

But Nāgārjuna, through his use of the phrase "the essence of entities" *(dngos-po rnams kyi rang bzhin)*, emphasizes a very important metaphysical consequence of this observation: Given that phenomena depend upon their conditions for their existence and given that nothing answering to an essence of phenomena can be located in those conditions and given that there is nowhere else that an essence could come from, it follows that phenomena that arise from conditions are essenceless. One might argue at this point that just as phenomena come into existence dependent upon conditions, their essences come into existence in this way. But what goes for phenomena[24] does not go for essences. For essences are by definition eternal and fixed. They are independent. And for a phenomenon to have an essence is for it to have some permanent independent core. So neither essences nor phenomena with essences can emerge from conditions.

The next two lines require a careful gloss, both because of the complexity of the philosophical point at stake and because of the Buddhist philosophical term of art I translate as "otherness-essence" (Skt: *parabhāva*, Tib: *gzhan dngos*). Let us begin by glossing that term. In its primary sense it means to have, as a thing's nature, dependence upon another for existence. So for a table, for instance, to have otherness-essence, according to a proponent of this analysis of the nature of things, might be for it to have as an essential characteristic the property of depending for its existence on some pieces of wood, a carpenter, and so forth. This way of thinking of the nature of things has great appeal—was used by those who defended the analysis of causation as production from other and the analysis of causes and their effects according to which they are linked by causal powers inhering in the causes—particularly for other Buddhist schools who would want to join with Nāgārjuna in denying essence to phenomena. For such a philosopher, it would be congenial to argue that the table has no essence of its own, but has the essential property of depending on its parts, causes, and so

---

24. Especially given the analysis Nāgārjuna will develop of phenomena as empty. See especially chapters XV, XVIII, XXIV.

forth—an essential property that depends critically on another. And it would then be important to note that this nature relies on the other having an intrinsic connection to the phenomenon in question, a connection realized in the causal powers (or other inherently existent relation to the effect) of that other and, hence, in the other's own nature. Moreover, it is crucial to such an analysis, if it is not to lapse into the absurdities that plague self-causation, that there be a real, substantial difference in entity—a difference in intrinsic nature between the dependent phenomenon and the conditions on which it depends. Absent such a difference, the otherness required in the analysis cannot be established.[25]

Given this understanding of otherness-essence, we can see the arguments Nāgārjuna is ostending in the last two lines of this verse. First, since all entities are without their own essences (that is, without essences that can be specified intrinsically without reference to anything else), the other with respect to which any phenomenon is purportedly essentially characterized will be without an essence, and so there will be no basis on which to build this otherness-essence. Second, without individual essences, there will be no basis on which to draw the absolute, essential distinctions necessary to establish phenomena as intrinsically other than their conditions. Without individual essences there are not substantial differences. Without substantial differences, there are no absolute others by means of which to characterize phenomena. Third, in order to characterize phenomena as essentially different from their conditions, it is important to be able to characterize them independently. Otherwise, each depends for its identity on the other, and they are not truly distinct in nature. But the whole point of otherness-essence is that things in virtue of having it are essentially dependent. So the view is in fact internally contradictory. Given that things have no intrinsic nature, they are not essentially different. Given that lack of difference, they are interdependent. But given that interdependence, there cannot be the otherness needed to build otherness-essence out of dependence.

Now, on the reading of this chapter that I am suggesting, we can see conditions simply as useful explanans. Using this language,

<hr/>

25. Streng (1967) makes a similar point. See pp. 44–45.

Nāgārjuna is urging that even distinguishing between explanans and explanandum as distinct entities, with the former containing potentially what the latter has actually, is problematic. What we are typically confronted with in nature is a vast network of interdependent and continuous processes, and carving out particular phenomena for explanation or for use in explanations depends more on our explanatory interests and language than on joints nature presents to us. Through addressing the question of the potential existence of an event in its conditions, Nāgārjuna hints at this concealed relation between praxis and reality.

Next, Nāgārjuna notes (I: 4) that in invoking an event or entity as a condition in explanation we do not thereby ascribe it any causal power:

4.   Power to act does not have conditions.
      There is no power to act without conditions.
      There are no conditions without power to act.
      Nor do any have the power to act.

This is the beginning of Nāgārjuna's attack on the causal power/ cement-of-the-universe view of causation and his contrastive development of his regularity view of conditioned dependent arising. Causal powers, according to those who posit them, are meant to explain the causal nexus—they are meant to explain how it is that causes bring about their effects, which is itself supposed to be otherwise inexplicable. But, Nāgārjuna argues, if there were a causal power, it itself, as a phenomenon, would either have to have conditions or not. If the former, there is a vicious explanatory regress, for then one has to explain how the powers to act are themselves brought about by the conditions, and this is the very link presupposed by the friend of powers to be inexplicable. One could posit powers the conditions have to bring about powers and powers the powers have to bring about effects. But this just moves one step further down the regress.

If, on the other hand, one suggests that the powers have no condition, one is stuck positing uncaused and inexplicable occult entities as the explanans of causation. If what is to be explained is how it is that all phenomena are brought about by causal processes, it is a bit embarrassing to do so by reference to unobserved entities that are explicitly exempted from this otherwise universal condition. Moreover, there is then no explanation of how these powers arise and why they come to be where they are. This is all startlingly anticipatory of Wittgenstein's famous echo of Hume in the *Tractatus*:

6.371   The whole modern conception of the world is founded on the illusion that the so-called laws of nature are the explanations of natural phenomena.

6.372   Thus people today stop at the laws of nature, treating them as something inviolable, just as God and Fate were treated in past ages. And in fact both are right and both are wrong: though the view of the ancients is clearer in so far as they have a clear and acknowledged terminus, while the modern system tries to make it look as if *everything* were explained.[26]

In the next two lines, as we will often see in the text, Nāgārjuna is speaking in two senses—first, from the conventional standpoint, and second, from the ultimate. In the third line of the verse, he notes that conditions can certainly, in a perfectly legitimate sense, be appealed to as the things that bring about their effects; in that sense, we can say that they are efficacious—that they have the power to act. But in the fourth line he emphasizes that we cannot, so to speak, quantify over this power, identifying it as a phenomenon or property possessed by the conditions. There are no powers in that sense. Just as we can act for someone else's sake, despite there being no sakes, we can appeal to the potency of conditions despite their being no such potency. The trick is to make correct

26. There is, as Tuck (1990) has noted, a current fashion of using Wittgenstein to explicate Nāgārjuna and other Mādhyamika philosophers. Most (e.g. Huntington [1983a, 1983b, 1989], Gudmunson [1977], and Thurman [1984]) emphasize connections to the *Philosophical Investigations*, indeed with good reason. But (as Waldo [1975, 1978] and Anderson [1985] as well as Garfield [1990, 1994, unpublished] have noted) the *Tractatus* is also a useful fulcrum for exegesis, particularly of Nāgārjuna's work. Tractarian ideas also inform my discussion of Nāgārjuna on positionlessness, the limits of expressibility, and the relation between the two truths below. None of this, however, should be taken either as implying that Nāgārjuna would agree with everything in the *Tractatus* (assuredly he would not) or that the parallels drawn between Mādhyamika philosophy and themes in the *Philosophical Investigations* are spurious. They are in fact often quite illuminating.

use of conventional locutions without reifying denotata for all of the terms. For example, we might ask a farmer, "Do these seeds have the power to sprout?" as a way of asking whether they are fertile. It would be then perfectly appropriate for him to answer in the affirmative. But if we then asked him to show us where in the seed the power is located, he would be quite justified in regarding us as mad.[27]

Our desire for light does not exert some occult force on the lights. Nor is there anything to be found in the flicking of the switch other than the plastic, metal, movement, and connections visible to the naked eye. Occult causal powers are singularly absent. On the other hand, Nāgārjuna points out in this discussion that this does not mean that conditions are explanatorily impotent. In a perfectly *ordinary* sense—not the sense that the metaphysicians of causation have in mind—our desire *is* active in the production of light. But not in the sense that it contains light potentially, or some special causal power that connects our minds to the bulbs.

What is it, then, about some sets of event pairs (but not others) that make them dependently related if not some causal link present in those cases but not in others?

> 5.   These give rise to those,
>   So these are called[28] conditions.
>   As long as those do not come from these,
>   Why are these not nonconditions?

One might answer this question, Nāgārjuna notes in the opponent's suggestion in the first two lines, by noting the presence of some relation of "giving rise to," realized in a power. But, he rejoins in the final two lines, this move is blocked: For having shown the absence and the theoretical impotence of such a link, it would follow that there would be no conditions. Nāgārjuna hence suggests here that it is the regularities that count. Flickings give

27. This example was suggested to me in conversation by the Ven. Geshe Lobzang Gyatso.
28. The verb here is *"grag"* (Skt: *kila*), which indicates that the embedded content is not endorsed. That is, the first two lines of this verse are in the mouth of the opponent.

rise to illuminations. So they are conditions of them. If they didn't, they wouldn't be. Period. Explanation relies on regularities. Regularities are explained by reference to further regularities. Adding active forces or potentials adds nothing of explanatory utility to the picture.[29]

In reading the next few verses, we must be hermeneutically cautious and pay careful attention to Nāgārjuna's use of the term "existent" (Tib: *yod-pa, Skt: sat*) and its negative contrastive "nonexistent" (Tib: *med-pa, asat*). For Nāgārjuna is worried here about *inherent* existence and *inherent* nonexistence, as opposed to *conventional* existence or nonexistence. For a thing to exist inherently is for it to exist in virtue of possessing an essence—for it to exist independently of other entities and independently of convention. For a thing to be inherently nonexistent is for it to not exist in any sense at all—not even conventionally or dependently. With this in mind, we can see how Nāgārjuna defends dependent arising while rejecting causation:

6.   For neither an existent nor a nonexistent thing
    Is a condition appropriate.
    If a thing is nonexistent, how could it have a condition?
    If a thing is already existent, what would a condition do?

He notes here that if entities are conceived as inherently existent, they exist independently and, hence, need no conditions for their production. Indeed, they could not be produced if they exist in this way. On the other hand, if things exist in no way whatsoever, it follows trivially that they have no conditions.[30] The follow-

---

29. The Mādhyamika position implies that we should seek to explain regularities by reference to their embeddedness in other regularities, and so on. To ask why there are regularities at all, on such a view, would be to ask an incoherent question: The fact of explanatorily useful regularities in nature is what makes explanation and investigation possible in the first place and is not something itself that can be explained. After all, there is only one universe, and truly singular phenomena, on such a view, are inexplicable in principle. This may connect deeply to the Buddha's insistence that questions concerning the beginning of the world are unanswerable.

30. See Bhattacharya (1979), esp. pp. 336–37, for a good discussion of this argument.

ing three verses make this point with regard to each of the four kinds of conditions:

7. When neither existents nor
    Nonexistents nor existent nonexistents are established,
    How could one propose a "productive cause?"
    If there were one, it would be pointless.

8. An existent entity (mental episode)[31]
    Has no object.
    Since a mental episode is without an object,
    How could there be any percept-condition?

9. Since things are not arisen,
    Cessation is not acceptable.
    Therefore, an immediate condition is not reasonable.
    If something has ceased, how could it be a condition?

In I: 7, Nāgārjuna is reasoning that since an inherently existent phenomenon is by definition independent, it could not have been produced by anything else. An inherently nonexistent phenomenon certainly cannot be produced; if it were, it would be existent. An existent nonexistent (for instance, something posited by a Meinongian ontology—existing in a logical space, though not in the actual world) cannot be produced since its actual production would contradict its nonexistence and its production in some other way would contradict the inherent existence of the other sort posited for it.

The argument in I: 8 is a bit different and is directed more specifically at the special status of simultaneous supporting conditions, such as those posited in perception, as discussed above. Nāgārjuna is making the following point: If we consider a particular moment of perception, the object of that perceptual episode no longer exists. This is so simply because of the mundane fact that the chain of events responsible for the arising of perceptual consciousness takes time. So the tree of which I am perceptually

---

31. The Tibetan is literally *"yod pa'i chos,"* or existent entity. But as both Tsong Khapa (pp. 31–32) and dGe-'dun-grub (p. 12) argue, the entity in question can only be a mental episode.

aware now is a tree that existed about one hundred milliseconds ago; not one that exists now. The light took some time to reach my eye; the nerve impulses from the eye to the brain took some time; visual processing took still more time. So if the story about how the tree is the percept-object condition of my perception according to which the tree exists simultaneously with the perception and exerts a causal power on my eye or visual consciousness were accepted, perception would be impossible. Moreover, the objects of many mental episodes are themselves nonexistent (like the golden mountain). But non-existents can't be causally responsible for anything.

Verse 9 contains two arguments. In the first half of the verse, Nāgārjuna is offering a quick reductio on the idea that immediately preceding conditions can exist inherently. By definition, an immediately preceding condition is a momentary element of a causal chain. And, by definition, something that is inherently existent is independent; hence, it cannot arise depending on something else and, therefore, cannot cease to exist. But immediately preceding conditions must arise and cease. In the final line of the verse, Nāgārjuna develops a related problem. Immediately preceding conditions must cease before their effect arises. If their existence and exertion of causal power is what explains the arising of the cause, the arising of the cause is then inexplicable. (This argument is also used by Sextus Empiricus in *Against the Logicians*.)

What is important about this strand of the argument? Nāgārjuna is drawing attention to the connection between a causal power view of causation and an essentialist view of phenomena on the one hand, and between a condition view of dependent arising and a conventional view of phenomena on the other. If one views phenomena as having and as emerging from casual powers, one views them as having essences and as being connected to the essences of other phenomena. This, Nāgārjuna suggests, is ultimately incoherent since it forces one at the same time to assert the *inherent existence* of these things, in virtue of their essential identity, and to assert their *dependence* and *productive* character, in virtue of their causal history and power. But such dependence and relational character, he suggests, is incompatible with their inherent existence. If, on the other hand, one regards things as dependent merely on conditions, one regards them as without essence and without power. And to regard something as without essence and without power is to regard it as merely conventionally existent. And this is to regard it as existing dependently. This provides a coherent mundane understanding of phenomena as an alternative to the metaphysics of reification that Nāgārjuna criticizes. Verse 10 is central in this discussion:

10. If things did not exist
     Without essence,
     The phrase, "When this exists so this will be,"
     Would not be acceptable.

Nāgārjuna is replying here to the causal realist's inference from the reality of causal powers to their embodiment in real entities whose essences include those powers. He turns the tables on the realist, arguing that it is precisely because there is no such reality to things—and hence no entities to serve as the bearers of the causal powers the realist wants to posit—that the Buddhist formula expressing the truth of dependent arising[32] can be asserted. It could *not* be asserted if in fact there were real entities. For if they were real in the sense important for the realist, they would be independent. So if the formula were interpreted in this context as pointing to any causal power, it would be false. It can only be interpreted, it would follow, as a formula expressing the regularity of nature.[33]

32. A formula familiar in the *suttas* of the Pali canon.
33. This verse is very often translated and interpreted in a diametrically opposed way: "Since things exist without essence the assertion 'When this exists, this will be' is not acceptable." Readings like this are to be found in Inada (1970), Streng (1967), Sprung (1979), and Kalupahana (1986). They may be suggested by Candrakīrti's comments to the effect that this phrase would make no sense were it asserted by the realist. But such a translation is not supported by the dialectical structure of the chapter and forces an excessively negative interpretation on the chapter as a whole. Moreover, as we shall see in Chapter XXIV, this would entail an untenable absolutism with respect to the ultimate truth and a corresponding untenable nihilism with respect to the conventional world. But see Nagao (1989) for a better reading:

The meaning of the traditional expressions "dependent upon this," or "if this exists then that exists" is not that when one essence exists, then some other essence exists apart from it. On the contrary, it is because both this and that do not exist as essences that, when this exists, then that also exists. (p. 7)

In the next three verses (I: 11–13), Nāgārjuna anticipates and answers the causal realist's reply:

11.   In the several or united conditions
        The effect cannot be found.
        How could something not in the conditions
        Come from the conditions?

Here the realist argues that the conclusion Nāgārjuna draws from the unreality of causal power—the nonexistence of things (where "existence" is read "inherent existence")—entails the falsity of the claim that things dependently arise. For if there are no things, surely nothing arises. This charge has a double edge: If the argument is successful it not only shows that Nāgārjuna's own position is vacuous, but that it contradicts one of the most fundamental tenets of Buddhist philosophy—that all phenomena are dependently arisen. Moreover, the opponent charges, on Nāgārjuna's view that the explanandum is not to be found potentially in the explanans, there is no explanation of how the former is to be understood as depending upon the latter. As Nāgārjuna will emphasize in I: 14, however, the very structure of this charge contains the seeds of its reply. The very emptiness of the effect, an effect presupposed by the opponent to be nonempty, in fact follows from the emptiness of the conditions and of the relationship between conditions and effect. Nāgārjuna will, hence, reply to the opponent's attempted refutation by embracing the conclusion of his reductio together with the premises it supposedly refutes.

12.   However, if a nonexistent effect
        Arises from these conditions,
        Why does it not arise
        From nonconditions?

How, the opponent asks, are we to distinguish coincidental sequence from causal consequence, or even from conventional dependence? And why don't things simply arise randomly from events that are nonconditions since no special connection is posited to link consequents to their proper causal antecedents?

13.   If the effect's essence is the conditions,
       But the conditions don't have their own essence,
       How could an effect whose essence is the conditions
       Come from something that is essenceless?

Finally, the opponent asks, since the phenomena we observe clearly have natures, and since those natures clearly derive from their causes, how could it be, as Nāgārjuna argues, that they proceed by means of a process with no essence, from conditions with no essence? Whence do the natures of actual existents arise? Nāgārjuna again will reply to this last charge by pointing out that since on his view the effects indeed have no essence, the opponent's presupposition is ill-founded. This move also indicates a reply to the problem posed in I: 12. That problem is grounded in the mistaken view that a phenomenon's lack of inherent existence entails that it, being nonexistent, could come into existence from nowhere. But "from nowhere," for the opponent, means from something lacking inherent existence. And indeed, for Nāgārjuna, this is exactly the case: Effects lacking inherent existence depend precisely upon conditions that themselves lack inherent existence.

Nāgārjuna's summary of the import of this set of replies is terse and cryptic. But unpacking it with the aid of what has gone before provides an important key to understanding the doctrine of the emptiness of causation that is the burden of this chapter:

14.   Therefore, neither with conditions as their essence,
       Nor with nonconditions as their essence are there any effects.
       If there are no such effects,
       How could conditions or nonconditions be evident?

First, Nāgārjuna points out, the opponent begs the question in asserting the genuine existence of the effects in question. They, like their conditions, and like the process of dependent origination itself, are nonexistent from the ultimate point of view. That is, they have no essence whatever. Hence, the third charge fails. As a consequence, in the sense in which the opponent supposes that these effects proceed from their conditions—namely that their essence is contained potentially in their causes, which themselves exist inherently—these effects need not be so produced. And so, finally, the effect-containing conditions for which the opponent charges Nāgārjuna with being unable to account are themselves unnecessary. In short, while the reificationist critic charges the Mādhyamika with failing to come up with a causal link sufficiently robust to link ultimately real phenomena, for the Mādhyamika philosopher the core reason for the absence of such a causal link is the very absence of such phenomena in the first place.

We are now in a position to characterize explicitly the emptiness of causation and the way this doctrine is identical with the doctrine of dependent origination from conditions adumbrated in this chapter. It is best to offer this characterization using the via media formulation most consonant with Nāgārjuna's philosophical school. We will locate the doctrine as a midpoint between two extreme philosophical views. That midpoint is achieved by taking conventions as the foundation of ontology, hence rejecting the very enterprise of a philosophical search for the ontological foundations of convention (Garfield 1990). To say that causation is nonempty, or inherently existent, is to succumb to the temptation to ground our explanatory practice and discourse in genuine causal powers linking causes to effects. That is the reificationist extreme that Nāgārjuna clearly rejects. To respond to the arguments against the inherent existence of causation by suggesting that there is then no possibility of appealing to conditions to explain phenomena—that there is no dependent origination at all—is the extreme of nihilism, also clearly rejected by Nāgārjuna. To assert the emptiness of causation is to accept the utility of our causal discourse and explanatory practice, but to resist the temptation to see these as grounded in reference to causal powers or as demanding such grounding. Dependent origination simply is the explicability and coherence of the universe. Its emptiness is the fact that there is no more to it than that.

Keep this analysis in mind, for when we reach Chapter XXIV, in which the most explicit analysis of emptiness itself and of the relation of emptiness to the conventional world is articulated, we will see that the principal philosophical move in Nāgārjuna's demystification of emptiness was this attack on a reified view of causality. Nāgārjuna replaces the view shared by the metaphysician and the person in the street, a view that presents itself as common sense, but is in fact deeply metaphysical, with an apparently paradoxical, thoroughly empty, but in the end commonsense view not only of causation, but of the entire phenomenal world. This theme—the replacement of apparent common sense that is deeply metaphysically committed with an apparently deeply metaphysical but actually commonsense understanding of the phenomenal world—will recur in each chapter of the text.

Chapter II

Examination of Motion

The target of Nāgārjuna's arguments in this chapter is any view of motion according to which motion is an entity, or a property with an existence independent of that of moving things, or according to which motion is part of the nature of moving things. These are versions of what it would be to think of motion as nonempty. It might be quite natural for a reificationist to reply to the arguments in Chapter I by proposing that such a view must be the case. For in Chapter I Nāgārjuna does presuppose, in developing the view that conventionally things do arise dependent upon conditions, that there is motion, or change. For if there were not, there would be no arising. And as we have seen, this would indeed be an absurd consequence for Nāgārjuna. So, one might think, even if the links between conditions and their consequences are empty, the change represented by the arising of these consequences must be real.

Nāgārjuna argues that from such a view a number of absurd consequences would follow: Things not now in motion, but which were in motion in the past or which will be in the future, would have to undergo substantial change, effectively becoming different things when they change state from motion to rest or vice versa; a regress would ensue from the need for the entity motion itself to be in motion; motion would occur in the absence of moving things; the moment at which a thing begins or ceases motion would be indescribable. Nāgārjuna concludes that a reification of motion is incoherent. Motion is therefore empty.

1. What has been moved is not moving.
    What has not been moved is not moving.
    Apart from what has been moved and what has not been
        moved,
    Movement cannot be conceived.

That is, if motion exists, there must be sometime at which it exists. Nāgārjuna in this opening verse considers the past and the future. This makes good sense. For motion requires a change of position, and a change of position must occur over time. But the present has no duration. So if motion were to exist, it would have to exist either in the past or in the future. But a thing that has moved only in the past is not now moving. Nor is a thing yet to be moved. One might, of course, suggest that there is a simple tense fallacy here—that things that were moving in the past were *then* in motion, that things that will move in the future will *then* be in motion. But this would be problematic. For that would mean that all motion would be in the past or in the future, and this could be said at any time. So there would be no time at which it would be true of any thing that it is in motion.[34] But this intuition is behind the opponent's reply in the next verse:

2. Where there is change, there is motion.
    Since there is change in the moving,
    And not in the moved or not-moved,
    Motion is in that which is moving.

This verse is important not only because it announces the obvious reply that motion exists in presently moving things, but because it introduces the connection between change in general and motion. Though this interpretative point is controversial, and several scholars have given widely different interpretations,[35] it is

34. The parallels to Zeno's paradoxes of motion, particularly that of the arrow, should be evident.
35. The Ven. Geshe Yeshes Thap-Khas, for instance, argues that the chapter should be interpreted as about change in general; the Ven. Gen Lobzang Gyatso,

highly plausible that Nāgārjuna is calling attention to the fact that the attack on motion as an inherently existent phenomenon is a general attack on seeing change or impermanence as inherently existent. This suggests that even the properties that according to Buddhist philosophy characterize all things—being dependently arisen and being impermanent—are not themselves inherently existent. Nāgārjuna replies:

> 3.   How would it be acceptable
> For motion to be in the mover?
> When it is not moving, it is not acceptable
> To call it a mover.

The point here is that if motion is thought of both as inherently existent and as a property of the mover, then it should, as inherently existent, continue to exist. For something that is inherently existent depends for nothing on its existence, and so it cannot be deprived of the conditions of its manifestation. That is because inherent existence is existence with an essence, as an independent entity whose identity can be intrinsically specified. (See Chapter XV for more detail.) But movers come to rest. It would seem then that it would have to be appropriate to call something a mover, even when it is at rest, since inherently existing motion could not cease.

> 4.   For whomever there is motion in the mover,
> There could be nonmotion
> Evident in the mover.
> But having motion follows from being a mover.

---

on the other hand, argues that though the arguments could indeed be applied to change in general, the chapter is specifically about motion through space. The Ven. Lobzang Norbu Shastri argues that it is in fact specifically only about walking, and that any further generalization is illicit (all personal communication). I side with the Ven. Geshe Yeshes Thap-Khas on this point since Nāgārjuna offers perfectly general arguments against change in properties. And it would seem especially elegant for Nāgārjuna, who is attacking the tendency to reify, to begin with the two properties most subject to reification in Buddhist philosophy, in virtue of their universal applicability to phenomena and centrality to the Buddhist metaphysical framework—dependent arising and change. While the canonical commentaries I have consulted do not extend the argument in this direction, they do not preclude such an extension.

In this verse Nāgārjuna begins his attack on the idea that motion is a property with an existence independent of movers. If, he asserts, one were to posit motion as such a property that simply happened to inhere in movers, it would follow from its independence that movers might not have it, but instead its contrary, namely, nonmotion. But that is not tenable. So it follows that motion can't be thought of as an independent property. This line of argument is continued in the next two verses:

5.   If motion is in the mover,
    There would have to be a twofold motion:
    One in virtue of which it is a mover,
    And one in virtue of which it moves.

6.   If there were a twofold motion,
    The subject of that motion would be twofold.
    For without a subject of motion,
    There cannot be motion.

Here Nāgārjuna develops a reductio on a position according to which motion is a property of the mover only at the time that the mover is in motion. This might seem to be a much more plausible view than the earlier discussed view of motion as an essential property. But Nāgārjuna argues that this can't work either. For it involves a multiplication of movements and agents of motion that is unacceptable to the proponent of such a theory. For if the motion is a property of the mover at all, both the mover and the motion must be moving. And this amounts to two separate motions. One motion—that in virtue of which the mover is a mover in the first place—is the motion posited by the theory. But if that motion were stationary, the mover would either also not be moving or it would "outrun" its motion and leave it behind. So there must also be a motion of the motion. Each of these two motions requires a subject. They can't be the same subject because then the mover and the motion would be identical, which would be absurd. So in explaining the motion of a single individual, the opponent is stuck with two movers.

This argument clearly can be understood as the start of an infinite regress. It is not at all clear whether Nāgārjuna so intended it, as the context in which the argument is formulated is one in which the consequence that two movers emerge in the analysis of the motion of a single mover is enough to refute the opponent.[36] But it is important to see that once this multiplication of explanatory motions and agents begins, it cannot be stopped, and so this argument constitutes a perfectly general attack on a view according to which motion is an entity associated with movers. It is also worth noting that the argument generalizes in other ways: It can be formulated as an argument against a parallel analysis of change as an independent property and, in general, as an argument against properties as entities that inhere in subjects—a twofold redness is required for a red shirt to be red because of the possession of redness. So this is, in fact, a "third man" argument.

7.   If without a mover
       It would not be correct to say that there is motion,
       Then if there were no motion,
       How could there be a mover?

Nāgārjuna is here emphasizing the codependence of motion and the mover. If there are no movers, there is no motion. If there is no motion, there are no movers. This has import at both the conventional level and with respect to any discussion of the inherent existence of either the mover or motion. At the conventional level, it means that any analysis of either motion or the mover that leaves the other out, or that does not involve codependence, will fail. Neither can be established as an independent basis for the analysis of the other. But it also means that neither, therefore, can be thought to inherently exist since to exist inherently would be to exist independently.

8.   Inasmuch as a real mover does not move,
       And a nonmover does not move,
       Apart from a mover and a nonmover,
       What third thing could move?

---

36. The commentaries I have consulted are silent on this issue, and there is no consensus among the Tibetan scholars with whom I have worked regarding this issue.

Here the terms "mover" and "nonmover" must be understood in the context of the previous arguments. Nāgārjuna is clearly talking about entities that are essentially in motion or in nonmotion. He has argued that we cannot think of a thing in motion as a thing whose nature is to move. And clearly a thing whose nature is not to move cannot be in motion. So if motion is thought of as a property that is either part of the nature of a thing or incompatible with a thing's nature, we are left with the conclusion that there is no motion. And so we have a philosophical problem: How is ordinary motion (and change) possible? Nāgārjuna emphasizes this in the following verses:

9.   When without motion,
     It is unacceptable to call something a mover,
     How will it be acceptable
     To say that a mover moves?

10.   For him from whose perspective a mover moves,
     There would be the consequence that
     Without motion there could be a mover.
     Because a mover moves.

These verses recapitulate the argument in II: 4 and II: 7. If we simply regard motion and mover as independent phenomena, we are forced to the absurd consequence that either could be present without the other.

11.   If a mover were to move,
     There would be a twofold motion:
     One in virtue of which he is a mover,
     And one in virtue of which the mover moves.

This last verse recapitulates the important argument in II: 6 in preparation for the attack on the possibility of the beginning and end of motion. The next few verses are reminiscent both of Zeno of Elea and Sextus Empiricus:

12.   Motion does not begin in what has moved,
     Nor does it begin in what has not moved,
     Nor does it begin in what is moving.
     In what, then, does motion begin?

13.   Prior to the beginning of motion,
        There is no beginning of motion in
        The going or in the gone.
        How could there be motion in the not-gone?

These two verses are alternative formulations of the same argument: If there is motion, it must begin sometime. But that moment
is inconceivable. For motion doesn't begin in a stationary thing.
And once a thing is in motion, it is too late. It can't always have
begun in the past or be yet to begin, and there simply isn't time to
go anywhere in the present.

14.   Since the beginning of motion
        Cannot be conceived in any way,
        What gone thing, what going thing,
        And what nongoing thing can be posited?

After having emphasized this point, Nāgārjuna points out that
all that has been said about motion (and hence implicitly about
change) applies, mutatis mutandis, to rest (and hence implicitly to
stasis). Things that are in motion cannot be simultaneously at rest.
But to say that a stationary thing is at rest, where rest is conceived
as a property or entity having independent existence, would involve us in the same paradoxes encountered above: The stasis itself
would have to be either in motion or at rest. If in motion, then the
static thing would have to be in motion, which is contradictory. But
if at rest, then it must be at rest in virtue of possessing stasis, and
we are off on the same regress:

15.   Just as a moving thing is not stationary,
        A nonmoving thing is not stationary.
        Apart from the moving and the nonmoving,
        What third thing is stationary?

16.   If without motion
        It is not appropriate to posit a mover,
        How could it be appropriate to say
        That a moving thing is stationary?

And, in the same fashion, all that applies to the initiation of motion applies mutatis mutandis, to its cessation:

17.　One does not halt from moving,
　　　Nor from having moved or not having moved.
　　　Motion and coming to rest
　　　And starting to move are similar.

Nāgārjuna now develops further problems with any view regarding motion as an entity; it must be either identical to or different from the mover. Both options, he will argue, turn out to be incoherent:

18.　That motion just is the mover itself
　　　Is not correct.
　　　Nor is it correct that
　　　They are completely different.

19.　It would follow from
　　　The identity of mover and motion
　　　That agent and action
　　　Are identical.

The identity of agent and action is absurd on its face. For then whenever an agent were to perform another act, s/he would become a distinct agent. There would be no basis for identifying individuals over time.

20.　It would follow from
　　　A real distinction between motion and mover
　　　That there could be a mover without motion
　　　And motion without a mover.

This is more complicated. It is important to recall that the target positions here are positions that reify motion as a distinct *entity*, however abstract. If motion were an entity, and were distinct from all movers, then it should be possible to separate motion from movers.[37] Then we should see motion when nothing is moving and movers that are not in motion. Noticing that this is a problem for Nāgārjuna's opponent provides us with a hint as to the positive account of conventional motion that we should take from this chapter to be discussed below: Motion can only be understood in relation to movers—as a relation between their positions at different times. Movers can only be understood as movers in relation to motion so understood. But to understand motion and movers this way is not to reify them as entities—and so to escape the dilemma of their identity or difference. Nāgārjuna emphasizes this moral in the next verse, where we must read "established" as meaning *established as existent entities*.

21.   When neither in identity
       Nor in difference
       Can they be established,
       How can these two be established at all?

22.   The motion by means of which a mover is manifest
       Cannot be the motion by means of which he moves.
       He does not exist before that motion,
       So what and where is the thing that moves?

In this verse and in the next, Nāgārjuna is simply emphasizing the interdependence of motion and the mover. In II: 22 he notes the absurdity of the supposition that the mover and the motion are known independently. If they could be, then the mover would have to have one motion in virtue of which he was a mover and a second independent motion in virtue of which he now moves. But since prior to being in motion, no mover exists, it cannot be that the mover exists as a mover independently of the motion. This then demands an answer to the question, What moves?

In II: 23 Nāgārjuna answers this in a very straightforward way: The mover who is a mover in virtue of his motion (and that motion is a motion in virtue of being carried out by a mover) is what moves. Hence, the mover is dependent for his identity as a mover

---

37. The principle here is the familiar Humean maxim of metaphysical analysis: Whatever is really distinct is in principle separable.

on the motion; the motion is dependent for its identity on the mover. Neither has an intrinsic identity, and both are empty of inherent existence:

23.   A mover does not carry out a different motion
        From that by means of which he is manifest as a mover.
        Moreover, in one mover
        A twofold motion is unacceptable.

24.   A really existent mover
        Doesn't move in any of the three ways.
        A nonexistent mover
        Doesn't move in any of the three ways.

The three ways in question are past, present, and future. Something that is inherently a mover has been shown to be incapable of motion in any of these periods. This is simply a way of emphasizing the moral of the entire chapter: Movers cannot be thought of as being movers intrinsically. Moreover, nonexistent movers—movers that are not even conventionally movers—certainly don't move. It must therefore be that neither do movers move intrinsically nor that there is no motion. There must be a sense in which motion and movers exist, but do not do so intrinsically. The final verse must hence be read with "entity," "nonentity," and "existent" as asserted in the ultimate sense:

25.   Neither an entity nor a nonentity
        Moves in any of the three ways.
        So motion, mover,
        And route are nonexistent.

So far so good. But then is motion completely nonexistent? Is the entire universe static according to Mādhyamika philosophy? If we simply read this chapter in isolation, that conclusion might indeed seem warranted. It would be hard to distinguish emptiness from complete nonexistence. We would be left with an illusory world of change and movement, behind which would lie a static ultimate reality. But such a reading would be problematic. For one thing, it would be absurd on its face. Things move and change. For another, it would contradict the doctrine of dependent origination and change that is the very basis of any Buddhist philosophical system, which Nāgārjuna has already endorsed in the opening chapter. How, then, are we to read this discussion more positively? Answering this question is hermeneutically critical not only for an understanding of this chapter, but for a reading of the entire text, which if not read with care, can appear unrelentingly nihilistic.

The positive account we are after emerges when we read this second chapter in the context of the first chapter: All phenomena, including motion, are dependently arisen and, hence, empty of inherent existence. The conclusion that motion is empty is simply the conclusion that it is conventional and dependent, like the putatively moving entities themselves. Since there is no implicit contrastive, inherently existent, ultimate reality—say of the static, or of stasis—this conclusion does not lead us to ascribe a "second class" or merely apparent existence to motion or to movers. Their nonexistence is simply their lack of existence as substantial entities. Existence—of a sort—is hence recovered exactly in the context of an absence of inherent existence.

But existence of what kind? Herein lies the clue to the positive construction of motion that emerges. The existence that emerges is a conventional and dependent existence. Motion does not exist as an entity on this account, but rather as a relation—as the relation between the positions of a body at distinct times and, hence, as dependent upon that body and those positions.[38] Moreover, it emerges as a conventional entity in the following critical sense: Only to the extent that we make the decision to identify, as a single entity, things that differ from each other in position over time, but are in other respects quite similar and form causal chains of a particular sort, can we say that whatever is so identified moves. And this is a matter of choice. For we *could* decide to say that entities that differ in any respect are thereby distinct. If we did adopt that convention for individuation, an entity here now and one there then would ipso facto be distinct entities. And so no *single entity* could adopt different positions (or different properties) at different times, and so motion and change would be nonexistent. It is this dependence of

38. See also Kalupahana (1986), p. 131.

motion on the moved, of the status of things as moved on their motion, and of both on conventions of individuation that, on this account, constitutes their emptiness. But this simply constitutes their conventional existence and provides an analysis of the means by which they so exist. The emptiness of motion is hence seen to be its existence *as conventional* and *as dependent,* not other than its conventional existence. In understanding its emptiness in this way, we bring motion, change, and movable and changeable entities back from the brink of extinction.[39]

---

39. Again, the affinities to Hume are intriguing: The Humean analysis of external physical objects and of personal identity appears at first to deny the reality of either. But what emerges from a more careful reading is that Hume shows that only the reified substantialist versions of objects and selves are nonexistent. The objects and selves with which we have actual perceptual and cognitive commerce, on his view, are perfectly existent, but only in virtue of being dependent upon conventions ("custom") for their identity and existence. It is a clear analysis of their conventional character that allows us to coherently assert their existence.

Chapter III

Examination of the Senses

In this chapter, which is most immediately about vision, Nāgārjuna really addresses the status of sense perception generally, as he makes clear in the opening and closing verses. Just as in Chapter II, where the target positions Nāgārjuna argues against are positions according to which motion and the mover inherently exist as distinct, independent, but somehow related entities, here he argues against positions according to which the sense faculties, the sense organs, the subject of sensory experience, and the sense object inherently exist and are distinct, independent, but somehow related entities. For we do perceive motion and change, and the argument for the conventional existence of motion did suggest that it could be seen as a relation between the positions at which we perceive objects at different times. So one can imagine an opponent saying, "Even if the motion we perceive is not real, the perception must be." Again, it will be important for Nāgārjuna that his analysis of perception as empty of inherent existence, and as merely dependently arisen, does not entail its complete nonexistence. He must, that is, steer a middle path between reification and nihilism using emptiness as his compass.

1. Seeing, hearing, smelling,
    Tasting, touching, and mind
    Are the six sense faculties.
    Their spheres are the visible objects, etc. . . . .

This is a standard Buddhist catalog of the sense faculties. It differs from the standard Western catalog only in that the Buddhists regard introspection literally as an inner sense with the same epistemic structure as outer senses and presumably subserved by analogous physical structures. Nāgārjuna will not dispute the reality of these faculties or of their respective spheres. But he will insist that that reality must be characterized interdependently and conventionally.

2. That very seeing does not see
    Itself at all.
    How can something that cannot see itself
    See another?

This cryptic argument is aimed at any theory according to which vision is inherently existent. The idea is this: If the visual faculty were to be inherently existent, then seeing would be its essence. Its action would hence require no distinct conditions and no external object to be seen. That is, if vision were inherently existent, vision would occur simply in virtue of the existence of the visual faculty. Suppose then that there is an inherently existent visual faculty and no external sense object for it. It would then have only itself as a possible object of sight, yet it would be seeing and so would have to be seeing itself. Therefore, Nāgārjuna argues, a view of vision as inherently existent would entail the possibility of visual apperception. But there is no such possibility. So the fact that vision can see other things cannot be in virtue of its containing percipience as an inherent property.

There is also a plausible Pyrrhonian interpretation of this verse: The point of a sensory faculty is to make knowledge possible. But that is only possible if the data the faculty provides are themselves perceived. But the data that the visual faculty delivers are visual. If they themselves are to be perceived, one would require either another visual faculty, hence generating a vicious regress, or apperception by vision, which is absurd. The point is not then that vision is impossible, but rather that visual perception—or any kind of perception—can only be completely explained and characterized by reference to things outside of the visual faculty itself. Vision is relational, and not an intrinsically identifiable phenomenon.[40]

3.   The example of fire
     Cannot elucidate seeing.
     Along with the moved and not-moved and motion
     That has been answered.

This is a reply to a standard substantialist counterexample to a Mādhyamika analysis, specifically: Fire burns other things, but does not burn itself. And it can be intrinsically identified. Perhaps then vision is like fire, in that it can see others but not itself, while it does not need to be relationally identified. This example is a standard in early Buddhist debates about intrinsic versus relational identity, and Nāgārjuna devotes an entire chapter to its refutation as a dialectical device (Chapter X), arguing there that fire cannot be intrinsically identified. But at this point, he is willing to grant the opponent that premise for the sake of argument. For, he claims, its utility as an analogy has already been undermined by the argument in the second chapter.

How? Whatever fire is burning must be burned in the past, the future, or the present. But, as with motion, burning cannot be, by its very nature, in the past, on pain of regress. Nor can it be in the future for the same reason. But burning cannot take place in the present either, for there is not enough time in an instant for anything to burn. Mutatis mutandis for vision. In the case of vision, for Nāgārjuna, there is a further problem with vision of another in the present. The visual process—and any sensory process—takes time. So if vision is seeing another thing, the other thing is already past. The only thing that vision could see in the present is a visual sense-impression. But then we are back to the problem of visual apperception. So even if fire were intrinsically identifiable, there is

40. I am indebted to the Ven. Gen Lobzang Gyatso for my reading of this verse. Kalupahana (1986) reads this quite differently—as an empiricist rejection of a Cartesian cogito argument. While I agree that Nāgārjuna has no sympathy with a Cartesian position, to see this verse as articulating an empiricist view with regard to self-knowledge seems unmotivated.

no point at which it could burn another. And if vision were intrinsically identifiable, there would be no moment at which it could see another.

4.   When there is not even the slightest
      Nonseeing seer,
      How could it makes sense to say
      That seeing sees?

When all there is to vision is visual perception, what is the motivation for positing an entity to undertake the process of perception? All there is to vision is the perceptual process: We don't need to posit an entity—the visual faculty over and above the set of interdependent phenomena that subserve vision. The desire to do so is of a piece with the more general substantialist imperative to posit an independent substratum to support every capacity or property.

5.   Seeing itself does not see.
      Nonseeing itself does not see.
      Through seeing itself
      The clear analysis of the seer is understood.

Perception is not accomplished by any independent entity known as vision. But that doesn't mean that things that are incapable of sight thereby perceive. In order to know what the proper subject of vision is, it is important to undertake a careful analysis of the perceptual process and not simply to posit a faculty with the nature of vision.

6.   Without detachment from vision there is no seer.
      Nor is there a seer detached from it.
      If there is no seer
      How can there be seeing or the seen?

On Nāgārjuna's analysis, we can't make sense of an autonomous subject of visual perception. For such a subject would by definition have its identity as a visual subject independent of perception. But there is no sense in calling something that does not see a seer. On the other hand, if we pack vision into its definition, we thereby fail to identify the subject nonrelationally. Vision and its subject are thus relational, dependent phenomena and not substantial or independent entities. So neither seeing nor seer nor the seen (conceived of as the object of sense perception) can be posited as entities with inherent existence. The point is just that sense perception cannot be understood as an autonomous phenomenon, but only as a dependent process.

7.   Just as the birth of a son is said to occur
        In dependence on the mother and father,
        So consciousness is said to arise
        In dependence on the eye and material form.[41]

Here the opponent offers yet another argument in favor of the inherent existence of the visual faculty (and, by extension, the other sense faculties): Consciousness is a consequence of vision, and it surely exists—in fact, its existence, one might say, is self-validating. Given the reality of the effect, the cause must also be real.[42] The final two verses reply to this objection and state the obvious generalization to all other senses, sense objects, sense faculties, and faculties of knowledge. The reply consists in pointing out that the other faculties and aggregates, including introspection and consciousness, exist and fail to exist in exactly the senses that vision and its objects exist and fail to exist: All are empty of inherent independent existence. But all exist conventionally. So the effect that, according to this interlocutor, exists inherently and demands an inherently existent cause does not so exist. And in the sense that it exists, its causes also exist:

8.   From the nonexistence of seeing and the seen it follows that
        The other four faculties of knowledge do not exist.

    41. The authenticity of this verse is a matter of dispute. It is not present in all editions of the text and may be a later interpolation.
    42. And from the standpoint of a Buddhist analysis of human existence there is more to it than this: In many presentations of the "twelve links of dependent origination," consciousness conditions craving for existence, which gives rise to existence in *saṃsāra*.

And all the aggregates,[43]etc.,
Are the same way.

9.   Like the seen, the heard, the smelled,
The tasted, and the touched,
The hearer, sound, etc.,
And consciousness should be understood.

Again, the point of this chapter is emphatically not that there is no perception, or that there are no sense faculties, sense organs, or sense objects. Rather the point is that none of these can be analyzed successfully as autonomous entities. They are interdependent phenomena that depend for their existence and their character on each other. None of them exists independently. They are all, hence, empty of inherent existence, and carving the process of perception into these components represents a conventional taxonomy of a process that does not present itself with natural joints demanding cleavage on their own.

---

43. The *skandhas* (literally "heaps" or "piles," but most often translated as "aggregates") are the basic constituents of the personality. Five are typically identified: form (really matter—the physical body), sensation, perception, disposition (behavioral and cognitive), and consciousness. But the term *"skandha"* indicates two features of this decomposition that must be born in mind to avoid confusion: The division is practical and empirical, and not philosophically principled, and the *skandhas* themselves are decomposible into further heaps, etc. These are not, hence, ontological fundamentals, but rather the first level of a psychology.

Chapter IV

Examination of the Aggregates

The five aggregates are the basic Buddhist categories of personal constituents. The first—that discussed as an example in this chapter—is in Sanskrit *rūpa*, in Tibetan *gzugs*. Unfortunately, given the lexicography of Western philosophy, this word has historically been translated as "form." This practice is so ubiquitous that I am loathe to depart from it, despite the confusion it engenders. For what the word means is *matter*. The other aggregates are sensation, perception, intellect, and the dispositions. It is important to realize that this taxonomy is to be understood pragmatically: There is no deep doctrinal or philosophical point that hangs on dividing the properties or capacities of humans up in just this way. In fact, most often the only important point about analysis in terms of the aggregates is that humans are composite. The precise nature of the best decomposition is of interest to psychology and to soteriological practitioners, but is at bottom, from the standpoint of the tradition, an empirical matter.[44]

This chapter is motivated by the natural suggestion that even if vision itself is empty, as was argued in the previous chapter, there must be a truly existent basis for vision in the person and his/her faculties. For the emptiness of vision was established in part by showing that perception depends upon the perceiver and the per-

44. That is not, of course, to say that it is arbitrary.

ceived. And that might seem to suggest that these bases—or at least the most essential one, the perceiver—truly exist. For then one could say that whereas vision itself is not inherently existent, it does exist as a relation between an inherently existent perceiver and an inherently existent object, or at least as a property of such a perceiver, even if there is truly no object.[45] Nāgārjuna aims to demonstrate the emptiness of all of the constituents of the person by taking form as an example and applying arguments that are general in scope. Form is taken as an example precisely because it is the most solid, apparently nonempty of the aggregates—the one that we are most likely to reify. So the program is to use arguments with application to any of the aggregates and to apply them to the hardest case. The conclusion Nāgārjuna is after is that no decomposition of the person will yield constituents that are themselves independent and nonempty.

1.   Apart from the cause of form,
       Form cannot be conceived.
       Apart from form,
       The cause of form is not seen.

Nāgārjuna begins by making use of the results of the first chapter. Nothing arises causelessly, and no cause is ineffectual. So if any form exists, it exists with a cause. And if the cause of any form exists, so does that form. But there is an interesting problem to be posed: How about form itself—matter considered in general, not in its specific instances? Does it have a cause or not? This question is important because it gets at the question of whether we can imagine ultimate ontological categories that exist independently. If form has a cause at all, it must be either the same or different from form. If the former, we have an infinite regress. If the latter, then we have the absurd conclusion that immaterial things can cause material things to come into

---

45. The reason for this second possibility is the possible presence of an idealist in the dialectical neighborhood, who might argue that even though neither seeing nor the seen inherently exists, both exist as illusions of the putative seer, who must exist, even if only as the subject of delusion.

existence. If it has no cause, then it cannot be said to exist at all.[46]

2.   If apart from the cause of form, there were form,
        Form would be without cause.
        But nowhere is there an effect
        Without a cause.

If form as such exists without any cause, we would have an example of an inherently existent category. But that would also violate the principle of dependent origination. That is, both Nāgārjuna and his opponent agree that all phenomena are dependently originated, and the discussion in the present chapter is in fact directed at figuring out just what material form depends on. So an attempt to posit material form as inherently existent on the grounds that it comes into existence causelessly is an ad hoc move that is unavailable to any participant in this debate.

Moreover, Nāgārjuna points out in the next verse, if we held form to be dependent upon a cause that was itself inherently existent, we would have an inherently existing cause without an inherently existing effect. That putative cause would, hence, fail to be a cause in the full sense. Between genuine causes and their effects there is a relation of dependence. For something to count as a cause independent of its producing an effect would be incoherent. But since in the context of inherent existence merely conventional existence counts as no existence at all, an inherently existent cause with a merely conventionally existent effect would count just as much as an ineffective cause. So neither can we make sense of an inherently existent cause of the existence of material form if material form is held not to be inherently existent.

46. We must understand "form" in this context to designate physical reality as a whole, including matter and energy. We can presume (bypassing hagiographic considerations) that Nāgārjuna was unaware of the relativistic understanding of the interchangeability of these two; but it is clear that, from the standpoint of "*skandha* theory," the operative contrast is between the physical and the nonphysical. (And here, given the antisubstantial metaphysics in play, "nonphysical" does not mean made of spook stuff.) Form is just whatever is succeptible of physical description and explanation. Many kinds of supervenience are compatible with the decomposition suggested by Buddhist psychology.

3.   If apart from form
       There were a cause of form,
       It would be a cause without an effect.
       But there are no causes without effects.

4.   When form exists,
       A cause of the arising of form is not tenable.
       When form is nonexistent,
       A cause of the arising of form is not tenable.

Any relationship between form and a putative cause is unintelligible, Nāgārjuna argues, following closely the reasoning in Chapter I. If form exists, the cause has ceased to exist. If form does not exist, the cause cannot have existed. This might seem at first glance to be a wholesale rejection of the possibility of dependency of effects on causal conditions. But if we recall the moral of Chapter I and keep the dialectical context of the current chapter firmly in mind we will see that this is not so: The paradox of causal contact arises—as Sextus also notes—only if we suppose that the causes we appeal to in explanation must have some special force by means of which they bring about their effects. That, as we have seen, is the view of the causal link as inherently existent and, hence, of causes as inherently existent. The opponent Nāgārjuna is attacking in this chapter is one who thinks that form/matter is inherently existent, but who has granted that all individual phenomena—all particular forms, such as human bodies, tables, and chairs—are dependently arisen. So the opponent agrees that all phenomena must be explicable. But the opponent wants to reify form, and that is to treat it as a phenomenon—albeit an inherently existent one. Therefore, it must, for the opponent, have an explanation of its existence, and since its existence is inherent existence, it must be an explanation in terms of inherently existent causation. So all that Nāgārjuna has to do is to remind the opponent of the incoherence of *that* notion in order to undermine the view that form as such is inherently existent. The coherence of conventional dependent origination is not at issue.

5.   Form itself without a cause
       Is not possible or tenable.

Therefore, think about form, but
Do not construct theories about form.

The moral of these arguments, Nāgārjuna concludes, is that we cannot think of form as such as an entity at all. Individual forms are entities—dependently arisen ones, hence, empty of inherent existence. But form itself is an abstraction, neither caused nor uncaused, but dependent upon the existence of material things with form. (Moreover, were one to argue that form itself exists as an entity, one would be faced with an uncomfortable dilemma: Its existence would be caused or uncaused. The latter alternative patently begs the question regarding the explanation of the existence of the material world. But the former issues in a further dilemma: The cause would either itself be material or immaterial. On the first horn, we have an infinite regress; on the second, the inexplicable causation of the material by the immaterial.)[47] So, he advises, think carefully about what form is and about the nature of particular material objects. But do not construct theories that purport to describe the essence of material form. For there is no such thing. It is simply a characteristic of individual material objects and, hence, something that depends upon their existence, with no essence of its own.

6.   The assertion that the effect and cause are similar
            Is not acceptable.
            The assertion that they are not similar
            Is also not acceptable.

We cannot say that nonmaterial things give rise to the existence of matter, for that would be an inexplicable miracle. Nor can we say that matter gives rise to matter, since that would beg the question. But there is no other possibility. So despite the reificationist's intuition that though individual material objects may be empty, the matter they are made of is nonempty, we see that we cannot even clearly conceive of the nature of matter as such independently of material objects. Matter, too, is hence dependent and empty of

47. See also Kalupahana (1986), p. 38, for a similar analysis.

inherent existence. Nāgārjuna immediately generalizes this to the other aggregates:

7. Feelings, discriminations and dispositions
    And consciousness and all such things
    Should be thought of
    In the same way as material form.

8. When an analysis is made through emptiness,
    If someone were to offer a reply,
    That reply will fail, since it will presuppose
    Exactly what is to be proven.

9. When an explanation is made through emptiness,
    Whoever would find fault with it
    Will find no fault, since the criticism will presuppose
    Exactly what is to be proven.

In these last two oft-quoted verses, Nāgārjuna claims that once a demonstration of the emptiness of a phenomenon or class of phenomena has been produced, any reply will inevitably beg the question. And this is meant to have been demonstrated by the argument in this chapter in the following way: Once we have shown something to be empty of inherent existence, we have, ipso facto, shown it to be dependently arisen and merely conventionally real. Anything an opponent would want to demonstrate to be inherently existent would fall prey to the causal paradoxes developed in this chapter. That is, he must either assume that the thing is completely independent and causeless, which is, upon analysis, exactly equivalent to the conclusion he is out to prove, or that it arises from another inherently existent phenomenon. But then in order to demonstrate that fact, he must demonstrate the inherent existence of that second phenomenon (as well as the inherent dependence relation between them—a kind of relation we have seen to be internally contradictory). And this is true no matter to which ontological category the putatively inherently existent phenomenon belongs.

That this is so should not be surprising, for the central thrust of Nāgārjuna's arguments thus far, and throughout *Mūlamadhyama-kakārikā,* is not that inherent existence is a property some things might have had but by global accident is uninstantiated or that emptiness just happens to characterize all phenomena. Rather he is arguing that inherent existence is simply an incoherent notion and that emptiness is the only possible analysis of existence. It would follow straightforwardly that arguments for inherent existence will be question begging.[48]

48. Kalupahana (1986), p. 145, sees a different question being begged. He writes:

> The argument in favor of dependence is experience. Hence, the person presenting a refutation of this idea should be in a position not only to negate "mutual dependence" but also to provide evidence for the establishment of a metaphysical substance (svabhāva). This has not yet been achieved. Thus, according to Nāgārjuna, what still remains to be proved is the thesis regarding "substance" rather than mutual dependence.

While this analysis is consistent with Kalupahana's interpretation of Nāgārjuna as a pragmatically inclined empiricist, I do not see it as an accurate rendering of the argument here. In particular, it ignores the emphasis on emptiness in these verses.

Chapter V

Examination of Elements

This chapter examines the ontological status of characteristics and the characterized, or in more familiar terms, properties and individuals. The question, as always, is this: Does it make sense to think of either as existing independently, substantially, or fundamentally? Or, on the other hand, are they mutually interdependent and therefore empty? The example Nāgārjuna chooses to focus on is space since it is one of the six primal elements according to classical Buddhist cosmology.[49] If he can show that these elements must be understood as neither inherently existing entities nor as inherently existing characteristics of entities, he will have shown that no ontological decomposition of phenomena into their primary constituents yields inherently existing constituents. Moreover, according to some early Buddhist schools, each of the primal elements has a distinguishing characteristic and, hence, an essence. So, Nāgārjuna is addressing his opponent on the opponent's home turf. If any entities or characteristics have essences, these do.

1.   Prior to a characteristic[50] of space
        There is not the slightest space.

49. The others are earth, water, fire, air, and consciousness.
50. The sense of "characteristic" (*mtsan nyid*) is that of a distinguishing characteristic, or a characteristic mark or signature of a thing. I therefore use the singular here. (I owe this suggestion to the Ven. Gareth Sparham.) But the points that Nāgārjuna makes are perfectly general and could as well be made using "characteristics," as Inada (1970) and Kalupahana (1986) do.

> If it arose prior to the characteristic
> Then it would, absurdly, arise without a characteristic.

Space cannot exist as a completely uncharacterized entity that then somehow acquires characteristics. Anything that exists has some properties and cannot be identified or characterized independently of them.

2.   A thing without a characteristic
       Has never existed.
       If nothing lacks a characteristic,
       Where do characteristics come to be?

So we can conclude that everything has characteristics. But maybe these characteristics exist inherently, independently of the things, and then come to be associated with them. On such a view, while individuals would not have inherent existence, properties would.

3.   Neither in the uncharacterized nor in the characterized
       Does a characteristic arise.
       Nor does it arise
       In something different from these two.

But there is a problem. If a characteristic were inherently existent, it would have to become instantiated in either a characterized or an uncharacterized object. But there are no uncharacterized objects, and if the object already is characterized, there is no need for the characteristic to become instantiated. So to think of individuals and properties as existing independently and then somehow coming together to constitute particulars makes no sense.

4.   If characteristics do not appear,
       Then it is not tenable to posit the characterized object.
       If the characterized object is not posited,
       There will be no characteristic either.

But if we were to go completely eliminativist with respect to characteristics, we would lose the ability to posit both actual objects with characteristics and characteristics that actual objects share.

5. From this it follows that there is no characterized
   And no existing characteristic.
   Nor is there any entity
   Other than the characterized and the characteristic.

In the first two lines of this verse, Nāgārjuna draws the conclusion that there are no inherently existent characteristics and no inherently existent characterized entities. Entities and their properties are mutually dependent and, hence, empty of inherent existence. But this does not mean, he emphasizes in the final two lines, that there is some other ontology of inherently existent basic types that could replace them. Indeed particulars can be thought of as characterized entities, with characteristics; but this does not entail the independent existence of entities of either of those types.

6. If there is no existent thing,
   Of what will there be nonexistence?
   Apart from existent and nonexistent things
   Who knows existence and nonexistence?

Here Nāgārjuna generalizes the conclusion and indicates its larger ontological implications. Having shown that there are no inherently existent things, it might seem that it follows that all things are inherently nonexistent. But existence and nonexistence, after all, are characteristics. So it follows that neither existence nor nonexistence can be said to exist independently and hence to characterize, inherently, anything. Moreover, since no particulars can be said inherently to exist, and thereby characterized as inherently existing things, none can be said to be inherently nonexistent. Existence and nonexistence are hence themselves dependent, relative characteristics. It is, of course, important to recall that this entire dialectic is aimed at nonrelative understandings of existence and nonexistence. Nāgārjuna is not arguing that nothing exists in any sense and that nothing fails to exist in any sense. Rather, he is arguing that nothing exists in virtue of instantiating an indepen-

dently existent property of existence. Similarly, things do not fail
to exist in virtue of instantiating the property nonexistence.

7.   Therefore, space is not an entity.
       It is not a nonentity.
       Not characterized, not without character.
       The same is true of the other five elements.

Nāgārjuna now returns to the example at hand to sum up the
conclusions of the chapter. Things cannot be analyzed ontologically as particulars existing independently of their properties. But
this does not mean that individual things do not exist. They do not
possess independently existing properties. But this does not mean
that things are all propertyless.

8.   Fools and reificationists who perceive
       The existence and nonexistence
       Of objects
       Do not see the pacification of objectification.

This is the soteriological import of this discussion of fundamental ontology: If one reifies phenomena—including such things as
one's own self, characteristics (prominently including one's own),
or external objects—and if one thinks that things either fail to exist
or exist absolutely, one will be unable to attain any peace. For one
will thereby be subject to egoism, the overvaluing of oneself and
one's achievements and of material things. One will not appreciate
the possibility of change, of the impermanence and nonsubstan-
tiality of oneself and one's possessions. These are the seeds of
grasping and craving and, hence, of suffering. The alternative,
Nāgārjuna suggests, and the path to pacification, is to see oneself
and other entities as non-substantial, impermanent, and subject to
change and not as appropriate objects of such passionate craving.

Chapter VI

Examination of Desire and the Desirous

This chapter represents a continuation of the discussion begun in the previous one. That is, while the chapter is nominally about desire, an example chosen for its obvious soteriological significance, it is in a larger sense a further discussion of the relation between entities and their properties, with specific attention to the relation between human beings and their psychological characteristics. Locating the discussion at this point is consonant with a tradition of Mahāyāna discussions of emptiness in which one first addresses external phenomena, which are both easier to analyze and less succeptible of reification than the self, and then generalizes the discussion to human psychological phenomena.[51] The chapter opens with an echo of the discussion of space:

1. If prior to desire
   And without desire there were a desirous one,
   Desire would depend on him.
   Desire would exist when there is a desirous one.

51. See, e.g., the *Heart Sūtra*, with its famous discussion of the emptiness of the aggregates that begins with form and then moves to the psychological aggregates.

One possibility for the relationship between the subject of desire and the desire is that the desirous one exists qua desirous one independently of the desire, which is then adventitious and dependent. That is, on this view the desirous one is inherently desirous, but the desire is merely dependent. This, however, is problematic, for then there is a real contrast in the mode of existence of the desirous one and the desire: The desirous one truly exists, but the desire does not truly exist. But if there is no real desire, in virtue of what is there a desirous one?

2.   Were there no desirous one, moreover,
      Where would desire occur?
      Whether or not desire or the desirous one exist,
      The analysis would be the same.

But if there is no desirous one, there is no ontological basis for the desire. So whether we posit an inherently existent desirous one or no desirous one at all, we cannot identify desire as existing. And, of course, this goes for any characteristic or psychological attribute and for any subject of any such attribute identified under any description. Moreover, the converse is also true: Whether or not we posit inherently existent desire, we cannot thereby establish the existence of a substantially existent desirous one. If the desire does not exist inherently but only dependently, that dependence in no way presupposes an independent basis. If on the other hand desire is posited as inherently existent, there would be no need for a basis in a desirous one at all. In neither case would the substantial existence of the entity in question (subject or attitude) have any import for the reality of the correlative entity (attitude or subject). And the reason for this is simply that inherent existence is not relational existence. Since desire and the desirous one must be understood as interrelated, they must be understood as mutually dependent.

3.   Desire and the desirous one
      Cannot arise together.
      In that case, desire and the desirous one
      Would not be mutually contingent.

Another possibility the opponent might suggest is this: Desire and the desirous one come into inherent existence at the same time. It is very important in following this argument to remember Nāgārjuna's dialectical task. The opponent against whom his reductios are aimed is one who attributes inherent existence either to the desirous one, to desire, or both. Nāgārjuna is only attempting to show that attributing to them that kind of existence is incoherent—not that there is no desire and that there are no desirous people at all. That would be crazy. Fundamental to the Buddhist conception of the predicament of human existence is the centrality of craving to the arising of suffering. But also fundamental is the conviction that there can be a release from craving. That is only possible, however, if craving is dependently originated since only then could the conditions that determine its arising be eliminated. So it is critically important from a Buddhist perspective to come to a complete understanding of the nature of desire, and the mode of its existence, and it would be inconceivable to deny its existence completely. But Nāgārjuna is emphasizing here that that understanding must reveal them as mutually dependent in order to avoid the absurd conclusion that either could exist without the other. That precludes the assertion that while they in fact always co-occur, that co-occurrence is not through interdependence, but through contingent simultaneity of independent phenomena.

Nāgārjuna's claim in VI: 3 is also the conclusion of the argument that is about to follow. It proceeds by means of a destructive dilemma. Given that the opponent must have desire and the desirous one arising simultaneously, they must be either identical or different. Nāgārjuna will show that neither alternative is coherent; VI: 4 spells out this strategy:

4.   In identity there is no simultaneity.
       A thing is not simultaneous with itself.
       But if there is difference,
       Then how would there be simultaneity?

In the first line of this verse, Nāgārjuna points out the relational character of simultaneity. If simultaneity is predicated, it must be predicated of two distinct things that arise at the same time. We don't say that a thing arises simultaneously with itself. But if things are completely distinct in nature, they cannot co-occur in the same place, that is, if desire and the desirous one had distinct essences, they could not be in the same place at the same time.

5.   If in identity there were simultaneity,
      Then it could occur without association.
      If in difference there were simultaneity,
      It could occur without association.

The first claim is meant to be a reductio on the view that simultaneous things can be identical. For suppose that there was an apparent pair of events whose simultaneity was in question, say William Clinton's uttering of the oath of office of the presidency and the inauguration of the first president from Arkansas. If there is every reason to believe that these events are distinct but occur at the same time, it is then appropriate to say that they are simultaneous. But if we know that there is in fact only one event, it is at best a joke to assert its simultaneity with itself. The proper thing to say then would be not that the oath taking was simultaneous with the inauguration but that it was identical to the inauguration. The term translated as "association" here (grogs-pa) can also mean friendship, or companionship—the idea is of something distinct but accompanying. For the inauguration and the oath taking to be associated would be for them to be, say, accompanying rituals that could in principle occur independently. But if they could occur independently, they cannot be identical. Simultaneity requires association of some kind. But identity is incompatible with association.

The second claim is meant to be a reductio on the view that simultaneous and associated things could be different in nature. Difference, like identity, is incompatible with association, though for a different reason. The kind of difference at issue here is essential difference. Nāgārjuna's claim is that things that are completely different from one another, that are completely independent, ipso facto, stand in no relation to one another and so are not associated. This is another application of the Humean (and Tractarian) argument Nāgārjuna has mobilized above: If phenomena are distinct—indeed, being simultaneous, they are not even argued to be causally related—they can be imagined to be separate. So they are then logically independent. But that would then entail that if desire and the desirous one were different in this strong sense, we could imagine a desirous one without desire, and vice versa. But that is of course absurd. So if desire and the desirous one are supposed to arise simultaneously, they can neither be identical nor different. Of course, since any inherently different entities, in virtue of having determinate natures, are either identical or different, it follows that desire or the desirous one are either nonsimultaneous or empty of inherent existence.

6. If in difference there were simultaneity,
   How could desire and the desirous one,
   Being different, be established?
   If they were, they would be simultaneous.

This last verse emphasizes and spells out the point scouted above: We are left with a hard choice once we conceive of desire and the desirous one as entities. If desire and the desirous one are conceived as substantially different but simultaneous, we would have to be able to establish the nature and existence of each independent of the other. That is no easy task. If we could accomplish it, simultaneity would be a satisfactory solution to the dilemma. But of course we cannot. Moreover, Nāgārjuna argues in the next verse, if they are completely different, we are left with the peculiar task of explaining why they always go together. And asserting their simultaneity forces this problem:

7. If desire and the desirous one
   Are established as different,
   Then why would you think
   That they are simultaneous?

8. Since difference is not established,
   If you assert that they are simultaneous,
   Since they are established as simultaneous,
   Do you also assert that they are different?

We have not established—nor could we—that desire and the desirous one are substantially different. But the opponent wishes to assert their simultaneity. Given the entailment of difference by simultaneity as per the argument above, this would force the opponent to assume the impossible burden of demonstrating this substantial difference.

The whole quandary is summed up in VI: 9. Since we can't establish their difference in entity, we can't establish the claim that desire and the desirous one arise as distinct, simultaneous phenomena. We don't even have two phenomena to serve as the relata of difference:

9.   Since nothing different has been established,
      If one is asserting simultaneity,
      Which different thing
      Do you want to say is simultaneous?

The conclusion, as stated in the special case in the preceding verse, is generalized in the final verse of the chapter. Once we think of entities and their properties—in particular, ourselves and our characteristics—as independently characterized things, we can make no sense of how they fit together temporally, logically, or ontologically. It is important that objects and their characteristics, persons and their states, be unified. But if we introduce essence and entity into our ontology, this will be impossible:

10.   Thus desire and the desirous one
      Cannot be established as simultaneous or not simultaneous.
      So, like desire, nothing whatever
      Can be established either as simultaneous or as
          nonsimultaneous.

As always, however, we must remind ourselves of the sense of the conclusion and of its dialectical context. There is no denial here of the possibility of simultaneity, of the existence of desire, or of the possibility of desirous persons. Rather, there is a denial that any of these things make sense in the context of inherent existence.

Chapter VII

Examination of the Conditioned

Having begun the text with an examination of the relation of dependency between phenomena, and having then conducted an analysis of the fundamental ontological constituents of reality, Nāgārjuna now brings these two analyses together in a long chapter investigating the nature of the world of conditioned things as a whole. The target position is the view that dependent arising itself, as well as dependently arisen things, are either inherently existent or completely nonexistent. There are really two positions here with which Nāgārjuna must contend: First, the reificationist opponent charges that even if we grant Nāgārjuna's earlier arguments for the conclusion that phenomena themselves are empty because they are dependently arisen, dependent arising itself must inherently exist. For only if phenomena are truly dependently arisen, one might argue, are they truly empty. Second, Nāgārjuna must answer the following objection: If dependent arising is empty, then arising, stasis, and cessation are nonexistent. Hence there are, in fact, no phenomena since phenomena are defined—particularly in a Buddhist context—as those things that arise, remain, and cease. But clearly there are actual empirical phenomena; indeed, such phenomena must exist for Nāgārjuna's claim that they are empty to make any sense at all. How can this be reconciled with the emptiness of dependent arising?

1.   If arising were produced[52]
        Then it would also have the three characteristics.
        If arising is not produced,
        How could the characteristics of the produced exist?

The three characteristics in question are arising, stasis, and cessation. On a standard Buddhist view, all phenomena come into being in dependence upon conditions, remain in existence dependent upon conditions, and cease to exist dependent upon conditions. This is the core of the two central doctrines of dependent arising and impermanence. Nāgārjuna here poses a problem: If dependent arising itself were produced by conditions, then it itself would have these three characteristics and, apparently paradoxically, be impermanent. This is prima facie paradoxical just because if dependent arising is impermanent, it would appear that sometimes things don't arise dependently, which contradicts the thesis that all phenomena are dependently arisen. Moreover, as Nāgārjuna will argue below, this assertion threatens a vicious regress—if arising arises, there must already be arising in virtue of which it does so.

But, Nāgārjuna asks in the third and fourth lines, if dependent arising is not produced, where did it come from? If one were to say that dependent arising were not produced and, hence, that it does not depend for its existence on anything else, this would appear to contradict the thesis that *everything* arises dependently. Dependent arising itself would then be the counterexample to the thesis.

2.   If the three, arising, etc., are separate,
        They cannot function as the characteristics of the produced.
        But how could they be joined
        In one thing simultaneously?

---

52. *"du byed."* This term is sometimes appropriately translated as "disposition," "action," or "compounded." Context is crucial in determining which rendering is best. In Buddhist metaphysics these meanings are closely connected. Kalupahana (1986) uses "conditioned," though he interprets this to mean "conditioned by dispositions." He argues that this chapter is closely connected to the previous chapter in that lust "is operative in the perceptual process especially in the formation of ideas derived from experience." He argues that this chapter is devoted to an examination of the way phenomena such as desire determine the formation of ideas from "the blooming, buzzing confusion" of sense experience (p. 159). I find this reading unsupported by the text.

These three characteristics, if they characterize the phenomenon of dependent arising itself, must either be present separately or together. This furnishes the basis of a destructive dilemma. If they are separate, then some parts of dependent arising have one of the three; some another. Some are arising; some abiding; some ceasing. But this is problematic since all phenomena are said to arise, to abide, and to cease.[53] So it would seem to be the case that if dependent arising itself has all three of these characteristics, it cannot have them separately, but must have them jointly and simultaneously.

But the three characteristics could not be present simultaneously since they are mutually contradictory. At any one point, dependent arising could have only one of them. The same thing cannot be—in the same sense, at the same time—arising and ceasing when these are understood in the sense at issue here, that introduced by the substantialist opponent. It is important in order to understand this argument to keep the dialectical context firmly in mind. The opponent throughout the text, whether on the nihilist side or on the reificationist side, considers existence to be inherent existence and predication to be the ascription of really existent properties to substantial bases. For the opponent Nāgārjuna has in mind here, dependent arising—if it is the nature of things at all—must inherently exist. It must therefore have the three characteristics inherently. To have a characteristic inherently is to have it essentially. But then dependent arising, for the opponent, would have a contradictory set of essential properties.

53. Moreover, one would not want to say that sometimes dependent arising is arising, sometimes abiding, sometimes ceasing. The whole Buddhist picture of impermanence is one according to which these processes are always co-occurring. But this dialectical move is not available to Nāgārjuna at this stage of the discussion. It would beg the question in a critical sense: The properties under analysis here, as well as dependent arising itself, are introduced by the opponent as candidates for inherent existence and as components of an analysis of the ultimate nature of phenomena. In the sense that they are deployed in a positive Buddhist account of the nature of conventional reality—the sense in which all phenomena are constantly arising in some sense, abiding through change in another, and ceasing in yet another—neither the phenomena to which these predicates are applied, nor the properties ascribed, are inherently existent. Quite the contrary; this is an analysis that is designed to demonstrate the lack of inherent existence of phenomena and their characteristics. It is important throughout the discussion that follows to bear in mind that Nāgārjuna is not subjecting this view to criticism, but its substantialist cousin.

3.   If arising, abiding, and ceasing
        Have characteristics other than those of the produced,
        There would be an infinite regress.
        If they don't, they would not be produced.

The other possibility is that dependent arising has some other characteristics—that is, characteristics other than those that all phenomena have in virtue of being dependently arisen. But we could then ask about the characteristics of those characteristics. Do those characteristics arise, abide, or perish? If so, the original regress has not been stopped. Another possibility is that arising, abiding, and perishing do not have characteristics at all. But if not, then they are not phenomena in any ordinary sense at all. While that would cut off the regress, it would do so without achieving any explanation, or any analysis of the kind originally sought, and would leave an uncomfortable paradox: We started seeking an understanding of dependent arising as inherently existent. But its inherent existence requires the inherent existence of arising, cessation, and stasis, all of which now come out to be ontologically sui generis. The further paradox is this: For dependent arising to exist inherently, these three should turn out to be essential properties of all phenomena. But on the alternative under consideration, they are not properties at all.

We might, of course, try to extend this horn of the dilemma by suggesting that although arising, abiding, and ceasing are not phenomena in the ordinary sense, they are characteristics of some special kind. We then seem to have a more curious regress; new ad hoc characteristics arise at each level of analysis. The regress here is an interesting one because its viciousness consists not in the same basis being required for each putatively basic posit, but in there being no principle available to determine a basis for any putative basic posit despite a principle that urges that there must be one. The point that Nāgārjuna is after, of course, is that this principle itself—that there must be an explanatory basis, an independent entity that has characteristics, as an explanation of the occurrence of any characteristic—is what generates the regress and must be rejected.

There is, of course, a third alternative. These three might neither have characteristics different from those possessed by ordinary phenomena nor have no characteristics at all: They might indeed have the very trio of characteristics that all ordinary phe-nomena have, namely, arising, abiding, and ceasing. It is this alter-native that occupies Nāgārjuna for the remainder of the chapter. This alternative is interesting dialectically in that, on the one hand, it represents the most natural way to approach an analysis of depen-dent arising, namely, by consistently predicating it of everything, hence suggesting that it is indeed a candidate for an essence of things. On the other hand, as we shall see, that very move pre-cludes treating it as a genuine essence since essences turn out to lack precisely the properties that we must universalize here.

4.   The arising of arising only gives rise
        To the basic arising.
        The arising of the basic arising
        Gives rise to arising.

This is the opponent speaking. He suggests that dependent aris-ing arises from a more basic arising. This basic arising comes to be, but not on the basis of anything else. The idea, defended by some earlier Buddhist schools, is this: There are two levels of dependent arising. The more superficial is the relationship of mutual depen-dence of all phenomena, issuing in their impermanence. But this interdependence, on this view, is itself dependently arisen. It de-pends on a basic arising—a mere fact of interdependent origina-tion, which gives rise to the more specific empirical relations we see. So in the first two lines of this verse, the opponent says that when arising itself is considered in isolation, all that we have is the basic arising. In the third and fourth lines, the opponent says that when that arising has arisen, it gives rise to the more superficial ordinary dependent arising. It is, then, that basic arising that is posited as ontologically foundational.

5.   If, as you say, the arising of arising
        Gives rise to the basic arising,
        How, according to you, does this,
        Not arisen from the basic arising, give rise to that?

But Nāgārjuna makes the obvious move in reply: Does the basic arising arise from a more basic arising, or is it somehow unarisen (eternal or inexplicable)? If the former, then we seem to have an infinite regress; if the latter, a petitio principii. Nāgārjuna makes some of the numerous difficulties that afflict this view explicit in the next two verses:

6.   If, as you say, that which is arisen from basic arising
      Gives rise to the basis,
      How does that nonarisen basis
      Give rise to it?

The account is either circular or regressive. If the basic arising is held to arise in dependence on other dependently originated phenomena, and dependent arising is explained as dependent upon the basic arising, then the basis is posited as dependent upon that which it explains, and we have a vicious circle. If on the other hand the phenomena on which the basis depends are other than those it explains, and the phenomena themselves depend upon yet another basis, we have a vicious regress.

In the next verse, Nāgārjuna points out the question-begging alternative reading of the enterprise. He notes that one may explain that dependent arising arises through basic arising without circles or regresses, but only by positing the basis as itself non-arisen. This, of course, flies in the face of the demand that motivates positing it in the first place—namely, the demand that every phenomenon, including dependent arising, be explained by some ontologically more fundamental phenomenon:

7.   If this nonarisen
      Could give rise to that,
      Then, as you wish,
      It will give rise to that which is arising.

The opponent now suggests another reply. Using the analogy of a lamp that illuminates both itself and others, he argues that arising can give rise to itself and to others. This would, from the standpoint of the reificationist, have the happy consequence that while other phenomena would be dependent on dependent arising, dependent arising would be independent and nonempty:

8.   Just as a butterlamp
        Illuminates itself as well as others,
        So arising gives rise to itself
        And to other arisen things.

Nāgārjuna now launches a lengthy critique of the example, arguing that the relation between the butterlamp and what it illuminates is not one that supports a notion of an inherently existent
basis on which things that are not inherently existent can depend:

9.   In the butterlamp and its place,
        There is no darkness.
        What then does the butterlamp illuminate?
        For illumination is the clearing of darkness.

Here Nāgārjuna is emphasizing a disanalogy between the relation between the butterlamp and what it illuminates, and the putative relation between dependent arising and what it depends upon.
The opponent who wields the example does so in order to demonstrate a difference in status between dependent arising and the
dependently arisen. Dependent arising is meant not to be dependently arisen, despite the fact that all dependently arisen phenomena are. So the appropriate analogy in the case of the lamp would
map this difference in status between being dependently arisen and
being independent onto the difference between being illuminated
and not being illuminated. The problem, though, is that in the
example there is nothing that is not illuminated: Everything in the
neighborhood of the lamp is illuminated just as is the lamp.

It was standard philosophical fare in the Buddhist tradition
within which Nāgārjuna was working to see darkness as a positive
phenomenon. So to the extent that one adopted a reified ontology,
darkness would be reified as easily as light. The attack on the
butterlamp analogy can thus effectively exploit the difficulties
Nāgārjuna has already developed for theories that require inherently existent things to be related to one another. But it is important to see that even if one is not disposed to reify darkness, and
regards it as the mere absence of light, to the extent that one reifies
light, Nāgārjuna can argue that one will be compelled to reify

darkness as well. For if light exists inherently, then wherever light is not present it is essentially not present. And the essential nonpresence of light is essential darkness.

10.   If the arising butterlamp
        Does not reach darkness,
        How could that arising butterlamp
        Have cleared the darkness?

Moreover, argues Nāgārjuna, the example itself does not bear close scrutiny as a case of an entity with some inherent power giving rise to a set of effects that depend upon it. For the task of the butterlamp is the clearing of darkness—or the production of illumination. Now the production of light and the clearing of darkness are, Nāgārjuna claims, equivalent. So, if the butterlamp illuminates objects by its light reaching them, it should clear darkness by means of its light reaching darkness. But that would be for light and darkness to be present in the same place, which is contradictory.

11.   If the illumination of darkness occurs
        Without the butterlamp reaching darkness,
        All of the darkness in the world
        Should be illuminated.

If it is not necessary, on the other hand, for the light of the butterlamp to reach darkness in order to dispel it, since there is a lot of darkness in the world not reached by any single butterlamp, that butterlamp should be capable of dispelling all of that darkness.

12.   If, when it is illuminated,
        The butterlamp illuminates itself and others,
        Darkness should, without a doubt,
        Conceal itself and others.

Finally, Nāgārjuna argues, if we are seriously to maintain that the butterlamp illuminates itself and others through a luminous essence, then since the essence of darkness is to conceal things, and things with such essences affect themselves and others, we should expect darkness to be self-concealing. But then we would not see darkness.

The point of all of this is not that we can't see lamps when they are lit or that we can when they aren't. Rather it is that the mechanism by which we see what we see when a lamp is lit is the same whether we are seeing the lamp or other things. To put it in contemporary terms, photons reach our eyes from the lamp or from its flame in the same way they do from the other physical objects in the neighborhood. And just as the visibility of the things in the neighborhood is dependent on a host of conditions, so is the visibility of the lamp. So we do not have even an analogy to a case where the status of dependent arising would be distinct from that of the dependently arisen.

13.   How could this arising, being nonarisen,
       Give rise to itself?
       And if it is arisen from another,
       Having arisen, what is the need for another arising?

Here Nāgārjuna is bringing us back to the original argument and reminding us of the reificationist's uncomfortable choice between a vicious regress and a begged question. If every arisen thing depends on an ontologically prior arising, we have an infinite regress. For each arising will require such a foundation. But if we cut off the regress by presupposing at some level a nonarisen dependent arising, we have to ask why *that* level is exempt from the need for explanation. Nāgārjuna now announces the conclusion he will defend in the next section of the chapter:

14.   The arisen, the non-arisen and that which is arising
       Do not arise in any way at all.
       Thus they should be understood
       Just like the gone, the not-gone, and the going.

Recall the analysis of motion: Nāgārjuna argued that no entity answering to "motion" could be found in an entity that was in motion in the past, nor in an entity yet to move, nor in a currently moving entity. Motion had to be understood relationally and not as an entity. Using similar reasoning, Nāgārjuna will now argue that arising cannot be found as an entity in something not yet arisen, nor in something that has already arisen, nor in something yet to arise. Arising will also fail to be an entity and will have to be understood relationally. This will provide the key both to the refutation of the position that underlies both extreme positions—that for arising to exist, it must exist inherently—and to the construction of a coherent positive account of dependent arising. The next three verses begin a sketch of dependent arising as empty, connecting this fact with the emptiness of dependently arisen phenomena:

15.   When there is arising but not yet
        That which is arising,
        How can we say that that which is arising
        Depends on this arising?

Nāgārjuna here suggests that the way the reificationist has gone about posing the philosophical problem about the status of dependent arising itself is all wrong. The initial presumption at the basis of this debate is that arisen entities arise from an independently existing process of dependent arising. But this is wrongheaded in at least two ways: First, phenomena arise from other phenomena, not from arising. So, for instance, if I strike a match, the fire emerges from the friction, the sulphur, the oxygen, my desire for light, and so forth, but *not* from dependent arising itself. That is a fact at a different level of analysis, which itself comprises the network of relationships just indicated. Second, if the existence of the process of arising antedates the existence of the arisen, it cannot be a sufficient condition or a complete explanation of the arisen. For if it were, the arisen would then exist. That being so, Nāgārjuna asks, "Why posit dependent arising itself as a phenomenon within the framework of dependent arising?"

16.   Whatever is dependently arisen,
        Such a thing is essentially peaceful.
        Therefore that which is arising and arising itself
        Are themselves peaceful.

The sense of "peaceful" (*zhi-ba*) here is important. Nāgārjuna is asserting that things are not, from the ultimate point of view, in the constant flux of arising, remaining, and decaying that characterizes them from the conventional point of view. This will be the conclusion of the extended argument that follows and is here merely announced in advance. But it is important at this stage to be clear about just what Nāgārjuna is asserting for it is indeed a delicate point: It is true that ordinarily and prereflectively, and sometimes as the result of bad philosophy, we tend to think of things as permanent and as having fixed essential natures. But a careful reflection on the nature of conventional phenomena shows them on analysis to be impermanent and, hence, to be characterized by the three properties of arising, stasis, and cessation.[54]

But while this takes us to a deeper understanding of the nature of phenomena, it does not take us all the way. For phenomena, having no essence, cannot have even these properties essentially. One way of seeing that is this: If we take the import of the three-fold nature of phenomena seriously, we see that the phenomena are themselves literally momentary. And if they are momentary, then there is literally no time for them to arise, to endure, or to decay. So from an ultimate point of view, the point of view from which they have no existence as extended phenomena at all, they do not possess these three properties. Hence no single real entity is in flux. In this sense they are peaceful. Nāgārjuna points out the other way of seeing phenomena in the next verse: It does not follow from the fact that there are no inherently existent arisen entities that there are non-arisen ones. All phenomena are arisen, but they arise as empty, and as dependent. Coming to be just is arising, and all arising is dependent arising.

Nāgārjuna now turns his attention to an analysis of the three characteristics of arising, stasis, and cessation, showing of each in turn that it cannot be understood as ontologically independent. He begins with arising:

17.   If a nonarisen entity
        Anywhere exists,
        That entity would have to arise.
        But if it were nonexistent, what could arise?

---

54. Such remarks also make it hard to sustain the nihilistic reading of the text Wood (1994) offers. For here Nāgārjuna is clearly committed to the claim that there are dependently arisen phenomena.

We can exclude nonarisen entities from the analysis since the only sense that we can make of the existence of any phenomenon is in terms of its having arisen. Arising is hence a ubiquitous characteristic of phenomena. This, of course, is part of what motivates treating it, as well as stasis and cessation, as inherently existent.

18.   If this arising
    Gave rise to that which is arising,
    By means of what arising
    Does that arising arise?

If we take arisen things to require ontological grounds, then ground them not in other arisen things (since that would generate an obvious regress within the phenomenal world), but in dependent arising itself, there remains the infinite regress to which Nāgārjuna alluded earlier. Assuming dependent arising is to be the ground, then if grounds are needed, it too needs a ground. Nāgārjuna makes this explicit in the following verse:

19.   If another arising gives rise to this one,
    There would be an infinite regress.
    If something nonarisen is arisen,
    Then all things could arise in this way.

The last two lines of this verse emphasize that the regress cannot ever be cut off by positing some nonarisen arising. That would, as Nāgārjuna argued above, patently beg the question.

20.   Neither an existent nor a nonexistent
    Can be properly said to arise.
    As it is taught before with
    "For neither an existent nor a nonexistent."

The reference of the last line is to I: 6:

    For neither an existent nor a nonexistent thing
    Is a condition appropriate.
    If a thing is nonexistent, how could it have a condition?
    If a thing is already existent, what would a condition do?

The implicit argument is, then, that inherently existent phenomena cannot be said to arise since they would exist eternally and independently; nonexistent phenomena cannot be said to arise since if they did, they would exist. Arising can hence only be a property of noninherently, but conventionally, existent phenomena. But it then follows that arising as a property can only be a noninherently existent, conventional property.

Nāgārjuna now turns his attention to the properties of cessation and endurance. He begins, though, with a final remark on arising as a transition, concerning the relation between arising and cessation. This next verse must be read along with VII: 23 and 26. Together they constitute an exhaustive discussion of the possible inherence of the three properties under discussion in ceasing entities:

21. The arising of a ceasing thing
    Is not tenable.
    But to say that it is not ceasing
    Is not tenable for anything.

The first alternative Nāgārjuna considers is that a ceasing thing is arising. But if a thing is already ceasing, it is therefore no longer arising. And since all phenomena are, when their impermanence is taken into consideration, ceasing, it would follow that nothing can be said to be arising.

22. A static existent does not endure.[55]
    A nonstatic existent does not endure.
    Stasis does not endure.
    What nonarisen can endure?

55. To translate the Tibetan *"gnas-pa,"* I have used "stasis (static)" as a noun form, "to endure" as a verb (and sometimes "to abide" to emphasize, where context makes it appropriate, the dynamic character of this process). One should bear in mind that these diverse English terms do not mark diverse Tibetan (or Sanskrit) terms in the original. I have tried to be consistent in preserving the connotations that are important in each context and to render the text in as smooth English as possible. This precludes the otherwise desirable lexical uniformity one would achieve by using one of these terms throughout.

Nāgārjuna now turns to stasis—the moment between arising and ceasing. This verse must be read along with VII: 23, 25, and 27, which together provide a complete examination of the status of stasis. Here he emphasizes that the moment between the arising and ceasing of a momentary phenomenon—an event— has no temporal extent. So a thing that we might conventionally refer to as static literally does not endure with identity through time. But of course neither does something that is not even conventionally static. And finally, since as a consequence of these two premises stasis is not instantiated in any phenomenon, it itself does not endure. So, Nāgārjuna concludes, stasis fails to exist over time in any sense and so is no candidate for an inherently existent phenomenon.

23.   The endurance of a ceasing entity
       Is not tenable.
       But to say that it is not ceasing
       Is not tenable for anything.

This verse plays a central role in each of two interwoven arguments. In the context of VII: 21 and 26, it provides part of the exhaustive analysis of the impossibility of arising, abiding and ceasing as instantiated in ceasing (hence in impermanent) phenomena. In the context of VII: 22, 25, and 27, it provides part of the analysis of the impossibility of locating endurance in any phenomenon, hence emphasizing the impermanence of all phenomena. Since to exist is to exist in time and things that are ceasing are by definition not in a state of continued existence, ceasing phenomena do not provide the kind of continuity with numerical identity that endurance demands. And all phenomena are, upon analysis, seen to be constantly ceasing. So endurance has no possibility of instantiation, and ceasing phenomena cannot have this property as an essential attribute.

24.   Inasmuch as the nature of all things
       Is aging and death,
       Without aging and death,
       What existents can endure?

Moreover, since all things decay, this analysis is perfectly general. Nothing exists in the way that it would have to in order to have endurance as part of its essence.

25.   Stasis cannot endure through itself
     Or through another stasis.
     Just as arising cannot arise from itself
     Or from another arising.

This verse recalls the discussion of VII: 13–19 and has an important echo in VII: 32. Nāgārjuna argued earlier that we cannot analyze arising either as sui generis or as dependent upon some other arising. In the first case, we beg the question; in the second we invite an infinite regress. He now points out that the same is true of stasis. We can't, in order to demonstrate the inherent existence of stasis, argue that it endures because of itself. If this kind of reflexive explanation were possible, we would not need to posit stasis in the first place as an explanation of the continued existence of empirical phenomena. Each could count as self-explanatory. But if we say that stasis, like other static things, is static because of its possessing a distinct stasis, we are off on a vicious regress.

26.   The ceasing of what has ceased does not happen.
     What has not yet ceased does not cease.
     Nor does that which is ceasing.
     What nonarisen can cease?

Nāgārjuna thus completes the tripartite argument for the impossibility of the instantiation of arising, abiding, and ceasing begun in VII: 21 and 23. Cessation, conceived of as an inherently existent, independent property, needs a substratum. We have seen in the previous two verses in this argument that neither arising nor static things can provide this substratum. The only alternative remaining is the ceasing. But these phenomena, passing out of existence, are by definition not inherently existent and so fail as candidates. And again, since all phenomena are ceasing, this means that ceasing as an independent property has no basis. The argument here is an obvious echo of the argument against the inherent existence of motion. So the conclusion to draw is not that there is no cessation or that there are no ceasing phenomena. That would be crazy. Rather, neither cessation nor any impermanent phenomenon can be identified independently as an entity itself. Their existence is purely relational. Nāgārjuna now turns to the cessation of the static:

27.   The cessation of what is static
        Is not tenable.
        Nor is the cessation of
        Something not static tenable.

Two points are being made here: First, if there were intrinsically real entities that could serve as ontological bases for cessation, they would have to have either remained stable or not. If the former, then in virtue of having the nature of stasis, they would be incapable of cessation. If the latter, since they never really existed, there is nothing to cease. But there is also a second point being made that depends upon the conventional reality of cessation. Since cessation is conventionally real and is incompatible both with inherently existent stasis and with there being no stasis at all, both of these alternatives with respect to stasis are eliminated. Cessation and stasis must be understood relatively and not absolutely. This point is reiterated in the following verse:

28.   Being static does not cease
        Through being static itself.
        Nor does being static cease
        Through another instance of being static.

This verse also echoes VII: 25 and that discussion of the impossibility of arising being either self-explanatory or always explained by reference to yet another arising. All things, having remained momentarily in existence, change constantly. This, however, cannot be explained by reference to the nature of stasis, either reflexively or regressively.

29.   When the arising of any entity
        Is not tenable,
        Then the cessation of any entity
        Is not tenable.

Since nothing arises inherently, nothing ceases inherently. Since upon careful examination nothing withstands analysis as an inherently existing phenomenon, nothing remains independent of conventional designation to be characterized as arising or ceasing. This is how it goes from the ultimate standpoint. From that standpoint—though achieved by noting the universality of arising and cessation of conventional phenomena—since there are no phenomena, there is no arising and cessation. But by contraposition we get the corelativity and mutual entailment of arising and ceasing at the conventional level.

30.   For an existent thing
        Cessation is not tenable.
        A single thing being an entity and
        A nonentity is not tenable.

This verse and the next reinforce the point about the ultimate nonexistence of cessation and, by implication, of arising and stasis. In the preceding, Nāgārjuna emphasizes that for an inherently existent entity to cease to exist would be for it to inherently exist and not exist. In the subsequent verse, he points out that it makes no sense for a nonexistent thing to cease to be, just as it makes no sense to behead someone a second time:

31.   Moreover, for a nonentity,
        Cessation would be untenable.
        Just as a second beheading
        Cannot be performed.

32.   Cessation does not cease by means of itself.
        Nor does it cease by means of another.
        Just as arising cannot arise from itself
        Or from another arising.

This verse has an exact parallel in VII: 25. Again, Nāgārjuna recalls the uncomfortable choice between a trivially begged question and a vicious regress presented originally in the context of the discussion of arising and recalled in the discussion of stasis. The argument applies, mutatis mutandis, to cessation. The conclusion of this trio of arguments is that we cannot conceive of any of the three characteristics of dependent arising as self-grounded. All must be understood dependently and hence as empty.

33.   Since arising, ceasing, and abiding
       Are not established, there are no compounded things.
       If all compounded things are unestablished,
       How could the uncompounded be established?

That is, arising, abiding, and ceasing are not entities at all—they are mere relations. Since these fundamental attributes of dependently arisen phenomena are empty of inherent existence, what could have inherent existence?

34.   Like a dream, like an illusion,
       Like a city of Gandharvas,
       So have arising, abiding,
       And ceasing been explained.

This chapter thus brings the first principal section of *Mūlamadhyamakakārikā* to a close, drawing together the threads spun in the earlier chapters to produce a thorough demonstration of the emptiness of the conventional phenomenal world. Having demonstrated the emptiness of conditions and their relations to their effects, change and impermanence, the elements, the aggregates,[56] and characteristics and their bases—in short, of all the fundamental Buddhist categories of analysis and explanation—Nāgārjuna has now considered the totality they determine—dependent arising itself and the entire dependently arisen phenomenal world—

---

56. Sometimes translated as "heaps," or "collections." These are the groups of more basic phenomena into which complex phenomena such as persons are decomposed in analysis. The decomposition is in principle bottomless—bundles of bundles of bundles. . . . See Chapters III and IV.

arguing that dependent arising and what is dependently arisen are themselves empty of inherent existence. This is a deep result. It again presages the doctrine of the emptiness of emptiness that is made explicit in Chapter XXIV, and it develops further the theme explored in Chapter I, namely, that when from the Mādhyamika perspective one asserts that a thing is empty or that it is dependently arisen, one is not contrasting their status with the status of some other things that are inherently existent. Nor is one asserting that they are *merely* dependent on some more fundamental independent thing. Nor is one asserting that instead of having an independent essence things have as their essence dependence or emptiness, either or both of which exist in some other way. Rather, as far as one analyzes, one finds only dependence, relativity, and emptiness, and their dependence, relativity, and emptiness.

But this is not to say either that emptiness, dependent arising or conventional phenomena are nonexistent—that they are hallucinations. Indeed it is to say the opposite. For the upshot of this critical analysis is that existence itself must be reconceived. What is said to be "like a dream, like an illusion" is their existence in the mode in which they are ordinarily perceived/conceived—as inherently existent. Inherent existence simply is an incoherent notion.[57] The only sense that "existence" can be given is a conventional, relative sense. And in demonstrating that phenomena have exactly that kind of existence and that dependent arising has exactly that kind of existence, we recover the existence of phenomenal reality in the context of emptiness. In the next major section, comprising Chapters VIII through XIII, Nāgārjuna addresses the emptiness of the subject of experience.

---

57. Compare Wood (1994), who misses the structure of this simile. The respect in which dependently arisen things are like a dream is this: They exist in one way (as empty) and appear to exist in another (as inherently existent). Just as dreams and mirages exist in one way (as illusions) and appear to exist in another (as objects of perception, or as water). But dreams and mirages are real dreams and mirages. So this verse should not be interpreted as asserting the complete nonexistence of all phenomena.

Chapter VIII

Examination of the Agent and Action

The discussion of external phenomena comprised by the first seven chapters of the text leads naturally to a discussion of the subject side of experience, a discussion that occupies the next six chapters. For it might be granted that the phenomenal external world is empty, but argued that it depends for its nominal existence on an inherently existing subject. This idealist tactic, familiar in the West through Berkeley and Hume (and criticized by Kant in the refutation of idealism), was adopted by some (the Cittamātra school) in the history of Buddhist philosophy. We can well imagine an opponent at this stage in the dialectic conceding to Nāgārjuna that external phenomena lack inherent existence and that the dependent arising that characterizes them lacks inherent existence, but that their very emptiness entails their nominal character and, hence, some subject capable of engaging in nominal imputation. So the subject as agent must exist.

1. This existent agent
   Does not perform an existent action.
   Nor does some nonexistent agent
   Perform some nonexistent action.

Nāgārjuna here announces that, with respect to agency and action as well, he will steer a middle course between inherent existence and complete nonexistence. Neither action nor agent will come out to be an inherently existing entity. Nor will either end up being completely nonexistent.

2.   An existent entity has no activity.
     There would also be action without an agent.
     An existent entity has no activity.
     There would also be agent without action.

If the agent were inherently existent, then it would be unchanging. Activity is always a kind of change. So if there were action in the context of an inherently existing agent, the action would be agentless, which would be absurd. Moreover, the agent would be inactive, which would also be absurd. This, of course, is just one more case of Nāgārjuna demonstrating the incoherence of a position that tries both to posit inherently existent, independent entities and then to get them to interact.

3.   If a nonexistent agent
     Were to perform a nonexistent action,
     Then the action would be without a cause
     And the agent would be without a cause.

However, if agent and action are totally nonexistent, there will be no cause for the action and no justification for calling the agent an agent.

4.   Without a cause, the effect and
     Its cause will not occur.
     Without this, activity and
     Agent and action are not possible.

Agent, the agent's activity, and the action all depend upon conditions. They are all, therefore, dependently arisen and empty. If, as the opponent would have it, these are inherently existent, there would be no action. But if we think of them as dependent, we can make perfectly good sense of agent, activity and action in interrelation.

5.   If activity, etc., are not possible,
          Entities and nonentities are not possible.
          If there are neither entities nor nonentities,
          Effects cannot arise from them.

If there were no action, then since entities arise from the action of previous events, there would be no entities and no effects. In short, without making sense of the possibility of actions and agency as empty, we can't account for the existence of any phenomena.

6.   If there are no effects, liberation and
          Paths to higher realms will not exist.
          So all of activity
          Would be without purpose.

And all of this has a moral and a soteriological dimension as well. For if there are no acts and no effects, then the practice of morality and of the Buddhist path will make no sense. There would be no point to life if human action is impossible. And again, its impossibility follows straightforwardly from the reification of either agent or action. It is ironic that it is the urge to guarantee more reality and significance for ourselves than emptiness appears to allow that leads to a view of life as perfectly impossible and pointless. That is, though we are led to ascribe inherent, independent existence to ourselves and to the world of phenomena we cherish—in part, in order to assign them the greatest possible importance—this very importance would be completely undermined by such inherent existence and independence. For in that case, all activity and all consequences of activity would be impossible. The resultant life would be static, detached, and utterly meaningless. Only in the context of emptiness—what might appear to be the greatest threat to meaningfulness—can a meaningful life be understood.

7.   An existent and nonexistent agent
          Does not perform an existent and nonexistent action.
          Existence and nonexistence cannot pertain to the same thing.
          For how could they exist together?

There is no way to escape from this dilemma by trying to have it both ways: The agent cannot be existent as an actor, but nonexistent as one who undergoes the action. Nor can the action be existent as an entity, but nonexistent as dependent upon the agent.

8. An actual agent
    Does not perform a nonactual action.
    Nor by a nonactual one is an actual one performed.
    From this, all of those errors would follow.

Nor is it coherent to suppose that the agent is existent, but the action nonexistent. For then there would be no reason to call the agent an agent. An agent, after all, is someone who performs an action. The next two verses put this point and those made in the opening verses together:

9. An existent agent
    Does not perform an action that
    Is unreal or both real and unreal
    As we have already agreed.

10. A nonexistent agent
    Does not perform an action that
    Is unreal or both real and unreal
    As we have already agreed.

11. An existent and nonexistent agent
    does not perform an action that
    Is unreal or both real and unreal
    As we have agreed.

Nāgārjuna now moves to assert his positive position on this matter: Agent and action are interdependent. Neither is logically or ontologically prior to or independent of the other. What it is to be an agent is to be performing an action. What it is to be an action is to be the action of an agent:

12. Action depends upon the agent.
    The agent itself depends on action.
    One cannot see any way
    To establish them differently.

13.   From this elimination of agent and action,
           One should elucidate appropriation in the same way.
           Through action and agent
           All remaining things should be understood.

By "appropriation," Nāgārjuna indicates any cognitive act by means of which one takes an attribute or entity as one's own, or as part of one's self. That includes the grasping of the aggregates as the self or of one's mental states as part of one's identity or of one's possessions as central to one's being. Appropriation in this broad sense is, hence, a central object of concern for Buddhist philosophy and psychology, and the relation between the appropriator and the act of appropriation is an important object of analysis. For in many ways the self that is constructed through appropriation presents itself as the subject of appropriation. But it is merely constructed, and its substantial reality is illusory. Then what indeed does the appropriation? And where there is no appropriator, how does appropriation occur? Nāgārjuna here suggests that this account of the relation between agent and action provides a model for understanding that relation. That is, this analysis provides a perfect paradigm for understanding the nature of subjectivity. In all cases of the relation between an agent of any kind and an act of any kind, the identity of the two will be seen to be mutually dependent, and each will come out as conventionally real, though not as inherently existent. We will see this paradigm articulated over the next five chapters as Nāgārjuna argues that we cannot make any sense of the self as an entity independent of its actions, perceptions, and interactions. Nor can we make any sense of the ontology of these phenomena as independent of the subject. This is a natural extension of the analysis of emptiness of the external world and demonstrates Nāgārjuna's determination to treat all phenomena on the same basis.

Chapter IX

Examination of the Prior Entity

Now one can surely imagine an opponent responding to the argument of the previous chapter by granting that agency and its corelative phenomena might be empty, yet still denying that awareness itself—the subjectivity that grounds perception—could be empty. For, one might argue, the emptiness of all phenomena still requires that there be a subject for whom they *are* phenomena. Nāgārjuna articulates this response in the opening verses of this chapter:

1.　Since sight and hearing, etc., and
　　Feeling, etc., exist,
　　He who has and uses them
　　Must exist prior to those, some say.

2.　If there were no existent thing,
　　How could seeing, etc., arise?
　　It follows from this that prior to this,
　　there is an existent thing.

That is, without a subject of experience, there can be no experience and no experienced objects. This argument has familiar instances in Descartes and Kant. But Nāgārjuna, siding with Hume on this issue, begins by asking how this entity could be an object of knowledge:

3.   How is an entity existing prior to
       Seeing, hearing, etc., and
       The felt, etc.,
       Itself known?

So first, Nāgārjuna points out, we have no direct evidence for the existence of such an entity because evidence of it would require that it could be an object, but is supposed by its proponent to be purely subjective. Moreover, Nāgārjuna points out, it is supposed to be independent of and ontologically prior to perception and the perceived. So:

4.   If it can abide
       Without the seen, etc.,
       Then, without a doubt,
       They can abide without it.

That is, independence is a two-way street. If the self is independent of its perceiving and perception, then its perceiving and perception are independent of it. Now there is one reading of this claim on which it is straightforwardly and foolishly fallacious. Nāgārjuna is *not* arguing that all relations are symmetric. It does not follow from the fact that this book is on your table that your table is on the book, and Nāgārjuna is not foolish enough to think that it does. The point is, rather, once again the Humean one that whatever is indeed logically independent is separable. The opponent wants to argue that the self is logically independent of its perceptions and their contents. But if so, then they are separable, and we can imagine not only a nonperceiving subject, but also unperceived perceptions. Just as we can imagine a clear table and a book not on a table. But, Nāgārjuna suggests, the idea of unperceived perceptions is both absurd on its face and contradictory to the opponent's theoretical framework.

5.   Someone is disclosed by something.
       Something is disclosed by someone.[58]

---

58. The Sanskrit strongly suggests that the "someone" is to be understood as the appropriator (in the sense discussed in the previous chapter) and that the "something" is to be understood as the appropriated object. Later commentators (e.g.,

Without something how can someone exist?
Without someone how can something exist?

Nāgārjuna here emphasizes the corelativity and interdependence of subject and object.[59] Subjectivity only emerges when there is an object of awareness. Pure subjectivity is a contradiction in adjecto. Moreover, the idea of an object with no subject is contradictory. The very concept of being an object is that of being the object of a subject. The affinities to Kant and Schopenhauer here are quite strong, but should not be pushed too far. Nāgārjuna would clearly have no truck with the substantialist flavor of their analysis of the subject and object.

6.   While prior to all of seeing, etc.,
      That prior entity doesn't exist,
      Through seeing, etc., by another one,
      That other one becomes disclosed.

An opponent might at this point argue that although there is no continuous prior entity that endures through time and stands behind all perception, we must posit an entity as the basis of each individual perceptual episode. The self on this model would be a succession of momentary but inherently existent subjects of moments of experience. But, Nāgārjuna argues in the next verse, the same argument against positing a single prior entity can be mobilized against each punctal prior entity:

7.   If prior to all of seeing, etc.,
      No prior entity exists,

Candrakīrti and Tsong Khapa see esp. pp. 210–11) generally treat the verse this way. This would be a reminder that perception is a special case of appropriation. (I thank the Ven. Gareth Sparham for pointing this out.)

59. But not their identity. Though subject and object as well as internal and external objects are, for Nāgārjuna, all ultimately empty and, in important senses, interdependent, they are not identical. Physical objects are, as Kant would emphasize, empirically external to the mind in a way that pains are not; and the conventional perceiver is not one with the perceived. When I see an elephant, it is not, thereby, the case that I have a trunk!

> How could an entity prior
> To each seeing exist?

That is, given that there is no need to identify an independent self as the basis of all seeing, there is no need to establish one as a basis for each one independently. The same arguments for the relativity and relational character of perception apply, mutatis mutandis, for each perceptual episode. Moreover, even if we did posit such entities, they would get us nowhere toward positing the self that the reifier of self really cares about—a continuous self with which we can really identity and whose fate we can care about.

8.   If the seer itself is the hearer itself,
        And the feeler itself, at different times,
        Prior to each of these he would have to arise.
        But this makes no sense.

Moreover, since this proposal is for a distinct prior entity for each perceptual episode, we would need distinct subjects for, for example, hearing and seeing. But as we can do these things at the same time, it would follow that there are multiple simultaneous selves. The unity of experience that is the putative explanandum and motivation for positing this entity in the first place (emphasized in the first two lines) would dissolve. Nāgārjuna emphasizes this conclusion at IX: 9:

9.   If the seer itself is distinct,
        The hearer is distinct and the feeler is distinct,
        Then when there is a seer there would also be a hearer,
        And there would have to be many selves.

10.   Seeing and hearing, etc.,
        And feeling, etc.,
        And that from which these are arisen:
        There is no existent there.

However, one should not be tempted to try to ground perception, the perceived object, and the perceiver in some more fundamental ontological ground—some intrinsically identical basis for their existence. For the need to develop a substantial foundation for these phenomena should vanish once one sees that not only do they have no ultimate ontic status, but that they need none. They, like all phenomena, emerge relationally and dependently.

11.   Seeing and hearing, etc.,
        And feeling, etc.,
        If that to which they belong does not exist,
        They themselves do not exist.

Not only has this analysis refuted the inherent existence of the self as a basis for experience, but in virtue of so doing, it has refuted the inherent existence of perception and the perceptual faculties.

12.   For whomever prior to,
        Simultaneous with, or after seeing, etc., there is nothing,
        For such a one, assertions like "it exists" or "it does not
            exist"—
        Such conceptions will cease.

Nāgārjuna here generalizes the point and offers a diagnosis of the confusion he has worked to resolve: Just as we want to say that the self as pure subject does not exist—nor do perception or perceptual objects exist as entities—yet want to affirm the conventional reality of perception, perceivers, and perceiveds, in general, we want to deny the inherent existence of phenomena and affirm their conventional reality. Just as we want to say that the self neither exists inherently nor that it is nonexistent inherently, we want to refrain from attributing inherent existence or inherent nonexistence to all entities. The apparent paradox involved in saying that things both exist and do not exist in one breath and saying that they neither exist nor do not exist in another—indeed of refusing in another sense to permit even these predications in another mood—arises, Nāgārjuna points out, from the conceptual imputation of inherently existent bases for these predications, which then have to be thought of as having contradictory properties. Absent the bases, we can see these assertions merely as useful analytical tools in various dialectical contexts to help us to see the ultimately empty and conventionally real nature of phenomena. And Nāgārjuna concludes this chapter by asserting that once one ceases hypostasizing the subjective self—that entity that might seem to be, as Descartes notes, the most obviously existent and most easily known entity of all—the temptation to hypostasize other entities dissolves.

Chapter X

Examination of Fire and Fuel

This chapter, the only one in this set of chapters ostensibly addressing an external phenomenon, is in fact concerned entirely with a standard counterexample to the kind of arguments Nāgārjuna offered in the two previous chapters on subjectivity in action and in perception. Recall that in those discussions Nāgārjuna argues that subject and object cannot be intrinsically and distinctly identified as entities because of their mutual dependence. Buddhist schools asserting substantial identity in the context of dependent co-origination, such as Vaibhāśika and Sautrāntika schools, used the example of fire and fuel to demonstrate the compossibility of substantial independent identity and dependent origination, as well as the possibility of the one-way dependence relation that these schools assert that actions and perception bear to the self. Just as fire depends on fuel but not vice versa, they would argue, and just as fire and fuel have distinct identities despite the fact that the former depends for its existence on the latter, action and perception can depend on the subject but not vice versa. Despite this dependence, proponents of this view would argue each relatum can be individually established as an entity.[60] In this chapter, Nāgārjuna undertakes the task of demonstrating that the example does not demonstrate these possibilities.

60. See Tsong Khapa's comments on this verse (p. 219).

1. If fuel were fire
   Then agent and action would be one.
   If fire were different from fuel,
   Then it could arise without fuel.[61]

The opponent does not want to assert the identity of fire and fuel, first, since it would contradict common sense, but second, since that, by the intended analogy, would identify agent and action, self and perception. On the other hand, if they are identified as intrinsically different—as having distinct and independent essential identities—they should be able to arise independently. Fuel should count as fuel even if there were no fire; fire should be possible without fuel. This follows from drawing the distinction at the level of intrinsic identity. Of course, distinguishing them conventionally permits their mutual dependence, but fails to establish the intrinsic identity intended by the reificationist.

2. It would be forever aflame;
   Flames could be ignited without a cause.
   Its beginning would be meaningless.
   In that case, it would be without any action.

The second and third verses spell out the consequences of attributing inherent existence to fire: It would be independent of all conditions, including its fuel; it would burn causelessly, since there would be no condition under which it would not burn. So all fire would, in that case, be eternal. Moreover, it would not consume anything, having no connection to the presence or absence of fuel. Moreover, Nāgārjuna asserts in the final two lines of X: 3, the activity of starting a fire would be nonsensical:

3. Since it would not depend on another
   Ignition would be without a cause.
   If it were eternally in flames,
   Starting it would be meaningless.

---

61. The intended sense of "fuel" here is material that is actually burning—not, for instance, firewood neatly stacked outside.

4. So, if one thinks that
    That which is burning is the fuel,
    If it is just this,
    How is this fuel being burned?

Nāgārjuna now sets up a destructive dilemma: Either the process of burning is identical to the fuel or different. In X: 4, he considers the possibility that they are identical. If so, he suggests, we have a problem in explaining how the fuel is consumed. The ordinary explanation of that is the presence of fire. But by identifying the burning process with the fuel, we have left the fire out of the picture. This analysis hence provides no explanation of combustion. After all, fuel by itself does not burn. It must be ignited, that is, fire must be introduced. If, as Nāgārjuna argues in X: 5, they are completely different, there won't be any fire at all. For then the burning would be dissociated from and independent of the fuel, and the unburned fuel would not be consumed by the burning. We could make no sense of the transition from unburned to burned fuel. The general moral is that we cannot make sense of interactive processes such as combustion without attending to the mutual dependence of the interacting phenomena that constitute those processes:

5. If they are different, and if one not yet connected isn't
        connected,
    The not yet burned will not be burned.
    They will not cease. If they do not cease
    Then it will persist with its own characteristic.

6. Just as a man and a woman
    Connect to one another as man and woman,
    So if fire were different from fuel,
    Fire and fuel would have to be fit for connection.

Here the opponent suggests that just as males and females are suited to connect in special ways in virtue of their particular anatomical structures, despite existing independently of one another, fire and fuel may be similarly suited to some special kind of connection. In that case, we would have the bizarre picture of fire being independent of fuel, yet peculiarly suited to coming together with it, and vice versa.[62] Moreover, since on this model fire and fuel are distinct from one another in nature, yet interactive (they "preclude" each other in the sense that causes and effects preclude one another—that is, in virtue of being connected yet incapable of simultaneous copresence), there must still be some account of how they connect, an account by no means easy to envisage:

7.   And, if fire and fuel
      Preclude each other
      Then fire being different from fuel,
      It must still be asserted that they connect.

Fire and fuel hence appear to be mutually dependent. Indeed the central point of Nāgārjuna's argument is that they are. But here the question arises: Don't they then have either to depend upon some third more fundamental thing or to be asymmetrically dependent, one of them established independently of the other?

8.   If fire depends on fuel,
      And fuel depends on fire,
      On what are fire and fuel established as dependent?
      Which one is established first?

If either is established as an entity first, without any reliance on the existence or nature of the other, that member of the pair would have a claim to being the basis in an asymmetrical dependency relation, and the opponent would have the counterexample necessary to refute the analysis in Chapters VIII and IX. The most obvious form that such an asymmetric dependence could take would involve the dependence of fire on fuel. Nāgārjuna argues that this is impossible to maintain:

9.   If fire depends on fuel,
      It would be the establishment of an established fire.
      And the fuel could be fuel
      Without any fire.

62. See also Kalupahana (1986), p. 199.

There are two arguments here. In the first two lines, Nāgārjuna argues that if fire were to depend upon fuel, fire would be doubly established. The point is that in order for the fuel to count as fuel, the existence of the fire must have already been established; indeed, the fuel depends upon the fire for its character as fuel. So to say then that the fire is dependent upon the fuel would be to argue that something whose existence is already presupposed if the fuel is to exist depends for its existence on that fuel. Note that this is only problematic for the opponent. That is, for one who accepts, as Nāgārjuna does, the mutual interdependence of phenomena, it is in fact true that fire depends upon fuel and that fuel depends upon fire. But the opponent at this stage in the argument argues that fire exists only dependently, but dependently on independent fuel. So Nāgārjuna only needs to show that position to be untenable. And the problem for the opponent is simply that the fuel he wants to exist independently can only do so in the presence of fire, which itself is merely dependent.

Second, Nāgārjuna argues, this would entail the absurd independent establishment of fuel as fuel. For fuel to be established independently as fuel in the absence of fire would be for there to be some characteristic of fuel that could be specified independently of fire that makes it fuel. But there is none. What makes fuel fuel is that it is combustible.

10.   If that on which an entity depends
        Is established on the basis
        Of the entity depending on it,
        What is established in dependence on what?

So in order to establish the existence of fuel as fuel, we must establish the existence of fire. In order for something to be fire, it must be consuming fuel. Neither depends asymmetrically on the other.

11.   What entity is established through dependence?
        If it is not established, then how could it depend?
        However, if it is established merely through dependence,
        That dependence makes no sense.

Now Nāgārjuna draws the general ontological moral from this discussion of the putative counterexample. If an entity is inherently existent, it must be independently established as an entity and with its own nature. So no entity could be established as inherently existent through dependence on any other entity. Only inherently existent entities could be independent. To establish something as inherently existent through its dependence on something else is incoherent. So since entities can be established neither through independence nor through dependence, there is no way to establish anything as an entity in its own right.

12.   Fire is not dependent upon fuel.
         Fire is not independent of fuel.
         Fuel is not dependent upon fire.
         Fuel is not independent of fire.

That is, neither fuel nor fire can be established as independent bases of predication separate from one another that then stand in accidental relations to one another. There are not two entities, fire and fuel, which then are related either by dependence or interdependence.

13.   Fire does not come from something else,
         Nor is fire in fuel itself.
         Moreover, fire and the rest are just like
         The moved, the not-moved, and the goer.

Though, as verse 12 grants, fire exists only in relation to fuel, it would not be correct to assert that fuel as an independent entity somehow produces fire. The analysis and the conclusion are strictly analogous to that regarding motion and the mover. We neither can say that motion is the same as the mover nor that they are different entities. We cannot say that motion is present in the unmoved, the moving, or the yet-to-move. Similarly we cannot say that fire is the same as the fuel nor that it is different. Nor can we say that it is present in the unburned, the burning, or the yet-to-be-burned fuel. The next verse emphasizes this point:

14.   Fuel is not fire.
        Fire does not arise from anything different from fuel.
        Fire does not possess fuel.
        Fuel is not in fire, nor vice versa.

15.   Through discussion of fire and fuel,
        The self and the aggregates, the pot and cloth
        All together,
        Without remainder have been explained.

The fire and fuel example is used as an analogy for a number of different cases of relations between bases and their attributes, including the relation between the putative self and its aggregates—that is, the components of the personality. But there are other stock examples—the relation between the pot and its properties and between the cloth and its thread—that are used to try to defend these asymmetrical dependence relations between inherently existent bases and the properties they support. Nāgārjuna is simply asserting the complete generality of this argument: It applies, mutatis mutandis, to all of these cases.

16.   I do not think that
        Those who teach that the self
        Is the same as or different from the entities
        Understand the meaning of the doctrine.

This colophon verse reminds us that when existence is understood in terms of emptiness and when entities are regarded as purely relational in character, identity and difference can only be understood conventionally. This applies not only with respect to apparently distinct entities, but also to the relation between parts and wholes, things and their attributes, events and their causes, and as Nāgārjuna emphasizes here, self and the objects of awareness. Strict identity and difference as determined by reference to phenomena themselves are only conceivable from the incoherent standpoint of inherent existence.

Chapter XI

Examination of the Initial and Final Limits

But suppose that one could see that the self, considered as agent or as subject, lacks inherent existence, and still one argued that nonetheless it must do so in virtue of its impermanence and being subject to change. Then, one might argue, birth, aging, and death must be real as the conditions of the self's unreality. This is the position with which Nāgārjuna concerns himself in this chapter. But he is also concerned with the generalization of this question to the birth, aging, and death of all of cyclic existence.[63] And it is this more general problem with which he actually opens the chapter, developing the account of individual impermanence as a special case:[64]

63. In Buddhist philosophy, the entire phenomenal world is referred to as cyclic existence (´khor-ba, Skt: saṃsāra). This term indicates not only the endless cycle of birth and death posited by the Buddhist doctrine of rebirth, but also the universally cyclic character of phenomena: Perception and action form a cycle; motivation and action form a cycle; the seasons are cyclic; chains of interdependence of phenomena are cyclic; interpersonal relations are cyclic; craving and acquisition are cyclic. It is this metaphor, suggesting that all of unenlightened existence amounts to going around in circles despite the illusion of progress, that most poignantly captures the sense in which all of human existence is suffering. See Sogyal Rinpoche 1992, pp. 18–22, for an excellent discussion.
64. This is, as the Ven. Sherab Gyatso pointed out in conversation, not the only possible reading of the import of this chapter. It could perfectly well be read simply as

1. When asked about the beginning,
    The Great Sage said that nothing is known of it.[65]
    Cyclic existence is without end and beginning.
    So there is no beginning or end.

The question about the existence and nature of the origin of the world is one of the questions that Sakyamuni Buddha declared to be unanswerable. Nāgārjuna here interprets that to mean that there is nothing coherent that can be said about the origin of the world. Given the striking similarity between the questions that the Buddha declared unanswerable and those that Kant argues to be unanswerable by reason in the Antinomies of Pure Reason, there is much to be said for this diagnosis.[66] So Nāgārjuna here claims that we cannot

---

a discussion of the problem of the beginning of personal existence and as an argument to the effect that cyclic existence and the predicament of suffering is beginningless, or at least that it is pointless or impossible to discuss and ponder its beginning. On the other hand, given the parallels between the analysis here and that in Chapter XXVII, where the questions concerning the finitude or infinitude of personal existence and of the world's existence are explicitly juxtaposed and receive identical treatment, there is good reason to see this chapter as implicitly addressing both as well.

65. *thub-pa chen-pos min zhes gsungs.* In an alternative Tibetan translation, this reads *thub-pa chen-pos mi gsungs zhu,*i.e.,— "The Great Sage did not answer." See the *Poṭṭhapāda Sūtra* 25:

Tell me, Is the world eternal? Is only this true and the opposite false? Poṭṭhapāda, I have not declared that the world is eternal and that the opposite view is false. Well, Lord, is the world not eternal? I have not declared that the world is not eternal. . . . Well, Lord, is the world infinite, . . . not infinite . . . ? I have not declared that the world is not infinite and that the opposite view is false. (Walsh, trans., 1987, p. 164)

There are three popular readings of the Buddha's refusal to answer the "unanswerable questions." On one reading this was an example of his great skill in teaching; any answer he would have given would have been misconstrued and would have had adverse consequences for the student. On another reading, by refusing to answer, the Buddha was indicating that asking these questions does not conduce to successful practice of the Buddhist path and that one should focus one's mind on more soteriologically efficacious issues. On a third reading—the one adopted here—these questions are in fact metaphysically misguided. They all involve incoherent essentialist presuppositions that, when rejected, render the questions meaningless.

66. The Buddha pronounced unanswerable questions regarding whether the world has an origin or an end in time or space, whether the individual continues to exist after entering nirvāṇa, whether there is some entity that transmigrates, and whether there is temporal beginning or end to the continuum of consciousness. Kant

make sense of the beginning or end of all of cyclic existence—
beginnings and ends are beginnings and ends of actual, conventionally designated and delimited processes within cyclic existence.

2.   Where there is no beginning or end,
      How could there be a middle?
      It follows that thinking about this in terms of
      Prior, posterior, and simultaneous is not appropriate.

The concept of a middle, Nāgārjuna argues, is bound up with
those of beginnings and ends. We can say that we and all phenomena are within cyclic existence, but to posit determinate absolute
spatiotemporal locations is senseless.

3.   If birth came first,
      And then old age and death,

---

pronounces unanswerable questions regarding the substantiality, simplicity, personal
identity, and primacy of the self, as well as questions regarding the finiteness or
infinitude of the world in space and time, the ultimate divisibility of the world, the
freedom of the will, and the existence of God. Murti (1985) makes a bit too much of
this parallel, however, arguing that Nāgārjuna follows Kant in asserting that

the aim in cosmological speculation (Rational Cosmology) is to reach the unconditioned ground of empirical objects by means of a regressive claim of reasoning
(i.e. arguing from effect to cause) stretched illegitimately, as Kant points out,
beyond the possibility of experience. . . .
      The question regarding the *Tathāgata* is in fact about the ultimate ground of
both the soul and objects—about the unconditioned in general. The *Tathāgata* as
the Perfect Man is the ultimate essence of the universe. His position is analogous
to that of God of Rational Theology. . . .
      The formulation of the problems in the thesis–antithesis form is itself evi-
dence of the conflict in Reason, that the conflict is not on the empirical level and
so not capable of being settled by appeal to facts is realized by the Buddha when
he declares them unsolvable . . ." (pp. xiii–xv).

While Nāgārjuna shares with Kant a critical approach to philosophy—each seeks
to limn the bounds of thought—and while Kant posits an unconditioned realm that
is the unknowable but necessary ground of the empirical world, Nāgārjuna eschews
just such a ground. His treatment of the unanswerable questions, then, differs from
Kant's, despite the many genuine parallels, in that while for Kant the antinomies
represent the application of concepts beyond their range, for Nāgārjuna they represent sheer nonsense: These antinomies are not for him insoluble problems, but
rather pairs of apparently coherent but in fact nonsensical verbal formulations.

Then birth would be ageless and deathless,
And a deathless one would be born.

Birth, old age, and death here are to be understood in an absolute sense. Of course, conventionally, the birth of a particular human being comes before her/his aging, which precedes her/his death. But that should not lead us to think of that birth as the origin of an entity, that aging as the midpoint in the life of that entity, or that death as the end of that entity. If one adopts a doctrine of rebirth, as does Nāgārjuna and as do all of his interlocutors, the point can be made quite straightforwardly: For any sentient continuum, every birth is preceded by an aging and a death, and so forth.

But even setting aside the particular doctrine of rebirth, we can elucidate this insight with equal force: To see particular entities as having determinate, nonconventional beginnings of existence and determinate, nonconventional termini and, hence, that there are distinct times at which there is a clear fact of the matter about whether or not they exist, independent of conventions for their individuation, is to see those entities as having necessary and sufficient characteristics for their identity, that is, as having essences. But the central thesis Nāgārjuna is defending is that this very conception of what it is to exist is incoherent—that things are empty of such essences and that the boundaries of objects are conventional and indeterminate. There is no fixed boundary between the existence of a seed, the tree to which it gives rise, a piece of wood from that tree, and a table fashioned therefrom or between the existence of an intact table, a broken table, wooden table parts, ashes, earth, the nutrients for a seed, that seed, the sapling to which it gives rise, and another tree.

Once we see the world from the standpoint of emptiness of inherent existence, the history of any conventionally designated entity is but an arbitrary stage carved out of a vast continuum of interdependent phenomena.[67] The arising of any phenomenon, hu-

---

67. One must not, however, take this to mean that for Nāgārjuna there is an inherently existent continuum out of which we carve the merely conventional. Rather just as any totality is dependent upon its parts, the totality of empirical

man, nonhuman sentient being, or inanimate object is the consequence of the disintegration of others. That disintegration succeeds their arising and aging. Once we give up the intrinsic identity of entities, the constant cycle of death, birth, aging, and rebirth of entities is unavoidable.

4.   If birth were to come after,
    And old age and death first,
    How could there be a causeless aging and death
    Of one not born?

But birth has to precede death as well, on pain of the absurdity of something that is unborn dying. And, as Nāgārjuna points out in the next verse, we must think conventionally of these things in sequence because any conventionally designated object undergoes them in order:

5.   Birth and age and death
    Cannot occur at one time.
    Then what is being born would be dying
    And both would occur without cause.

6.   When the series of the prior, simultaneous, and posterior
    Is not possible,
    Why are you led to posit
    This birth, aging, and death?

The birth, aging, and death that the opponent has in mind can be represented at two levels: At the most general level, it is the birth, aging, and death of cyclic existence, the examination of which frames this discussion. At that level, Nāgārjuna is pointing out that

---

reality depends upon its empty components and, so, is itself empty. Ontology presupposes conventional categories. Nor is this to say that the conventions we adopt are from our perspective arbitrary. They reflect our needs, our biological, psychological, perceptual, and social characteristics, as well as our languages and customs. Given these constraints and conventions, there are indeed facts of the matter regarding empirical claims and regarding the meanings of words. But there is no transcendent standpoint, Nāgārjuna would insist, from which these conventions and constraints can be seen as justified.

these conceptions, having legitimate employment only within the empirical realm, are nonsense. But the opponent could also be interpreted as positing birth, aging, and death as determinate, intrinsically identifiable moments in the evolution of empirical phenomena or, specifically, of sentient beings. Nāgārjuna rejects that as well, arguing that moments intrinsically prior to, simultaneous with, or posterior to the existence of entities cannot be identified, given the lack of intrinsic identity of the entities themselves. So long as one in conceiving of phenomena thinks of them as temporally determinate and bounded, and thinks of the identity of things as intrinsic to them, one will have to identify their beginnings, middles, and ends. But this leads to paradox, given the indeterminateness, interdependence, and interpenetration of things. Nāgārjuna hence advises the rejection of this ontology:

7.   Not only is cyclic existence itself without beginning,
      No existent has a beginning:
      Neither cause and effect;
      Nor character and characterized . . .

The alternative, both with respect to cyclic existence as a whole and with respect to individual entities, is to reject the ontology of entities and characteristics altogether, along with the boundaries and determinate relations that ontology requires:

8.   Nor feeling and the feeler;
      Whatever there is;
      All entities
      Are without beginning.

Chapter XII

Examination of Suffering

The first of the Four Noble Truths is that "all this is suffering." So one can imagine an interlocutor granting all that has gone before, but in defense of Buddhist orthodoxy, insisting that suffering is inherently existent. After all, the Four Noble Truths are, from a Buddhist perspective, *truths*. Nāgārjuna, of course, is a Buddhist and accepts the Four Noble Truths. (In fact, the principal chapter of this work, Chapter XXIV, is devoted to an exposition of the Four Noble Truths from the standpoint of emptiness and to the argument that only on Nāgārjuna's analysis can these truths be maintained at all.) So he must, without denying the reality of suffering, explain its emptiness.

> 1. Some say suffering is self-produced,
> Or produced from another or from both.
> Or that it arises without a cause.
> It is not the kind of thing to be produced.

These are the four possibilities with regard to inherently existent suffering. The echo of I: 1 is obvious, and the argument here will depend heavily upon the analysis of dependent arising developed in that chapter and in Chapter VII.

> 2. If suffering came from itself,
> Then it would not arise dependently.

For those aggregates
Arise in dependence on these aggregates.

Self-arising suffering would indeed be a candidate for inherent existence. But for the proponent of a Buddhist analysis of suffering, that is little help since suffering on a Buddhist analysis is the consequence of delusion, attachment, craving, action, and so forth. So such an analysis is not open to anyone wanting to defend the inherent existence of the suffering explored in the Four Noble Truths.

3. If those were different from these,
    Or if these were different from those,
    Suffering could arise from another.
    These would arise from those others.

The next alternative—that suffering arises from another— requires that there be essential difference. For since suffering does arise from previous conditions, if there is genuine otherness, that would characterize the relation between suffering and its grounds.

4. If suffering were caused by a person himself,
    Then who is that person—
    By whom suffering is caused—
    Who exists distinct from suffering?

But who is that other? It must be the sufferer himself at another stage, or another individual altogether. If it is the person himself, then as the cause of suffering, he must be distinct from suffering. This poses two problems: First, as per the analysis of motion, desire, and agency in Chapters II, VI, and VIII above, we cannot conceive of the sufferer as inherently different from the suffering he experiences. For part of his identity is constituted by that very suffering, and that suffering is his suffering. But second, given the framework of the first of the Four Noble Truths, a Buddhist philosopher such as Nāgārjuna would share with any Buddhist interlocutor the assumption that in saṃsāra sentient beings not only suffer, but are literally constituted of suffering—that every aggregate of a sentient being's existence is a cause, an effect, and a basis

of misery. So on either score, to distinguish sufferer from suffering
for the purpose of such an analysis would be impossible.

5.   If suffering comes from another person,
     Then who is that person—
     When suffering is given by another—
     Who exists distinct from suffering?

Another alternative is that the suffering is caused not by earlier
stages of one's own life, but by another individual. That other individual of course could be someone else entirely, in the ordinary
sense, or it could be an earlier moment of what is ordinarily regarded as oneself, but which is for the purposes of this analysis
regarded as substantially other. That is, taken in this way, Nāgārjuna can be seen to be arguing on each side of a dilemma with regard
to the identity of persons across time. But if this were so, it would
have to be the case that the person in whom suffering was caused by
that other could be identified and that that person could be distinguished from her suffering. But then the same problems developed
above apply. Nāgārjuna emphasizes this in XII: 6:[68]

6.   If another person causes suffering,
     Who is that other one
     Who bestowed that suffering,
     Distinct from suffering?

7.   When self-caused is not established,
     How could suffering be caused by another?
     Whoever caused the suffering of another
     Must have caused his own suffering.

But the suffering of that other person must either be caused by
someone else or be self-caused. The former alternative leads to a
regress: The whole point from the standpoint of the opponent who
is the target of this argument is to find the independent explana-

68. In this case, there is a second difficulty as well: For one person to cause
suffering for another, that first must already be suffering. For to cause suffering is a
very serious wrong, which could only be done by someone who him/herself is
suffering. So there is a possible regress.

tory ground for suffering. The second alternative leads back to the problem scouted in the opening verses: Self-caused suffering is both inconceivable within a general Buddhist soteriological framework and runs afoul of the arguments against self-causation generally. Finally, it is rather embarrassingly ad hoc. Nāgārjuna sums this up in the next verse:

8.   No suffering is self-caused.
     Nothing causes itself.
     If another is not self-made,
     How could suffering be caused by another?

But, as Nāgārjuna points out in XII: 9, it can't be caused by both since we have seen that neither can be causally relevant at all to inherently existent suffering of a kind relevant to Buddhist doctrine. And it is absurd to suppose that it is uncaused:

9.   If suffering were caused by each,
     Suffering could be caused by both.
     Not caused by self or by other,
     How could suffering be uncaused?

10. Not only does suffering not exist
     In any of the fourfold ways:
     No external entity exists
     In any of the fourfold ways.

The fourfold analysis is, of course, that in terms of the tetralemma of causation. And Nāgārjuna is simply emphasizing that this refutation of the existence of inherently existing suffering is perfectly general. No entity can arise from itself, from another, from both, or from a noncause. This was the burden of the first chapter. We must, of course, recall that this is not a refutation of the existence of the suffering we all experience and wish to avoid. Rather it is a demonstration of its emptiness of inherent existence. For just as the analysis in Chapter I has provided the key to dismissing the inherent existence of suffering, the positive side of that same analysis can be used to recover its conventional existence. If by suffering we mean something dependently arisen, impermanent, and conventional, existing only as imputed and only in relation to its empty subjects, there is plenty of suffering to go around.

But moreover, not only is the existence of suffering rendered comprehensible on this analysis, but so is the possibility of the alleviation of suffering. For if the proponent of the inherent existence of suffering were correct, while it might seem that suffering would then have a more solid status than that vouchsafed it by Nāgārjuna's analysis in terms of emptiness, that very substantial existence and hence independence of other conditions would make its alleviation impossible. For if it exists independently, then there are no conditions in the absence of which it fails to exist. So Nāgārjuna's analysis not only makes good sense of the first truth—that of suffering—and by implication of the second—that of the cause of suffering—but also opens the door for an analysis of the third and fourth truths—those of cessation and of the means to cessation.

Chapter XIII

Examination of Compounded Phenomena

In this chapter, Nāgārjuna begins to develop the idea of emptiness more explicitly. Up to this point, he has been arguing that phenomena are empty, but has not been characterizing emptiness itself, or its relation to entitihood or to conventional reality, except by example and by implication. At this point, through a general discussion of all compounded phenomena—that is, all phenomena constituted of parts or brought into being dependent upon causes—he argues explicitly both that emptiness is the lack of essence and that emptiness itself is wholly negative in character. It is not an essence that things have instead of whatever essence naive common sense or sophisticated reification might have thought they had—rather, it is the total lack of essence or inherent existence. This is, hence, an anticipation of the explicit discussions of the emptiness of emptiness to follow.

1.   The Victorious Conqueror has said that whatever
       Is deceptive is false.
       Compounded phenomena[69] are all deceptive.
       Therefore they are all false.

69. Kalupahana (1986) translates this term (Skt: *saṃskāra*, Tib: *'du byed*) as "dispositions." That is often correct. But it can also refer to compounded phenom-

This is an important verse for any understanding of the relation of the two truths—the conventional and the ultimate—to one another. That relation is vexed because the conventional truth is sometimes referred to as a truth and sometimes as wholly false. Conventional phenomena are sometimes referred to as empirically real and not imaginary and sometimes as wholly imaginary.[70] So it is important to see that the sense of "falsehood" in play when the conventional is characterized as false is "deceptive." That is, insofar as conventional phenomena present themselves as more than conventional— as inherently existent—they deceive us. We take them to be what they are not—to be intrinsically identified, inherently existent entities. In that sense, they are false. But to the extent that we understand them as dependently arisen, empty, interdependent phenomena, they constitute a conventional truth. Yet one must bear in mind that, according to Nāgārjuna, perception untutored by Mādhyamika philosophy and rigorous practice delivers objects to consciousness as inherently existent. In *this* sense, the things that we see are wholly false. For most of us, the best that we can do is reason our way into knowing, but not seeing, their true nature. The goal of meditation on emptiness is to bring this knowledge into perceptual experience and, hence, to see things as they are.

2.   If whatever is deceptive is false,
       What deceives?
       The Victorious Conqueror[71] has said about this
       That emptiness is completely true.

---

ena in general. Given the structure of the argument in this chapter, I (as do Tsong Khapa and his followers) prefer this reading. Kalupahana (p. 48) argues that it makes sense to follow a chapter on suffering with one on dispositions, inasmuch as the latter plausibly give rise to the former. He is right. But it also makes sense to follow a chapter on suffering with one on compounded phenomena since positing them as self-existent is what gives rise to suffering. Dispositions and compounded phenomena are—as the homonymy in question demonstrates—closely linked in Buddhist metaphysics. Dispositions are themselves compounded phenomena; but more importantly, they are what lead us to the conceptual compounding that gives phenomena their status as conventional entities.

70. This, of course, is partially responsible for the kind of nihilistic misreading of the text one sees, e.g., in Wood (1994).

71. An epithet of the Buddha. (The translation reflects the sense of the Tibetan. The Sanskrit would read "Blessed One.")

The opponent then asks what we are deceived about. Here is what motivates the question: If there are no real tables, for instance, then when I believe that there is a table in front of me and am therefore deceived, what is deceiving me? We don't want to say that a nonexistent phenomenon is pretending to be existent since it would have to exist in order to pretend. Nāgārjuna replies that what actually exists is an empty table. (That is not to say, however, that that empty table is *inherently existent*—only that the correct way to characterize the entity that exists conventionally is as an "empty table.") That empty table is misperceived by an ordinary mind as a truly existent table. To the extent that it appears *as empty,* it appears as it truly is. In the first two lines of the next verse, Nāgārjuna notes that it is the absence of essence that permits change:

3.   All things lack entity (hood),
        Since change is perceived.
        There is nothing without entity
        Because all things have emptiness.

It is emptiness that makes change possible. If things had essences, they would be incapable of real change. But since they are seen to change, Nāgārjuna argues, they must be empty of essence. The opponent, though, rejoins: Since according to Nāgārjuna all things are empty and since this is their ultimate nature, all things in fact do have a kind of entitihood, namely, *existence as empty phenomena.* Nāgārjuna is here anticipating the charge that he has rejected *other* essences only to posit emptiness as an essence, subject to all of the problems he has already adumbrated for essentialist metaphysics.

The opponent then asks (XIII: 4), "If everything lacks being, and is therefore empty, what could change?" Change would seem to have to be change of something, and the doctrine of emptiness seems to rob us of those somethings. Nāgārjuna, hence, presents himself, in the voice of the opponent, with a dilemma: He seems to have propounded, his protestations to the contrary notwithstanding, a theory of the essence of all phenomena. That theory, according to this hypothetical objection, is that emptiness just is the essence of all phenomena. He could deny having propounded such a theory, of course. But the consequence of such a denial, the opponent charges, would be no better. For then, the very basis of the argument here offered for emptiness—the reality of change—would have to be rejected. This is because without real entities there would no longer be a possible subject of change. Nāgārjuna replies in the third and fourth lines of XIII: 4 that the opponent has things backward: If there was entitihood—if things were nonempty—change would be impossible. It is emptiness itself that makes change comprehensible:

4.   If there is no entity (hood),
        What changes?
        If there were entity,
        How could it be correct that something changes?

Now Nāgārjuna begins a brief explanation of how to understand change in the context of emptiness and of why entitihood would preclude change. This discussion is certainly grounded in the analysis in Chapter II, but is more explicitly tied to the doctrine of emptiness at this point in the text:

5.   A thing itself does not change.
        Something different does not change.
        Because a young man doesn't grow old,
        And because and an old man doesn't grow old either.

When we imagine change, we imagine one thing retaining its identity, but changing its properties. But if identity is understood strictly, it is only possible as an internal relation that a thing bears to itself. To the extent that a thing changes, it becomes, strictly speaking, a different thing. But the relation between two things is not the change of a thing—it is simply the difference between two nonchanging entities. A young man does not grow old. When he is old he is no longer a young man. The relation between the young man and the old man is simply the difference of two things. But an old man doesn't grow old either. He is already old. So if change

and things that change are thought of nonrelationally, we can make
no sense of change at all.

6.   If a thing itself changed,
      Milk itself would be curd.
      Or curd would have come to be
      An entity different from milk.

If we think of identity persisting through change, there is a single
thing that changes as conventionally, milk becomes curd. Since
that thing is identical to milk and to curd, by transitivity we would
have to say that curd and milk are identical. But no one would
want to put curd in his/her tea! The only way to avoid this result
while retaining the idea that milk and curd are entities would be to
consider them to be wholly different entities. In that case, there is
still no change in an entity—only the difference between two unre-
lated phenomena.[72]

7.   If there were even a trifle nonempty,
      Emptiness itself would be but a trifle.
      But not even a trifle is nonempty.
      How could emptiness be an entity?

Verses 7 and 8 are critical for any understanding of the subtle
doctrine Nāgārjuna is developing of the emptiness of emptiness. In
XIII: 7, Nāgārjuna is emphasizing that emptiness is not one of the
many properties that a thing might or might not have. It is not that
some things are empty and some are nonempty, or that all things
happen to be empty although they might have been otherwise.
Emptiness is important because it is the only way that things can
exist. Moreover, emptiness is not an entity. It is not a distinct
phenomenon to which other phenomena are related. It is exactly

---

72. My reading of these last two verses appears to conflict with that of Inada
(1970), who reads Nāgārjuna as here denying that there is change. Rather, I take it,
Nāgārjuna denies that there is any inherently existent change or any substantial
entity that could be the subject of change, in virtue of the conventional reality of
change and the changed.

the emptiness of all phenomena.[73] The conventional character of conventional entities and their emptiness are one and the same.

8. The victorious ones have said
    That emptiness is the relinquishing of all views.
    For whomever emptiness is a view,
    That one will accomplish nothing.

The sense of "view" (Tib: *lta-ba*, Skt: *dṛṣṭi*) at work in verse 8 is crucial. By a view, Nāgārjuna here means a theory on the same level of discourse at which reificationist-nihilist debates proceed. A view in this sense is a view about what does or does not exist when existence is taken to mean inherent existence, or about the nature of phenomena, presupposing that the idea of a nature is coherent. So both the theory that compounded phenomena exist in virtue of having natures and identities and the theory that since they don't have such natures and identities they don't exist at all are views in this sense. Both presuppose that things exist at all if and only if they do so inherently. But the analysis in terms of emptiness is not a view at all in this sense. For the claim is *not* that things exist in virtue of having the property of emptiness as an essence. Rather it is the claim that they are empty *because* they have *no* essence.

It is also very important to see that this understanding of what a view is is closely bound up with Nāgārjuna's account of assertion and of the role of language in Mādhyamika dialectic. For Nāgārjuna, assertion in the literal sense is always the ascription of a property to an entity. As long as we are talking from the conventional standpoint, there is no problem here. There are plenty of conventional entities and conventional properties to go around and, so, lots of available conventionally true assertions. That is the basis of conventional truth. It is also important to note here that

---

73. So here I agree with Wood (1994, p. 174) when he concludes that the purport of this verse is that emptiness is not an entity. But unlike Wood, I do not think that entails a nihilism with respect to emptiness. It remains a characteristic of all phenomena (including itself) and, hence, like them, is conventionally real. See also Siderits (1989).

corresponding to these conventional assertions are real propositions that make them true or false—entities with or without the
ascribed properties. Again, as long as we remain and are aware
that we remain within the framework of conventional designation
and conventional assertion, this poses no problems.

But, when we start to do metaphysics, it is easy to slip into
nonsense: For now, when we want to characterize the essence of a
thing, we take ourselves to be positing a non-conventional thing
and ascribing to it an essential property. And there not only are no
such things, but there are not even *possibly* such things. There is
no ultimate *way the world is* that we are characterizing, truly or
falsely.

The danger to which Nāgārjuna is here adverting with respect to
Mādhyamika philosophy (of treating Mādhyamika as a view) is
then connected to assertion in the following way: If one were to
think that in asserting that things are empty that one is positing
entities and ascribing to those independent entities the property of
emptiness, one would be treating the language of Mādhyamika as
making literal assertions. But from the standpoint from which
these would be true, there are no entities and no characteristics,
and a fortiori, there are no entities having the characteristic of
being empty. The language must hence be understood, from the
ultimate perspective, not as making assertions, but rather as
ostending—indicating that which cannot be literally asserted without falling into nonsense—as Wittgenstein puts it in the *Tractatus*,
showing that which cannot be said.

Nāgārjuna makes this much more explicit in his discussion of
positionlessness in *Vigrahavyāvartanī* XXI-XXVIII, where he explicitly denies that the Mādhyamika assert any propositions, in
virtue of there being no entities or properties presupposed by their
use of language existing independently and corresponding to the
words used. Āryadeva makes the same point at *Catuḥśataka* XVI:
21. Candrakīrti in his comments on these verses compares one who
treats emptiness as an essential property—as opposed to the lack
of any essential property, thus treating Mādhyamika language as
assertoric in the sense of asserting the view that all things have the
essential nature of emptiness—to one who, upon entering a shop

and learning that there are no wares for sale, asks the shopkeeper to sell him the "no wares."[74,75]

To hold a view of emptiness—to reify it and then attribute it to phenomena—would then involve simultaneously reifying those phenomena as having a fixed nature and denying their existence at all, in virtue of disparaging their conventional reality as unreality by contrast with the reality of emptiness. It is this incoherence, so characteristic of essentialist philosophies, that leads Nāgārjuna to assert that one holding such a view is completely hopeless—incapable of accomplishing anything, philosophically or soteriologically.[76,77]

74. Murti (1985) puts this point nicely: "Criticism of theories is no theory. Criticism is but the awareness of what a theory is, how it is made up, it is not the proposing of a new theory. Negation of positions is not one more position" (p. xxiii).

See also Siderits (1989) for an interesting discussion of the connection between Nāgārjuna's claim to positionlessness and contemporary antirealism. Siderits puts the point this way:

[Nāgārjuna] neither asserts nor intimates any claims about the ultimate nature of reality, for he takes the very notion of a way that the world is independently of our cognitive activity to be devoid of meaning. . . . The slogan 'The ultimate truth is that there is no ultimate truth' is merely a striking way of putting the point that an acceptable canon of rationality will have to reflect human needs, interest, and institutions. (p. 6)

I am neither completely comfortable with Siderits's construction of the contemporary realism-antirealism debate nor with his location of Nāgārjuna on the antirealist side. (I rather think that Nāgārjuna would reject the presupposition of that debate—that the relevant sense of "real" is coherent in the first place.) But the connection he establishes between positionlessness and the rejection of a realist ontology is instructive.

All of this will become much more explicit (if not much clearer) in the discussions in XXII, XXIV, XXV, and XXVII below. I discuss this at greater length in Garfield (unpublished).

75. Ng (1993), however, argues that this verse should be read "all false views." So he claims that, according to Nāgārjuna, to understand emptiness is to relinquish all false views and that anyone who holds false views about emptiness is incurable. But Nāgārjuna doesn't say this, and the interpretation seems unfounded. See pp. 18–25.

76. The Tibetan "bsgrub-tu-med-pa" (will accomplish nothing) translates the Sanskrit term "asādhyān," which can also be translated "incurable."

77. This does not entail, however, pace Sprung (1979, p. 9, 15-16), that nothing is intelligible. Nāgārjuna spends a good deal of time developing quite lucid analyses of conventional phenomena and their relation to emptiness. What fails to be intelligible is, rather, the idea of inherent existence. But since no phenomena exist that way, and since emptiness is intelligible, the actual nature of phenomena is intelligible.

This argument against the coherence of any understanding of emptiness as itself an essence is tied very tightly to the analysis in Chapter XXIV: 18–40 of the emptiness of emptiness and of the connection between emptiness, dependent arising, and convention and tied most directly to the concluding verse of the text, XXVII: 30. (The commentaries on XXIV: 36 and XXVII: 30 below may be useful in elucidating this verse as well.) It is clearly an early anticipation of the powerful and climactic conclusions drawn in those two discussions.

Chapter XIV

Examination of Connection

The word here translated as "connection" (*phrad-pa*) is the term denoting the relation between the components that are compounded in any compounded phenomenon. It can also describe the relation between two things coming together in space and time or colliding, or two things fitting together, and while this can be taken fairly literally in the context of physical objects when they are understood as compounded of their parts, the relation is actually much more general than that. In fact, the example that Nāgārjuna takes as central, and one that is used by some earlier Buddhist theorists as an example of a case of connection in this sense, is visual perception. In such a case, according to the proponent of the reality of meeting, or compounding, the subject, the sensory organs, the sensory faculty, and the object join together, or "connect," not in a literal physical sense of spatiotemporal coincidence, but rather in the sense of forming an ensemble. Sense perception is, on this view, the entire compound ensemble.

So, dialectically, this chapter follows quite naturally on the heels of the examination of compounded entities. For we can imagine an opponent might reason as follows: Nāgārjuna may be right in denying the inherent existence of compounded entities in virtue of their dependence upon their parts and upon their parts being compounded, but surely since these phenomena depend upon being compounded that relation—the connection—exists. This chapter is aimed at replying to this position.

1. The seen, seeing, and the seer:
   These three—pairwise or
   All together—
   Do not connect to one another.

First, he claims, these things simply don't occur in the same place at the same time. There is no literal sense in which they connect.

2. Similarly desire, the desirous one, the object of desire,
   And the remaining afflictions
   And the remaining sources of perception
   Are understood in this threefold way.

In the various chapters on the relation between characteristic and characterized, Nāgārjuna has argued that it makes no sense to think of the relation between individuals and their properties or between entities as any kind of relation between independent entities at all, and that these phenomena cannot be understood as the same, as different, or as neither.

3. Since different things connect to one another,
   But in seeing, etc.,
   There is no difference,
   They cannot connect.

In order to have things that connect in the relevant sense, they must be different from one another, but as we saw in the chapters on characteristics, on desire, on seeing, on action, on motion, and on the self, the differences of the relevant kind are not found on analysis.

4. Not only in seeing, etc . . .
   Is there no such difference:
   When one thing and another are simultaneous,
   It is also not tenable that there is difference.

This problem emerges not only in the analysis of intuitively unitary phenomena like vision, but is perfectly general. Things that are separate from one another cannot be coherently thought of as inherently different entities either. For without any inherent identity, there is no basis for inherent difference. This recalls the argument of Chapter I.

5.   A different thing depends on a different thing for its
              difference.
          Without a different thing, a different thing wouldn't be
              different.
          It is not tenable for that which depends on something else
          To be different from it.

For there to be substantial difference, it must be possible to independently establish the identity and natures of the relata. But this, Nāgārjuna has argued repeatedly, is impossible.

6.   If a different thing were different from a different thing,
          Without a different thing, a different thing could exist.
          But without that different thing, that different thing does not
              exist.
          It follows that it doesn't exist.

That is, the only way that difference or the identity of a different thing as different could be shown to exist inherently would be for that difference to be present independently of the existence of another different thing. But that is not so. The only alternative would be to argue that difference is present independently in single things. But this ignores the relational character of difference.

7.   Difference is not in a different thing.
          Nor is it in a nondifferent thing.
          If difference does not exist,
          Neither different nor identical things exist.

So difference cannot be located either as a relation between things or as a unary property of individual things. So there is no inherently existent difference. But it is the existence of inherent difference that grounds the problem of connection. So there is no such relation, and no problem to be solved.

8.   That does not connect to itself.
          Nor do different things connect to one another.
          Neither connection nor
          Connected nor connector exist.

The conclusion is a powerful one and, especially when conjoined with the conclusion of the previous chapter, goes to the heart of any Buddhist (or non-Buddhist, for that matter) ontology that seeks to reify the entities that appear at any stage of ontological analysis. It is quite tempting when examining dependent, compound phenomena to think that while they themselves might not be inherently existent, and might not be the ultimate entities of the empirical world, it must at least be a fundamental fact that their being constituted of parts, or dependent upon their location in a causal and mereological nexus, exists as a fact. That would seem, in fact, to be the natural way to interpret the doctrine of dependent origination and the emptiness of macroscopic entities. But Nāgārjuna here pulls the rug out from any such analysis, pointing again to the emptiness of emptiness: Not only are compounded phenomena empty of inherent existence, but so is the relation among their constituents and determinants in virtue of which they are compounded.

Chapter XV

Examination of Essence

This chapter continues the discussion begun in Chapter XIII and carried on in Chapter XIV of the fundamental nature of things and the relation between emptiness and existence. Here Nāgārjuna rejects the coherence of the concept of essence and explores its ramifications for the concept of inherent existence, the concept of an entity, and the concept of a nonentity. This chapter is also aimed at dispelling any nihilistic interpretation of the Mādhyamika philosophical orientation and in explaining the deep connection between the analysis of phenomena as empty of essence and the demonstration of the possibility of empirical reality.

1. Essence arising from
    Causes and conditions makes no sense.
    If essence came from causes and conditions,
    Then it would be fabricated.

Essence by definition is eternal and independent. So it can't arise dependently. Chapter XV: 1, 2 develop this point directly. But since all entities arise dependently, it follows that none of them have essence.[78]

---

78. But see Bhattacharya (1979), pp. 341–42, for a contrary view. Bhattacharya argues that we can make sense of dependent, changeable essences. Perhaps. But

2.   How could it be appropriate
     For fabricated essence to come to be?
     Essence itself is not artificial
     And does not depend on another.

In these first two verses, Nāgārjuna indicates the three cardinal characteristics of an essence: An essence (or an entity that exists in virtue of possessing an essence) is uncaused, independent of other phenomena, and not fabricated from other things. It is important to bear this in mind in any Mādhyamika analysis of emptiness. For when Nāgārjuna argues that phenomena are all empty, it is *of* essence in this sense that they are empty. Hence, when Nāgārjuna argues that all phenomena originate in dependence upon conditions, that all phenomena are interdependent, and that all phenomena are fabricated (both in virtue of being compounded from parts and in virtue of acquiring their identity as particulars through conceptual imputation), he is thereby arguing quite directly for their emptiness.

3.   If there is no essence,
     How can there be difference in entities?
     The essence of difference in entities
     Is what is called the entity of difference.

This is an echo of the argument about difference presented in Chapter I. Essential difference presupposes essences of individuals. So any argument against individual essence will count as an argument against essential difference.

4.   Without having essence or otherness-essence,
     How can there be entities?
     If there are essences and entities
     Entities are established.

The concept of an inherently existent entity is the concept of an entity with an essence. So without essence, there are no inherently existing entities.

---

these are not the essences Nāgārjuna has in mind and are not those that lie behind the kind of pernicious reification or its counterpart, nihilism, that he is out to extirpate.

5.   If the entity is not established,
        A nonentity is not established.
        An entity that has become different
        Is a nonentity, people say.

By a nonentity, Nāgārjuna means something inherently different from some existing entity. A nontable in this sense would be inherently different from a table. But a nonexistent in general would be a Meinongian subsistent which is available as a basis of predication but is intrinsically different from what it is to be an existent—a real thing possessed of the property of being nonexistent. Just as a table must be established as a determinate entity in order to establish the nature of nontables, existence must be established as an inherently existent property in order to establish the parallel status of nonexistence. But neither tables nor existence can be so established. By the same token, then, there are no inherently established nontables, nor any inherently established nonexistents in their stead. So even though it might appear that an analysis through emptiness would leave us only with nontables and nonexistent phenomena, it doesn't even leave us with that (inherently), though it leaves us with plenty of tables, nontables, existents, and nonexistents (conventionally).

6.   Those who see essence and essential difference
        And entities and nonentities,
        They do not see
        The truth taught by the Buddha.

If the only way that one can think about phenomena is to think of them as things with inherent natures and to think of things without such natures as thereby nonexistent, none of the Buddhist doctrines of impermanence, emptiness, or liberation will make any sense.

7.   The Victorious One, through knowledge
        Of reality and unreality,
        In the *Discourse to Kātyāyana*,
        Refuted both "it is" and "it is not."

In the *Discourse to Kātyāyana*, the Buddha argues that to assert
that things exist inherently is to fall into the extreme of reification,
to argue that things do not exist at all is to fall into the extreme of
nihilism, and to follow the middle way is neither to assert in an
unqualified way that things exist nor in an unqualified way that
things do not exist. It represents one of the fundamental *sutta*s of
the Pali canon for Mahāyāna philosophy. In the *sutta*, the Buddha
claims that reification derives from the failure to note impermanence and leads to grasping, craving, and the attendant suffering.
Nihilism, he claims, is motivated by the failure to note the empirical reality of arising phenomena. It leads to suffering from failure
to take life, others, and morality seriously enough. The middle
path of conventional existence leads to engagement in the world
without attachment.[79]

8.   If existence were through essence,
      Then there would be no nonexistence.
      A change in essence
      Could never be tenable.

If for a thing to exist were for it to be a determinate entity with
an essence, then no thing would ever cease to exist or change in
any way. For an essential property is a necessary property, and it is
incoherent to say that a thing loses a necessary property.

9.   If there is no essence,
      What could become other?
      If there is essence,
      What could become other?

In the first half of this verse, the opponent replies that since the
argument in the previous verse presupposes the reality of change,

79. Kalupahana (1986) relies on this verse to argue that the entire *Mūlamadhyamakakārikā* is a "grand commentary on the *Discourse to Kātyāyana*" (pp. 81,
232). While this *sutta* is clearly important for Nāgārjuna, nothing in the text justifies
this global interpretation. The range of topics Nāgārjuna considers far exceeds the
scope of that *sutta*, and no other passage from that *sutta* is mentioned in the
Mūlamadhyamakakārikā.

it must presuppose the reality of the changer. If it presupposes the reality of change, it presupposes the reality of things that change and, hence, that persist through time. In order to remain the same, there must be some essence that accounts for this identity. Nāgārjuna replies, however, that if this persistence through time were determined by essence, the change it putatively explains would be impossible. Only conventional existence over time can explain change. Nāgārjuna summarizes, paraphrasing the *Discourse to Kātyāyana*:

10.   To say "it is" is to grasp for permanence.
        To say "it is not" is to adopt the view of nihilism.
        Therefore a wise person
        Does not say "exists" or "does not exist."

11.   "Whatever exists through its essence
        Cannot be nonexistent" is eternalism.
        "It existed before but doesn't now"
        Entails the error of nihilism.[80]

To say that if something exists, it does so in virtue of having an essence and hence cannot change or pass out of existence would entail the absurd position that everything is eternal. To say of something that it existed in this strong sense—with an essence—in the past, but does not do so now, is absurd. For if for something to exist is for it to do so inherently, and if it is not now existent, it could never have been. So since everything we observe is impermanent, if the only existence that there could be were inherent existence, nothing could exist at all. That would be nihilism. The upshot of this chapter is that the very concept of an essence, and hence the very concept of an inherently existent entity at all, is incoherent. No coherent conception of the phenomenal world can be one in which things are posited other than conventionally.[81]

80. The verse ends "*...thal-bar 'gyur.*" This form indicates that the nihilism is taken as the unacceptable consequence that would provide a reductio on the claim "it existed before but doesn't now."
81. See Ng (1993), pp. 25–27, 34–36, for a nice discussion of the connection between this rejection of extremes and the emptiness of emptiness.

Chapter XVI

Examination of Bondage

So there are no entities. But still, from a Buddhist perspective, we are bound: bound to our conceptions of entities and essence, bound to our selves, bound to objects, and principally, bound to cyclic existence itself. Surely, the opponent might ask, mustn't the bondage that accounts for the illusions so ruthlessly analyzed in the previous chapter be intrinsically real? If not, what is the causal basis for all of these illusions and all of this suffering? In a Buddhist framework, this bondage to cyclic existence is instantiated in endless transmigration in saṃsāra, and freedom from bondage would be liberation from cyclic existence into nirvāṇa. We will postpone a discussion of the precise nature of that liberation and of nirvāṇa until we reach the chapters where that topic is discussed, namely, XXII and XXV. Nāgārjuna begins with an examination of transmigration and the entity that transmigrates:

1. If compounded phenomena transmigrate,[82]
    They do not transmigrate as permanent.

82. The Tibetan term translated as "transmigrate" ('khor, Skt: saṃsār) is a cognate of the term "saṃsāra," or cyclic existence. It literally means go around and could also be translated with justice as "flow." But the root idea here is that of cycling or circulating or participating in a phenomenal reality conceived as multicyclic. In this chapter, as in Chapter XIII, I opt to translate " 'du byed" as "compounded phenomena," rather than, as Kalupahana (1986) does, "dispositions." This follows the Tibetan commentarial tradition and makes better sense of the argument.

If they are impermanent they do not transmigrate.
The same approach applies to sentient beings.

Nāgārjuna sets up a by now familiar destructive dilemma: Either compounded phenomena—of which sentient beings, the beings who are bound, are instances—are permanent or impermanent. Let us just consider the compounded phenomena who are sentient and hence who transmigrate: If they are thought of as permanent, they cannot transmigrate because transmigration involves, by definition, change. And what is permanent, as we have seen, cannot change. But if they are impermanent, then they do not endure through time and, hence, cannot transmigrate. So no sentient being considered as an inherent entity can be conceived of as a transmigrator in cyclic existence.

2.   If someone transmigrates,
        Then if, when sought in the fivefold way
        In the aggregates and in the sense spheres and in the elements,
        He is not there, what transmigrates?

Given that no inherently existent person can be found upon analysis as the bearer of the aggregates, as identical to the aggregates, as different from the aggregates, as the collection of the aggregates, or as the arrangement of the aggregates, and mutatis mutandis for other possible modes of analysis in terms of domains of knowledge or experience and in terms of basic elements, it follows that there is no inherently existent subject of transmigration. If the transmigrator cannot be identified on analysis, though, neither can the transmigration itself. It will follow that there is no inherently existent transmigration and, hence, no inherently existent bondage to cyclic existence.

3.   If one transmigrates from grasping[83] to grasping, then
        One would be nonexistent.
        Neither existent nor grasping,
        Who could this transmigrator be?

83. This term (nye-bar-len-pa) is used in a quite general sense: To grasp could be to cling to a possession, to regard attributes or experiences as part of oneself, or to grasp an object in consciousness.

"Grasping" here refers primarily to grasping the aggregates as one's self. Transmigration—or for that matter continuation within one life, which from the Mādhyamika perspective is exactly the same kind of process—involves moving from grasping one set of phenomena as one's self to grasping another in the same way. That is one of the most fundamental delusions from a Buddhist standpoint. But grasping can also be the grasping of an object as an object, or the clinging to possessions. Life in saṃsāra, Nāgārjuna would insist, can equally well be characterized in any of these ways. But if in order to exist as an individual one would have to retain one's identity over time since on this view it is of the very nature of cyclic existence that one constantly changes from one moment to another, then it would follow that no subject exists. But if there is no subject of grasping, there can be no grasping. So, on the supposition that to exist and to transmigrate is to exist as a continuing entity, there is no way to make sense of the phenomenal world. So an inherently existent grasper, posited in order to guarantee the reality of cyclic existence, in fact makes the reality of cyclic existence incoherent.

4.   How could compounded phenomena pass into nirvāṇa?
      That would not be tenable.
      How could a sentient being pass into nirvāṇa?
      That would not be tenable.

If compounded phenomena are permanent, grasping is permanent. And if grasping is permanent, saṃsāra is permanent. And if saṃsāra is permanent, then nirvāṇa is impossible. But the philosopher who is positing inherently existent bondage is doing so in order to defend a Buddhist perspective on cyclic existence and nirvāṇa. This is precisely the motivation for the reification—the worry that saṃsāra and nirvāṇa are, if not inherently existent, nonexistent. So this conclusion is inadmissible for such an opponent.

5.   All compounded phenomena are arising and ceasing things:
      Not bound, not released.
      For this reason a sentient being
      Is not bound, not released.

Neither bondage nor release can be seen as inherently existent, nor as inherent properties of sentient beings. This is the conclusion of the argument that follows. Nāgārjuna first considers bondage as an inherent property, and then liberation:

6.   If grasping were bondage,
       Then the one who is grasping would not be bound.
       But one who is not grasping is not bound.
       In what circumstances will one be bound?

If grasping is identified with the property of bondage, then the continuity of bondage across transmigration is inexplicable: The problem is that grasping is not only the cause, but is also the effect of bondage. Delusion by which we are bound, from a Buddhist perspective, leads us to grasp at things; that grasping perpetuates delusion and bondage. To the extent that we grasp onto external phenomena or onto the self as inherently existent, we are bound to the delusions that constitute and ground saṃsāra. To the extent that we are bound in delusion, we continue to grasp. The bondage is hence not only conditioned by, but overarches, particular instances of grasping. But we don't want to infer from the fact that grasping and bondage are not identical that the relinquishing of all grasping would not free one. The task is then to figure out the nature of bondage, which must be conceived as relational.

7.   If prior to binding
       There is a bound one,
       There would be bondage, but there isn't.
       The rest has been explained by the gone, the not-gone, and the
       goer.

The only way that bondage itself could be an inherently existent phenomenon would be if it could exist prior to and independently of a bound sentient being. But then the case would be strictly analogous to motion (as well as to several other analysands we have considered so far). That is, just as there is no motion apart from the mover, there is no bondage apart from the bound. The argument can be applied in a strictly parallel way.

8. Whoever is bound is not released.
    Whoever is not bound does not get released.
    If a bound one were being released,
    Bondage and release would occur simultaneously.

Nāgārjuna then recalls another argument from Chapter II, the argument against the possibility of the beginning of motion. There, Nāgārjuna argued that motion could not begin in a stationary object since it is not moving, nor in a moving object since it is already in motion. And there can be no moment when a thing is both moving and stationary, nor any moment when an entity is neither. Similarly, nirvāṇa cannot arise in one in saṃsāra, nor in one already in nirvāṇa. One cannot be simultaneously in saṃsāra and nirvāṇa. Nor is there any third option.

9. "I, without grasping, will pass beyond sorrow,
    And I will attain nirvāṇa," one says.
    Whoever grasps like this
    Has a great grasping.

There is a stylistic feature in this verse that deserves note: The pronoun "I" (*bdag*) is uncharacteristically fronted in the sentence and is emphasized with the focus particle (*ni*). Nāgārjuna is hence drawing attention to the fact that the individual in whose mouth this verse is put is grasping to his own identity as an agent and as a continuing subject both through saṃsāra and into nirvāṇa. This grasping onto self, he suggests, precludes the nirvāṇa the speaker craves. But Nāgārjuna presents another argument as well: It is also possible to grasp after nirvāṇa—to reify it as a state and to crave it as a phenomenon inherently different from saṃsāra and as highly desirable since it is indeed characterized as liberation from suffering. But this grasping onto the end of grasping is itself a grasping and so precludes the attainment of nirvāṇa. Nirvāṇa requires, according to Nāgārjuna, a complete cessation of grasping, including that onto nirvāṇa itself. While that might seem paradoxical, it is not: To grasp onto something in this sense requires, inter alia, that one reify it. By refusing to reify liberation, in virtue of seeing it as the corelative of bondage, which itself is not inherently existent, it

is possible to pursue the path to liberation without creating at the
same time a huge obstacle on that path—the root delusion with
regard to nirvāṇa itself. Possible, that is, but perhaps not that
easy.[84,85]

10. When you can't bring about nirvāṇa,
    Nor the purification of cyclic existence,
    What is cyclic existence,
    And what is the nirvāṇa you examine?

Anyone who is subject to either of these pathologies—grasping to
one's self or grasping for nirvāṇa—is incapable of attaining that
peace. So, Nāgārjuna urges, in order to make such progress possible, one should reexamine one's conception of the nature of phenomena in cyclic existence (both oneself and external phenomena)
and nirvāṇa itself. By coming to see their ultimate emptiness, he
suggests, one can relinquish that grasping and attain that liberation.
Neither nirvāṇa nor saṃsāra are inherently existent. Ultimately
both are nonexistent. So, what, Nāgārjuna asks rhetorically, are
they? The answer is that they are conventionally real, dependently
arisen phenomena that are empty of inherent existence. In virtue
of that fact, it is possible to escape the former and to attain the
latter. But that escape would be impossible were they inherently
existent and is impossible for anyone who takes them to be so.

84. In *Yuktiṣaṣtikā* 11, Nāgārjuna asserts "This is nirvāṇa in this very life!" He
emphatically rejects the positing of nirvāṇa as a distinct entity divorced from
saṃsāra. This will emerge much more explicitly in the discussion of nirvāṇa in XXV
below.
85. It is also important to note that this indicates a difference in kind between
grasping for nirvāṇa and an aspiration to attain buddhahood. For it is central to
Mahāyāna Buddhist practice to develop the altruistic aspiration to attain buddhahood for the sake of all sentient beings—to enhance one's knowledge, skill, and
compassion so as to maximally benefit others. But this aspiration can be cultivated
without reification of self, of the goal, or of the objects of compassion or action and,
hence, without grasping of the kind at issue.

Chapter XVII

Examination of Actions and Their Fruits

Arguing for the emptiness of bondage and liberation, however, raises a further question that demands an answer: If there is no real bondage and no real release, what are the effects of our actions? For it would appear, at least given standard Buddhist moral theory and the doctrine of karma on which it is grounded,[86] that meritorious actions conduce to liberation and that morally wrong actions increase bondage. Given the emptiness of these latter, an analysis of the consequences of action is in order. Nāgārjuna begins with Buddhist moral truisms, accepted by the Mādhyamika as well as by members of other Buddhist schools. It is important to note that the first nineteen verses of this chapter represent the views of four distinct opponents in order of increasing similitude to the Mādhyamika understanding. Despite the fact that Nāgārjuna sets these views up as targets, however, some of the views the opponents put on the table are, suitably interpreted, shared by Nāgārjuna. Each

---

86. That is, broadly speaking, that our actions, words, and intentions have consequences that determine the future course of our lives. Karma from the Buddhist standpoint is a straightforwardly deterministic process and not a matter of accounts being kept by a cosmic accountant. The doctrine can be applied both within a single life or across rebirths and with respect both to individuals and to groups of individuals.

can be seen as, despite being inadmissible as a characterization of a nonconventional basis for the relation between action and its effects, a reasonable empirical assessment of at least part of the conventional reality in this domain.

1. Self-restraint and benefiting others
   With a compassionate mind is the Dharma.
   This is the seed for
   Fruits in this and future lives.

2. The Unsurpassed Sage has said
   That actions are either intention or intentional.
   The varieties of these actions
   Have been announced in many ways.

The classification to which Nāgārjuna refers is a partition of actions into mental and physical. Mental actions are mere intentions on this view; physical actions and speech (generally distinguished in Buddhist psychology and action theory) are properly intentional. That is, the latter two involve a mental and a nonmental component; the mental actions only involve a mental component. Verse 3 clarifies this:

3. Of these, what is called "intention"
   Is mental desire.
   What is called "intentional"
   Comprises the physical and verbal.

In the next verse, an opponent uses these truisms as a platform for the defense of the view that actions themselves must remain in existence until their consequences are observed. Actions that derive from renouncing the world are different from those that derive from worldly concerns. This difference in nature, he argues, must explain the difference in their consequences:

4. Speech and action and all
   Kinds of unabandoned and abandoned actions

And resolve[87]
As well as . . .

5.   Virtuous and nonvirtuous actions
     Derived from pleasure,
     As well as intention and morality:
     These seven[88] are the kinds of action.

The kinds of actions to which Nāgārjuna's imaginary opponent refers are simply the various kinds of virtuous and nonvirtuous actions. In general, morally good actions are done for the sake of pleasure for others; morally bad actions sacrifice others' good for one's own pleasure. The opponent, however, goes further, pointing out that these actions have diverse long-term consequences that must be explained:

6.   If until the time of ripening
     Action had to remain in place, it would have to be permanent.
     If it has ceased, then having ceased,
     How will a fruit arise?

The problem is this: Given that the consequence of an action may be far in the future, something must persist to connect the action to the result. This is a kind of karmic analog of doubts about action at a distance. It is the same kind of move that lies behind trace theories of memory in recent philosophy of mind. So this first position is that there must be some permanent entity that remains in existence until the consequences of an action occur.

A second possibility is that some third thing mediates the relation between action and consequence—a kind of karmic link that is generated by the action and remains in the psychophysical contin-

---

87. *rnam rig byed min pa* (Skt: *avijñaptaya*). A technical term that can refer to such things as a monk's vows or a resolution to perform some action.

88. The arithmetic here is none too clear. Tsong Khapa has it like this: (1) good and bad speech; (2) good and bad physical action; (3) abandoned and unabandoned actions; (4) meritorious actions; (5) nonmeritorious actions; (6) the intention to do good actions; (7) the intention to do bad actions. Just what the principle of partition is here is not obvious. Clearly the categories overlap (pp. 300–301).

uum until the consequence is produced. The interlocutor then offers an analogy popular in Buddhist philosophy:

7.   As for a continuum, such as the sprout,
       It comes from a seed.
       From that arises the fruit. Without a seed,
       It would not come into being.

That is, just as every actual fruit requires an actual seed as its predecessor and a sprout to mediate between them, the opponent reasons, every consequence of action requires an actual action and an actual karmic link between the action and the consequence. The next three verses extend this analogy:

8.   Since from the seed comes the continuum,
       and from the continuum comes the fruit,
       The seed precedes the fruit.
       Therefore there is neither nonexistence nor permanence.

That is, this interlocutor points out, the position developed in XVII: 5–6 requires that actions either be permanent or nonexistent. His own view, on the other hand, allows actions to exist as impermanent and is, hence, more plausible:

9.   So, in a mental continuum,
       From a preceding intention
       A consequent mental state arises.
       Without this, it would not arise.

10.   Since from the intention comes the continuum,
       And from the continuum the fruit arises,
       Action precedes the fruit.
       Therefore there is neither nonexistence nor permanence.

In the next verse, another opponent offers an orthodox formulation from a substantialist Buddhist school, arguing that particular kinds of action are described as the methods of attaining realization and that particular rewards for the practicioner are mentioned as consequences of realization. The implication is that, since these are specified in *sūtra*s as real, they must be inherently existent:

11.   The ten pure paths of action
        Are the method of realizing the Dharma.
        These fruits of the Dharma in this and other lives
        Are the five pleasures.

"The ten paths" simply denotes the totality of virtuous actions as characterized by one of the Buddhist botanies of morally worthy action.[89] The five pleasures are the pleasures appropriate to the various sense faculties. According to the opponent, all we need to do in order to reach enlightenment and to lead good lives is to act virtuously. The principal consequence of this is that we will enjoy temporal happiness.

Yet another interlocutor replies that this wholly misunderstands the Buddha's explanation of the relation between action and its consequences. While it is the case that acting well is an important ingredient in Buddhist practice and in any account of what it is to lead a good life, and while it is true that when one lives well, one in general is rewarded with material happiness, this hardly indicates that action, the agent, or the consequences of action are inherently existent. Rather, this more sophisticated opponent suggests, the nature of the link is completely abstract, like a legal obligation:[90]

12.   If such an analysis were advanced,
        There would be many great errors.
        Therefore, this analysis
        Is not tenable here.

89. Refraining from killing, stealing, adultery, lying, deception, slander, gossip, avarice, hatred, and philosophical error.
90. Kalupahana (1986) misreads XVII: 12–19 as Nāgārjuna's own view. This is understandable, as Nāgārjuna is providing four rival accounts of the relation between action and its karmic consequences. Each on his view contains a kernel of truth; each is indeed accurate in a sense, though misleading in the sense in which it is intended. This final position is closest to Nāgārjuna's position and can easily be confused with it, but to read it this way misses the significance of the transition at XVII: 20.

13.   I will then explain what is tenable here:
             The analysis propounded by all
             Buddhas, self-conquerors
             And disciples according to which . . .

14.   Action is like an uncancelled promissory note
             And like a debt.
             Of the realms it is fourfold.
             Moreover, its nature is neutral.

Using the metaphor of a promissory note, the defender of this view compares action and its consequences to a document attesting to a particular debt or other legal action: Though the act to which the document attests was in one sense momentary, its consequences, and the evidence of its reality, are unlimited in duration. So the consequences of any action—however local that action might appear to be—reverberate through all realms of existence.[91] Moreover, the fundamental nature of action and its consequences is neutral. That is, simply considered as such, on this view, neither action nor its consequent trace is either positive or negative. Any particular action or trace may of course be so—but action itself is equally capable of being positive or negative in character. We now turn to specific advice to enable one to realize the nature of reality and to abandon the mundane concerns and attachments that lead to binding actions (advice with which Nāgārjuna would not take issue):

15.   By abandoning, that is not abandoned.
             Abandonment occurs through meditation.
             Therefore, through the nonexpired,
             The fruit of action arises.

Simply by resolving to abandon attachment one cannot thereby succeed in shedding it. It is difficult to accomplish this. Attachment arises as a consequence of the persistent, pervasive psychological, verbal, and physical habits that together constitute what Buddhist philosophers call the "root delusion," the ignorance of the true

---

91. The four realms reflect traditional Buddhist cosmology: the desire realm, the form realm, the formless realm, the realm of freedom.

nature of things. That delusion consists in confusing existence with inherent existence and issues inevitably in one of the two extreme views—reification or nihilism. Only through extensive meditation on the nature of phenomena and on the nature of emptiness can these habits be abandoned, and only through an understanding of the ultimate nature of things can the fruit of actions done through abandonment—that is, liberation from the suffering of cyclic existence—be attained. The promissory note metaphor is at work here as well. The idea is that one cannot simply cancel a promissory note on one's own without paying the debt. One must do something more substantial to discharge one's obligation to one's creditor.

16.   If abandonment occurred through abandoning, and
        If action were destroyed through transformation,
        The destruction of action, etc.,
        And other errors would arise.

If one thought that one could just resolve to abandon attachment and delusion and succeed, that would be to treat attachment and attached action as trivial entities—even as illusory in the full sense. Just as when one sees a mirage, one can, knowing that it is a mirage, stop seeing it as water. That is possible for illusory things, but not so for empirically real ones. It takes effort to see an actual puddle as empty—not of conventional water, but of nonconventional inherent existence—and it takes effort to stop reifying habits. Again, though this is articulated in defense of the opponent's view, this is a sophisticated opponent, and Nāgārjuna in fact agrees with much of this.

17.   From all these actions in a realm,
        Whether similar or dissimilar,
        At the moment of birth
        Only one will arise.

One performs countless various actions in one's life. And the confluence of the karmic consequences of all of them, on this view, are realized in the beginning of a single individual at the moment of rebirth (the one who arises). This comment is, of course, most directly about rebirth and the mechanism of karma in transmigration. Here is a way to understand that explicit point: The mechanism by which karma operates in rebirth is not that each individual action in a continuum designated as an individual remains permanently in place or leaves a substantial trace that lies dormant until it produces its consequence. This is indeed how karma is often conceived by substantialist Buddhist schools. Rather, each moment of such a continuum, including the moment of rebirth, is a consequence, through the mechanism of dependent arising, of all of the previous moments of that continuum (and, of course, of much else besides). Those karmic consequences are, as it were, "summed up" in the total state of the individual at birth.

But of course the implications of this are more general and concern every moment of any life. They can hence be made independently of any discussion of transmigration, though of course they help to demystify that Buddhist doctrine, at least as it is conceived in Mahāyāna philosophy. The point is this: Every moment of our lives represents the causal consequences of, inter alia, all of our prior actions. No action "lies dormant" waiting for its consequences to emerge. Nor does any action somehow become "canceled" when some salient consequence is noticed. There is no accounting kept, and no debit and credit system, either from the causal or the moral point of view in the continuum of human action and experience. Rather, at each moment we are the total consequence of what we have done and of what we have experienced. And the only sense in which some past action may determine some future reward is one in which that past action, as well as other conditions, have determined a state now that, together with other future conditions, will determine that reward. Mutatis mutandis, of course, for negative consequences. This sober empiricist account of these matters forms the basis for Mahāyāna moral theory and its account of the nature of soteriological practice.

18.   In this visible world,
        All actions of the two kinds,
        Each comprising action and the unexpired separately,
        Will remain while ripening.

But here the opponent slides over into the substantialism that Nāgārjuna will criticize. For although he has characterized actions as impermanent, he has retained the seed-and-sprout metaphor that has the actions identifiable over time and, hence, as having an independent existence and identity. Moreover, he suggests, their consequences are determinate in time, delimited by death or nirvāṇa:

19.   That fruit, if extinction or death
        Occurs, ceases.
        Regarding this, a distinction between the stainless
        And the stained is drawn.

Nāgārjuna now mounts a reply against all of these positions collectively:

20.   Emptiness and nonannihilation;
        Cyclic existence and nonpermanence:
        That action is nonexpiring
        Is taught by the Buddha.

All phenomena, including action, its result, and the connection between them, will come out to be empty of inherent existence, yet conventionally real; they will be part of cyclic existence, but will be impermanent. This is not surprising. But Nāgārjuna also says that no action expires (retaining the promissory note metaphor). Obviously, he cannot mean that actions are permanent. Rather, we should understand this to assert two related theses: First, it indicates that the consequences of actions do not cease at some point. All actions have ramifications into the indefinite future, due to dependent arising. Second, actions themselves, being empty of inherent existence are not entities capable of passing out of existence, when passing out of existence is interpreted to mean the cessation entirely of something that once existed inherently. Since actions are not inherently existent, they are not suitable bases for inherent cessation. And this resolves the final apparent paradox: The tension between the assertion that nothing is permanent and that all action is nonexpiring. All phenomena are indeed impermanent, but that entails both that they do not inherently cease and that their effects are indefinite in scope.

21. Because action does not arise,
     It is seen to be without essence.
     Because it is not arisen,
     It follows that it is nonexpiring.

This verse emphasizes the second reading of the thesis of the nonexpiration of action and echoes the arguments from Chapter VII.

22. If action had an essence,
     It would, without doubt, be eternal.
     Action would be uncreated.
     Because there can be no creation of what is eternal.

Moreover, Nāgārjuna reminds us, again drawing heavily on the arguments reviewed and redeployed in Chapter VII, things with essences don't arise and cease, and can't be related causally to other things. If action existed inherently, it couldn't be initiated. So, if one were trying to preserve the reality of action and karma against the analysis in terms of emptiness (because one viewed that analysis as undermining their genuine existence), it would be pointless to defend the existence of action and karma as inherent existence.

23. If an action were uncreated,
     Fear would arise of encountering something not done.
     And the error of not preserving
     One's vows would arise.

Nāgārjuna here and in XVII: 24 draws some of the moral consequences of the nihilistic view of action that seems to follow from the conditions set on its existence by the reificationist: Actions would not come into being through agency and so would have no regular relation to any agents. And so one might find oneself experiencing the consequences of some action one had not performed, or find that it was, in some sense, one's own action. One would not take action seriously as one's own responsibility and would not worry about moral infractions. Monks and nuns would break their vows. Since morality depends on a distinction between morally positive and morally negative acts, if there were no actions, or if actions could not be thought of as initiated by their agents, there would be no morality. From another perspective, the preservation of vows would be an impossibility anyway since preserving the vows requires taking action, which would be impossible if action were uncreated.

24.   All conventions would then
        Be contradicted, without doubt.
        It would be impossible to draw a distinction
        Between virtue and evil.

Moreover, Nāgārjuna argues in the next verse, if actions had essences, they could not cease, and if their karmic consequences had essences since they would need no conditions to arise, they would just keep arising:

25.   Whatever is mature would mature
        Time and time again.
        If there were essence, this would follow,
        Because action would remain in place.

26.   While this action has affliction as its nature
        This affliction is not real in itself.
        If affliction is not in itself,
        How can action be real in itself?

Moreover, Nāgārjuna continues, afflicted action is, for the opponent, done essentially in affliction. But given that affliction has already been shown to be empty in the chapter on suffering (XII), how could it serve as an essence for action?

27.   Action and affliction
        Are taught to be the conditions that produce bodies.
        If action and affliction
        Are empty, what would one say about bodies?

The opponent replies, however, that action and affliction are referred to in *sūtra*s as the causes of different kinds of rebirth and of different characteristics in rebirths. And since beings are indeed reborn and do indeed have characteristics, how, from the standpoint of a Buddhist view of rebirth, could empty actions and empty karmic consequences explain this?

28.   Obstructed by ignorance,
         And consumed by passion, the experiencer
         Is neither different from the agent
         Nor identical with it.

Nāgārjuna focuses in his reply on the nature of the individual who is the putative agent of these actions and experiencer of their consequences. The present objection rests on the presupposition that they exist inherently. That is why the problem arises about how empty actions and empty karmic links could be sufficient to link their properties. So Nāgārjuna emphasizes that neither an analysis in terms of inherent identity nor one in terms of inherent difference between agent and action will suffice. Both presupposes, incoherently, the inherent existence and hence the possession of an essence, of each term in the putative relation. But this of course recalls the problem posed near the end of Chapter I: How can actual effects arise from empty conditions? And Nāgārjuna's reply echoes the reply developed there:

29.   Since this action
         Is not arisen from a condition,
         Nor arisen causelessly,
         It follows that there is no agent.

Since the action does not arise inherently, it lacks inherent existence. Since, as per the discussion of agent and action in Chapter VIII, empty actions entail empty agents, there is no inherently existing agent of the kind presupposed by the objector. But the objector continues:

30.   If there is no action and agent,
         Where could the fruit of action be?
         Without a fruit,
         Where is there an experiencer?

That is, if we deny the reality of the action and the agent, we seem to deny the reality of the consequences of the action and, hence, the experiencer, whether "without understanding and consumed by passion" or not. But Nāgārjuna's view is not that these things are non-existent, as he emphasized in XVII: 20—only that they are empty. So it does follow that the consequences are *empty*—but that does not entail in any way that they are nonexistent. And it follows that the consequence and the karmic link are empty. From this it follows that the reborn individual whose existence and characteristics are determined by this causal sequence is also empty of inherent existence. And if so, there is no problem about how his/her genesis is dependent upon an empty sequence. Nāgārjuna introduces an analogy to explain this situation:

31.   Just as the teacher, by magic,
            Makes a magical illusion, and
            By that illusion
            Another illusion is created,

32.   In that way are an agent and his action:
            The agent is like the illusion.
            The action
            Is like the illusion's illusion.

That is, we can understand the entire sequence of agent, action, consequences of action, and arising of new agent, whether within a single lifetime or—in the context of Buddhist ontology and doctrine—across lifetimes, as an entirely empty sequence with entirely empty stages. But that does not prevent its being perceived, or its reality for those who participate therein.

33.   Afflictions, actions, bodies,
            Agents, and fruits are
            Like a city of Gandharvas and
            Like a mirage or a dream.

Again, it is important to emphasize that emptiness, rather than being a kind of nonactuality contrasting with empirical reality, is in fact the very condition of empirical reality and hence the only kind of genuine actuality. Mirages and dreams are actual phenomena, which actually appear and which have consequences. But that does not mean that they appear to us in a nondeceptive way. Mirages are not water and do not quench thirst, and dream-elephants carry no loads. By analogy, saṃsāra, action, karmic link, and consequence, Nāgārjuna argues, are real empirical phenomena, but are empty of anything more than conventional existence. While they may appear to exist inherently, either as persistent phenomena, as processes or elements of processes, or as abstract phenomena—as per the various opposing views considered in this chapter—they do not so exist. For to exist in those ways would in fact be incoherent. This analysis hence does not entail the nonexistence of agent and action, except from the ultimate point of view. Rather it explains how it is possible for them to exist at all.

Chapter XVIII

Examination of Self and Entities

A good deal of the confusion Nāgārjuna diagnoses in the previous two chapters concerns the presupposition that the self, as an afflicted being capable of liberation from suffering, must be thought of as an inherently real entity. In this chapter, therefore, Nāgārjuna turns to an examination of the self, per se, apart from its relation to such things as perception, action, suffering, affliction, and so forth, as he has examined it in prior chapters.

1. If the self were the aggregates,
   It would have arising and ceasing (as properties).
   If it were different from the aggregates,
   It would not have the characteristics of the aggregates.

If there is an inherently existent self, it must either be identical to or different from the aggregates. The aggregates are the more basic components into which the individual divides upon analysis. In standard Buddhist analysis, they include the physical body, sensation, perception, dispositions, and consciousness or cognition. It is important to note, though, that this particular analysis has no deep philosophical significance. It reflects an essentially empirical psychological theory about the best explanatory framework to use in comprehending human behavior and the most useful way for a Buddhist practitioner to attend to his/her experience. As we have seen already, the aggregates are themselves empty, and as much Buddhist psychology emphasizes, they, too, are subject to further decomposition. But Nāgārjuna's argument proceeds independently of any particular decomposition. No matter how one analyzes the human being, if we are to posit over and above the components into which it divides an inherently existent self, that self must be either identical to or different from those components. (This argument, by the way, appears in virtually the same form in *On Man* by Sextus Empiricus.)

But if the self is identical to the aggregates, it will be constantly changing, constantly arising and ceasing, since the aggregates are constantly arising and ceasing. This is so whether one takes the self to be identical to some one of the aggregates or to the whole collection of the aggregates. If, on the other hand, one takes the self to be distinct from the aggregates, the relation between them becomes completely mysterious; the self becomes unknowable, and the fate of the aggregates becomes irrelevant to the fate of the self. This is because the only objects ever given to us in introspection are the aggregates (a familiar Humean insight), and the self we presumably care about is one we *know*. And it would be a bit bizarre to suggest that whatever happens to my mind, body, memory, sensory experience, and so forth, is independent of what happens to *me*.

One must, of course, keep in mind that this destructive dilemma depends upon the attempt to identify a single inherently existent self and does not undermine the possibility of a conventionally identified self posited on the basis of the aggregates. So what Nāgārjuna is emphatically *not* doing is arguing that there are no aggregates in any sense or that there are no persons, agents, subjects, and so forth. The hypothesis for reductio is that over and above (or below and beneath) any composite of phenomena collectively denoted by "I" or by a proper name, there is a single substantial entity that is the referent of such a term.

But, the proponent of the inherently existent self asks, what is the bearer of the self's properties and the thing that possesses those aggregates? The first half of XVIII: 2 raises this question. The second half begins Nāgārjuna's reply, which occupies the remainder of the chapter and constitutes a substantial portion of his positive view on the nature of self from the standpoint of ontology and soteriology:

2.   If there were no self,
            Where would the self's (properties) be?
            From the pacification of the self and what belongs to it,
            One abstains from grasping onto "I" and "mine."

Nāgārjuna replies that once one stops trying to posit an independent self, the problem posed simply vanishes. That is, the worry about the possessor of the aggregates and properties of the self occurs only given that one conceives of them as properties and aggregates that are essentially *of* something. The insight is a bit abstract, but it is the same one that Hume was after in the Fig argument in the *Treatise*.[92] Much of the motivation for positing a substantial self is the intuition that since its properties and components exist, they must exist *somewhere*—that there must be a substratum in which they inhere. But once we give up that conception of what it is for a property or a component to exist (as Nāgārjuna has argued that we must in Chapters V, VI, and IX above), the drive to posit a substratum vanishes. And when the drive to posit the substratum vanishes, we simply, Nāgārjuna urges, think of the aggregates and properties as associated aggregates and properties, not as *my* aggregates and properties.

3.   One who does not grasp onto "I" and "mine,"
            That one does not exist.
            One who does not grasp onto "I" and "mine,"
            He does not perceive.

These are corelative. When one stops grasping the aggregates and the self as independent entities or as the possessions of independent entities, one recognizes one's own lack of inherent existence. One also recognizes the lack of inherent existence of the aggregates, as in the case of perception. This is not to say that one ceases conventionally to exist or that one goes blind—rather it is

92. See Hume (1975), pp. 235–39.

that one comes to understand one's own existence and that of other entities in the context of emptiness and, hence, to regard that existence as necessarily relational and conventional.

The relation between the second and third verses of this chapter is also important from the standpoint of the relation between theory and practice, philosophy and soteriology: Nāgārjuna emphasizes the two-way streets in this neighborhood. Understanding emptiness leads one to grasp less, to become more detached. Relaxing one's tendency to grasp leads to a realization of emptiness. Philosophy, meditation, and the practice of the moral virtues that issue in the relaxation of grasping are conceived from this vantage point as necessarily mutually supportive.

4.   When views of "I" and "mine" are extinguished,
        Whether with respect to the internal or external,
        The appropriator ceases.
        This having ceased, birth ceases.

When one completely relinquishes the view of entities and the self as inherently existent and when all habits of reification have been eliminated, Nāgārjuna urges, liberation from cyclic existence and suffering have been achieved. Nāgārjuna defers the precise characterization of nirvāṇa to the chapter devoted to its examination and that devoted to the examination of the status of the Tathāgata (XXV and XXII, respectively).

5.   Action and misery having ceased, there is nirvāṇa.
        Action and misery come from conceptual thought.
        This comes from mental fabrication.
        Fabrication ceases through emptiness.

The diagnosis, though, of the predicament of saṃsāra and the corresponding prescription are clear: Grasping, contaminated action, and suffering are rooted in delusion, and this delusion comes from cognitive error. The root delusion—the fundamental cognitive error—is the confusion of merely conventional existence with inherent existence. The realization of emptiness eliminates that fabrication of essence, which eliminates grasping, contaminated action, and its pernicious consequences.

6.   That there is a self has been taught,
And the doctrine of no-self,
By the buddhas, as well as the
Doctrine of neither self nor nonself.

There are many discussions of the way to think about the self in the Buddhist canon. For those who are nihilistic about the self (such as contemporary eliminative materialists or classical Indian Cārvākas), it is important to explain the conventional reality of the self. For those who tend to reify the self, the doctrine of no-self is taught, that is, the doctrine of the emptiness of the self. But, Nāgārjuna claims, as a preamble to the next verse, there is a deeper view of the matter—a doctrine of neither self nor nonself. That doctrine is closely tied to that of the emptiness of emptiness. Both the terms "self" and "no-self" together with any conceptions that can be associated with them, Nāgārjuna claims, are conventional designations. They may each be soteriologically and analytically useful antidotes to extreme metaphysical views and to the disturbances those views occasion. But to neither corresponds an entity—neither a thing that we could ever find on analysis and identify with the self, nor a thing or state that we could identify with no-self. The terms and the properties they designate are themselves empty, despite the fact that they are used to designate emptiness. To say neither self nor no-self is, from this perspective, not to shrug one's shoulders in indecision but to recognize that while each of these is a useful characterization of the situation for some purposes, neither can be understood as correctly ascribing a property to an independently existent entity. And if they cannot be understood in this way, what are we really saying?

7.   What language expresses is nonexistent.
The sphere of thought is nonexistent.
Unarisen and unceased, like nirvāṇa
Is the nature of things.

This insight is developed further in this verse. Here Nāgārjuna begins to move towards his famous and surprising identification of nirvāṇa with saṃsāra, and of emptiness with conventional reality. This identification of what in earlier Buddhism were regarded as wholly different from one another and this characterization of the mundane in terms heretofore reserved for the putatively transcendent are among Nāgārjuna's most radical and original moves and are central to the development of a distinctively Māhāyana outlook. In the first two lines, he reiterates that there are no actual convention-independent entities that correspond to the ostensible referring terms or predicates in our language. But, he argues, from the emptiness of things, it follows that they never either arise or cease. This does not mean that they are permanent, of course. Rather it means that while arising and ceasing and consequent impermanence are features of all conventional phenomena and are among the features that make them empty, from the ultimate point of view, as was argued in Chapter VII, there is no ultimate basis for arising and ceasing. But if nirvāṇa is liberation from cyclic existence and hence from arising and ceasing, it follows that, from the ultimate standpoint, all things in saṃsāra are actually just as they are in nirvāṇa.

8.   Everything is real and is not real,
      Both real and not real,
      Neither real nor not real.
      This is Lord Buddha's teaching.

This is the positive tetralemma regarding existence. Everything is conventionally real. Everything is ultimately unreal (that is, not unreal in just any sense, but unreal when seen from the ultimate standpoint). Everything has both characteristics—that is, everything is both conventionally real and ultimately unreal. Nothing is ultimately real or completely nonexistent. That is, everything is neither real in one sense nor not-real in another sense.[93,94]

93. My reading contrasts with that of Inada (1970, p. 113), who argues that here Nāgārjuna intends to deny these four possibilities. See also Sprung (1979) and Wood (1994) for interpretations that fail to appreciate completely the positive tetralemma and its role in Nāgārjuna's enterprise (though to be sure Wood takes note of the positive mood of this instance). Ruegg (1977) interprets this verse as suggesting gradations of progressively more sophisticated teachings—progressing from a mundane analysis of existence to a teaching of emptiness, to a teaching of their compatibility, to an indication of the inability of predication. Ng (1993), pp. 93–97, agrees. While such a purport would be something with

Interestingly, the tetralemma can also be asserted in a negative form with some of the same force: Nothing is real (ultimately). Nothing is not-real (everything has a kind of reality). Nothing is both real and not-real (in the same sense—that would be contradictory). Nothing is neither real nor not-real (the law of the excluded middle). Both forms of the tetralemma are found in this text. See XXII: 11.[95,96]

9. Not dependent on another, peaceful and
   Not fabricated by mental fabrication,
   Not thought, without distinctions,
   That is the character of real*ity* (that-ness).

That is, independent of conceptual imputation there are no objects, no identities, and so, no distinctions. But of course, as Kant would agree, there is no way that we can think such a reality.

---

which Nāgārjuna would agree, it seems out of place in this discussion. Wood, on the other hand, takes this verse to indicate that straightforward contradictions (existence and nonexistence) follow from the supposition that anything exists at all, in any way, and, hence, to form part of a nihilistic analysis. While such a reading would make sense if one only attended to this chapter, taken in the context of the work as a whole, and especially Chapter XXIV, that nihilistic reading is very hard to sustain.

94. That is, of course, everything that is conventionally real in the first place. Santa Claus is not among the objects of analysis here.

95. It is interesting to note—and we will return to this point in XXII below—that Nāgārjuna typically resorts to positive forms of the tetralemma when emphasizing claims about conventional phenomena and to negative forms when emphasizing the impossibility of the literal assertion of ultimate truths. Ng (1993), pp. 99–105, notices this point as well.

96. Here I take issue with philosophers such as Sprung (1979), who argue that the tetralemma is insignificant for Mādhyamika thought. Indeed, as I indicate in several places in this commentary, it is, both in its positive and negative moods, often an indispensable analytic tool. It is indeed "used as a means of investigation" (p. 7) here and elsewhere in the text. And as I argue here and below it is often quite useful. Sprung may be led to this conclusion by the fact that he overlooks the contrast between positive and negative tetralemmas, focusing exclusively on the latter. Moreover, he confuses its logical structure. See Ruegg (1977) and Matilal (1977) for divergent but each interesting and helpful investigations into the structure of the tetralemma, as well as Wood (1994) for what I regard as a serious misunderstanding of the tetralemma and of its deployment in Mādhyamika philosophy (see esp. pp. 64–77).

Nonetheless, Nāgārjuna argues (and Kant still agrees), we must see that that is the ultimate truth about things, though it might in its nature be inexpressible and inconceivable.[97]

10. Whatever comes into being dependent on another
     Is not identical to that thing.
     Nor is it different from it.
     Therefore it is neither nonexistent in time nor permanent.

Here Nāgārjuna recapitulates a brief analysis of what it is for a phenomenon to be dependently arisen. But in the context of the deeper understanding of emptiness and of the relation between the ultimate and the conventional developed in this chapter, a deeper reading of this verse is in order: Our attention is called to the fact that the analysis of dependency developed here—and consequently of the conventional reality and ultimate nonexistence of the dependent—is at the same time a correct conventional characterization of the nature of phenomena and an ostention of the fact

97. His Holiness the Dalai Lama, in oral remarks (Columbia University, 1994), notes that "whenever we examine physical, mental, or abstract entities, we find as a result of a reductive analysis nothing but their unfindability. So you can't really speak coherently of identity or of entities. This is the fundamental teaching of Mādhyamika." See also Nagao (1989), pp. 67–68, for useful remarks on XVIII: 7–9. But this interpretation can be carried too far, with the consequence that Nāgārjuna is seen as a thoroughgoing Kantian absolutist regarding the ultimate truth. Murti (1985) endorses just such a view:

Origination, decay, etc . . . are imagined by the uninformed; they are speculations indulged in by the ignorant. The real is utterly devoid (śūnya) of these and other conceptual constructions; it is transcendent to thought and can be realised only in nondual knowledge—prajñā or Intuition, which is the Absolute itself. . . . The distinction between two truths, Paramārtha and Saṃvṛti, is emphasised. . . .
. . . It as generally accepted [by Nāgārjuna and his followers] that the real is Absolute, at once Transcendent of Empirical Determinations and Immanent [in] Phenomena as the innermost essence. (p. xi [capitalization in original])

Kalupahana (1986) adopts another extreme reading, arguing that this verse in fact says nothing about the character of reality, but rather "the means by which a conception of truth is arrived at." He argues that it merely admonishes one to be independent in one's thinking, unbiased and calm in one's philosophical inquiry. It is hard to see how this reading could be justified apart from a strong antecedent commitment to seeing Nāgārjuna as a pragmatist.

that it is only a conventional designation of a nature that must remain uncharacterizable.[98]

11.   By the buddhas, patrons of the world,
       This immortal truth is taught:
       Without identity, without distinction;
       Not non-existent in time, not permanent.

That is, this doctrine itself is also empty. It is conventionally real, ultimately nonexistent, dependent, impermanent, and has a nature in itself that can never be characterized. The final verse is an admonishment to meditate seriously on this argument. For by understanding clearly the nature of the self and of the entities to which it is related, Nāgārjuna believes that one can attain buddhahood. That is why he emphasizes that with a correct view, even without a teacher or a buddha to instruct one, a patient meditator can attain his/her own awakening.

12.   When the fully enlightened ones do not appear,
       And when the disciples have disappeared,
       The wisdom of the self-enlightened ones
       Will arise completely without a teacher.

98. Kalupahana (1986) reads these final verses very differently, as having nothing to do with the ultimate truth, but rather as suggesting that freedom from suffering "does not necessarily mean the absence of a subject-object discrimination. It means the absence of any discrimination based upon one's likes and dislikes, one's obsessions" (p. 59). It is, however, very hard to square this reading of XVIII: 10, 11 with any defensible reading of XVIII: 8, 9.

Chapter XIX

Examination of Time

Another response to the attack on the reality of action and its consequences might to be argue that, nonetheless, the time in which action and its consequences are realized must be real. Nāgārjuna in this chapter argues that time cannot be conceived of as an entity existing independently of temporal phenomena, but must itself be regarded as a set of relations among them. His arguments are closely akin to those of Zeno, Sextus, and McTaggart.

1.   If the present and the future
       Depend on the past,
       Then the present and the future
       Would have existed in the past.

   Nāgārjuna's method is to divide time into the past, the present, and the future and then to argue that none of these can be said to inherently exist. In these first two verses, he considers one horn of an implicit dilemma: The present and the future either depend upon the past or they do not. In these two verses he considers the possibility that they do depend upon the past. But if they depend upon it in any sense that could plausibly guarantee their inherent existence, they must somehow emerge from it as a basis. If so, he argues, they must have existed in the past. For if they did not, then we would have the situation where when the time on which they ostensibly depend exists they do not exist, or a situation where at the time they exist that on which they ostensibly depend does not exist. We would then either have the situation in which the ostensibly dependent exists, but in the absence of that on which it depends, or in which the necessary condition exists, but without that of which it is the condition.

This raises two difficulties, one general and one specific to the case at hand: First, by the arguments developed concerning the temporal relations between causes and their effects in Chapters I and VII, we have two incoherent situations from the standpoint of anyone who considers the causal relation or its relata to be inherently existent. There must be a real relation between the cause and the effect in which the effect is contained potentially in the cause, and this would unfortunately entail the past existence of the present and the future. But second, there is a little regress to be developed. For if the present and the future depend upon the past, they must succeed or be simultaneous with it. But they must succeed or be simultaneous with it in time. That requires a super-time in which the parts of time are related, and so on, ad infinitum.

2.   If the present and the future
      Did not exist there,
      How could the present and the future
      Be dependent upon it?

That is, if we deny that the present and the future existed potentially in the past and were somehow coexistent with it, there is no way to understand the mechanics of the dependency relation. By the time the present comes around, the past isn't around to give rise to it. And when the past was around, the present didn't occur.

3.   If they are not dependent upon the past,
      Neither of the two would be established.
      Therefore neither the present
      Nor the future would exist.

If, on the other hand, one argued that the parts of time are independent, there would be no sense in which they would be determinately ordered and in which they would be part of the same time. Time is by definition an ordering of events in which moments stand in determinate relations to one another, in virtue of which the location of any moment depends on the location of all of the others. The present is the present only because it is poised within the past and the future. If it were not, it would not be the present. So either the present is in the past, in which case it is nonexistent, or it is independent of the past and the future, in which case it is nonexistent.

4.   By the same method,
      The other two divisions—past and future,
      Upper, lower, middle, etc.,
      Unity, etc., should be understood.

That is, we can generalize this argument about the dependency of the future and present, whose narrow purpose is to demonstrate the nonexistence of the present, to demonstrate the nonexistence of the past and future as inherently existent entities. Moreover, Nāgārjuna notes, this argument applies, mutatis mutandis, to spatial relations.

5.   A nonstatic time is not grasped.
      Nothing one could grasp as
      Stationary time exists.
      If time is not grasped, how is it known?

This is a second destructive dilemma: Time, if it exists as an entity, is either stationary or changing. To say that it is changing is incoherent; we would need to posit a super-time in which that change occurs. But to say that it is static is incoherent as well. That suggests that past, present, and future coexist. So there is no coherent conception of time as an entity.

6.   If time depends on an entity,
      Then without an entity how could time exist?
      There is no existent entity.
      So how can time exist?

Finally, Nāgārjuna argues, we cannot suppose that time exists as one entity dependent on some other as its ground if we want time to exist inherently. This is because, in the previous arguments in the text, we have already argued that none of the entities that exist in time are inherently existent. So none would form a suitable ontological basis for an inherently existent time.

But this final verse is double-edged, and its positive reading contains Nāgārjuna's positive account of the nature of time. Nāgārjuna points out that with no entities to be temporally related, there is no time. That is, the only mode of existence that time has is as a set of relations among empirical phenomena. Apart from those phenomena and those relations, there is no time.[99] But that means that, given the lack of inherent existence of phenomena, there can be no inherent existence of time. Time is thus merely a dependent set of relations, not an entity in its own right, and certainly not the inherently existent vessel of existence it might appear to be.

---

99. This insight is foundational for Dōgen's later analysis of *Uji*, or being-time.

Chapter XX

Examination of Combination

This chapter examines the possibility that, while no effect could be inherently dependent upon any single cause, it might be that the correct understanding of dependent arising and the thoroughgoing interdependence of phenomena that Nāgārjuna urges involves the inherent dependence of any phenomenon on the combination of all of its conditions. Thus, while every phenomenon would, as Nāgārjuna has been arguing, be completely dependent on all others, this dependence itself would be inherently existent. Much of the argument is a reprise of arguments that we have seen already, particularly in Chapters I and VII. But the temporal analysis of Chapter XIX is also in evidence.

1. If, arising from the combination of
   Causes and conditions,
   The effect is in the combination,
   How could it arise from the combination?

2. If, arising from the combination of
   Causes and conditions,
   The effect is not in the combination,
   How could it arise from the combination?

In the opening verses, Nāgārjuna sets up the destructive dilemma that frames the first part of this chapter: Either the effect is already present in the combination on which it is supposed by the reificationist to inherently depend or it is not. If it is, he will argue, there is no sense in which it really arises from them at all. If not, on the other hand, he will argue that there is no sense in which whatever dependence there is could be inherent dependence. Nāgārjuna alternates in the subsequent verses between these alternatives, developing a number of difficulties for each.

3. If the effect is in the combination
    Of causes and conditions,
    Then it should be grasped in the combination.
    But it is not grasped in the combination.

First, suppose that the effect already exists somehow in the combination of phenomena on which it depends. Then in grasping—that is, in conceiving or perceiving—that collection, we should, ipso facto, grasp the effect. But we do not. Consider the set of conditions of a match lighting. There is the presence of sulphur, friction, oxygen, and so forth. But neither in virtue of conceiving of these things nor in virtue of seeing them do we see fire.

4. If the effect is not in the combination
    Of causes and conditions,
    Then actual causes and conditions
    Would be like noncauses and nonconditions.

On the other hand, Nāgārjuna argues, if the proponent of inherently existent dependence argues that the effect is not present in the combination, he would have to say that there is no difference between actual conditions of an effect and an arbitrary collection of phenomena with no relation at all to it. Because the very point of this analysis is to explain how a particular set of conditions determines an effect. For Nāgārjuna, as we should be able to see by recalling his treatment of dependent origination and the relation between conditions and their effects in Chapter I, this is no problem: There is simply no general metaphysical answer to such a question for a Mādhyamika philosopher. A collection of conditions determines its effect simply because when those conditions are present, that effect arises. That fact may in turn be empirically explicable by other regularities. But there is no independent foundation for the network of regularities itself. However, for the substantialist there must be some analysis of the collection of conditions itself that answers the question regarding *how* that collection has the power to produce that effect. And the answer the opponent proposes is that it does so because the effect is inherently present in some sense in that collection.

5.   If the cause, in having its effect,
      Ceased to have its causal status,
      There would be two kinds of cause:
      With and without causal status.

At this point, Nāgārjuna turns to the temporal relation between the effect, the cause, and the combination of conditions that together with the primary cause of the effect bring about the effect. The position that he is worrying about is this: Effects depend upon particular causes, but those causes need the cooperation of supporting conditions in order to be efficacious. The familiar example in this context is that of the seed and the sprout. The seed, according to the proponent of such a position, causes the sprout, but only if there is soil, water, air, and so forth, to support it. Nāgārjuna then complains that on this view the word "cause" is being used equivocally: In one sense it is used to refer to things—the primary causes—that really don't cause anything. In the other sense, it is used to refer to those that really have causal status—namely, the entire assemblage of conditions that are necessary and sufficient for the arising of the effect.

6.   If the cause, not yet having
      Produced its effect, ceased,
      Then having arisen from a ceased cause,
      The effect would be without a cause.

But, he urges, if we want to assert that the cause, instead of changing from a cause to a noncause, simply ceases at the moment when it produces its effect, we still have a problem. Because by the time the effect emerges, the cause will have vanished, and the effect will then have emerged without a cause and so will be a causeless effect.

7.   If the effect were to arise
      Simultaneously with the collection,
      Then the produced and the producer
      Would arise simultaneously.

Turning now to the entire collection as determinative of the effect, Nāgārjuna points out that the effect cannot be simultaneous with the occurrence of a collection of its conditions for all of the reasons that he has advanced previously against the simultaneity of causes and their effects.

8.   If the effect were to arise
      Prior to the combination,
      Then, without causes and conditions,
      The effect would arise causelessly.

But neither, of course, can the effect arise before the conditions are met since the effect would then arise spontaneously, and this possibility has been refuted earlier.

9.   If, the cause having ceased, the effect
      Were a complete transformation of the cause,
      Then a previously arisen cause
      Would arise again.

Nāgārjuna now responds to the following possible reply: The effect in question is not an entity distinct from the cause or the collection of conditions that serve as its ground. Therefore these questions about the temporal relations between events involving distinct entities do not arise. The sprout is not distinct from the seed, but is merely a complete transformation of it. But, Nāgārjuna argues, it is also not possible to characterize the effect as a simple change of nature of a single entity that was the cause before the transformation. For then we would have to say that the cause remains in existence after the effect arises and so would have to keep producing the same effect over and over again. This argument might seem not to have much bite. After all, one might think, the alternative being proposed seems quite like Nāgārjuna's own view that we should not think of causes and their effects as distinct entities. But this would be wrong. This argument succeeds because the opponent denies the distinctness in entity between cause and effect by positing an identity in essence and by appealing to that essence to explain the causal potential of the cause. If the essence of the entity is what determines its causal potential, then if that essence remains, the potential should remain as well. If the essence does not remain, then the language of transformation must be abandoned. If the essence remains, and the language of transformation is retained at an accidental level, the claim that there is an essential causal principle must be rejected.

10.   How can a cause, having ceased and dissolved,
       Give rise to a produced effect?
       How can a cause joined with its effect produce it
       If they persist together?

Nāgārjuna now returns to the temporal trilemma. As he has argued before, just as a cause cannot follow or be simultaneous with its effect, the precedence of cause over effect is problematic as well. For when there is a cause, there is no effect. When there is an effect, there is no cause. And if we appeal to temporal overlap, we inherit all of the problems with precedence, simultaneity, and collections. In introducing the idea of a cause being "joined" with its effect ('brel-ba), Nāgārjuna is introducing a putative causal link into the discussion. One who proposes simultaneity or temporal overlap of cause with effect might be doing so in order to make possible such a link. But Nāgārjuna here claims that positing that link does not overcome the temporal difficulties he has presented.

In XX: 11–15, Nāgārjuna summarizes the results of these arguments. Causes, whether single or composite, cannot precede, coincide with, or follow their effects; causes cannot produce their effects in isolation, nor can collections of causes inherently produce their effects:

11.   Moreover, if not joined with its cause,
        What effect can be made to arise?
        Neither seen nor unseen by causes
        Are effects produced.

Here Nāgārjuna returns to his critique of the idea of a causal nexus. He points out that though that idea has been shown to be incoherent, it is the only way that one can make sense of a real causal link or of inherently existent production. So in its absence, we cannot make sense of the production of an effect by its cause. In the last two lines, Nāgārjuna makes use of the strange metaphor of a cause seeing its effect to denote this link (*thongs-ba*).[100] This is clearly a metaphor for this link, suggesting that whether it is forged by contiguity or by some other means at a distance, it will be explanatorily impotent.

12.   There is never a simultaneous connection
        Of a past effect
        With a past, a nonarisen,
        Or an arisen cause.

13.   There is never a simultaneous connection
        Of a an arisen effect
        With a past, a nonarisen,
        Or an arisen cause.

14.   There is never a simultaneous connection
        Of a nonarisen effect
        With a past, a nonarisen,
        Or an arisen cause.

15.   Without connecting,
        How can a cause produce an effect?
        Where there is connection,
        How can a cause produce an effect?

At this point, Nāgārjuna turns directly to the connection between emptiness and the dependence of effects on collections of condi-

---

100. Inada, with some philosophical justification, translates this as "projected." But I see little lexical merit in that choice.

tions. The opponent now asks how a cause or collection of causes that does not contain the effect in any way can produce that effect:

16.   If the cause is empty of an effect,
        How can it produce an effect?
        If the cause is not empty of an effect,
        How can it produce an effect?

Nāgārjuna, echoing the argument of Chapter I, replies that only if cause and effect are empty can production be understood. The next verse explains this in more detail:

17.   A nonempty effect does not arise.
        The nonempty would not cease.
        This nonempty would be
        The nonceased and the nonarisen.

If the effect were nonempty, as the opponent presupposes in wondering how the effect could be produced from empty causes, then since the inherently existent depends on nothing, the effect would be unproduced and would never cease. But there are no such things. So the putative problem case, the nonempty effect of empty causes, is not even possible.

18.   How can the empty arise?
        How can the empty cease?
        The empty will hence also
        Be the nonceased and nonarisen.

Nāgārjuna emphasizes here the double edge of the ontology of emptiness. Even though it is in virtue of the fact that conventional entities are constantly arising and ceasing that they are empty, their emptiness entails that they do not, from the ultimate standpoint, arise, cease, or abide at all. This is an eloquent statement of the interpenetration of the ultimate and the conventional truths: The very ground on the basis of which emptiness is asserted is denied reality through the understanding of emptiness itself. The emptiness of phenomena is, after all, asserted on the basis of their momentary impermanence. But that impermanence and the very existence of the impermanent objects asserted to be empty is not even present from the ultimate standpoint. Yet that, rather than constituting a self-refutation, constitutes a self-confirmation. For if anything were apparent from the ultimate standpoint, that phenomenon would be nonempty. It is the absence of any such phenomenon—not its presence—that confirms the analysis and that prevents it from lapsing into a view, in the pernicious sense.[101]

19.   For cause and effect to be identical
         Is not tenable.
         For cause and effect to be different
         Is not tenable.

Nāgārjuna here returns to the business of mobilizing destructive dilemmas against the view that any dependence of effects on collocations of conditions could be inherently existent. The argument in XX: 20 is based on the dichotomy of identity or difference of cause and effect and is drawn from Chapter I:

20.   If cause and effect were identical,
         Produced and producer would be identical.
         If cause and effect were different,
         Cause and noncause would be alike.

For the relation at issue in this chapter to be inherently existent, the collection of conditions would have either to be identical in nature or different in nature from the effect. If identical, we would have the absurd consequence that the effect was self-caused. But if the effect is totally different in essence, we have no explanation of how *that* collection of conditions produced *that* effect.

21.   If an effect had entitihood,
         What could have caused it to arise?
         If an effect had no entitihood,
         What could have caused it to arise?

This attack on the inherent status of the relation between conditions and effects focuses on arising itself. The effect must either

101. See the discussion of XXVII: 30 for more on this point.

have entitihood or not. If it does, its being caused to arise is self-contradictory. If not, though, from the ultimate standpoint it does not arise. It would follow from either that there is no inherently existent arising and, so, no inherent production from a collection of conditions. The next verse makes this same point from the side of the collection. If the effect produced is not inherently produced, the collection does not inherently produce it. If not, it is not an inherently productive collection:

22.   If something is not producing an effect,
       It is not tenable to attribute causality.
       If it is not tenable to attribute causality,
       Then of what will the effect be?

23.   If the combination
       Of causes and conditions
       Is not self-produced,
       How does it produce an effect?

The ground of an inherently existent relation of production must be inherently existent. But then it could depend on nothing else. It would have to be self-produced. But this is not claimed for the collection of conditions or the relation between them and the effect by the opponent here. It couldn't be. For the whole point of moving to a collection is to avoid the problems of production from a single cause. But collections depend upon their parts and upon the causes of those parts. So no such collection can be self-produced. So, while Nāgārjuna can certainly grant that effects are dependent upon collections of conditions, it cannot be that those collections or that dependence exist inherently.

24.   Therefore, not made by combination,
       And not without a combination can the effect arise.
       If there is no effect,
       Where can there be a combination of conditions?

Combinations of conditions, just like individual conditions and just like their effects, can only be conceived of as empty of inherent existence.

Chapter XXI

Examination of Becoming and Destruction

In this chapter, Nāgārjuna examines the phenomenon of momentary impermanence. At this point in the dialectic, one might suggest that since the emptiness of phenomena derives directly from their decomposition into momentary time-slices and from the fact that they are constantly coming into existence and being destroyed, that process of momentary arising and destruction itself ought to be real in the strong sense. Nāgārjuna, by way of completing the discussion of the nature of conventional phenomena, demonstrates the emptiness of even arising and destruction themselves as a prelude to the final section of the text, that discussing the nature of the ultimate and its relation to conventional reality.

1. Destruction does not occur without becoming.
   It does not occur together with it.
   Becoming does not occur without destruction.
   It does not occur together with it.

This first verse announces the final stage in the argument to be developed. Nāgārjuna will show that destruction and becoming are both mutually incompatible and that they are mutually entailing. It will then follow that if they are inherently existent, they have contradictory properties.

2.   How could there be destruction
      Without becoming?
      How could there be death without birth?
      There is no destruction without becoming.

Nāgārjuna argues that, absent something coming into being, there is no sense in which it can be destroyed. So destruction presupposes becoming.

3.   How could destruction and becoming
      Occur simultaneously?
      Death and birth
      Do not occur simultaneously.

But they cannot exist simultaneously. For then the same entity would have contradictory properties.

4.   How could there be becoming
      Without destruction?
      For impermanence
      Is never absent from entities.

Since all phenomena are impermanent, as has been forcefully argued in earlier chapters, anything that comes into existence passes out of existence.

5.   How could destruction
      And becoming occur simultaneously?
      Just as birth and death
      Do not occur simultaneously.

6.   How, when things cannot
      Be established as existing,
      With, or apart from one another,
      Can they be established at all?

This is the argument to this stage: Becoming and destruction are mutually contradictory. So they cannot be properties of the same thing at the same time. But everything that is coming into existence is at a stage in a process that culminates in its destruction. So everything that is becoming is at the same time being destroyed. Everything that is being destroyed is in a later stage of a process that earlier resulted in its coming into existence and, indeed, is coming to exist in some other form. So everything that is being destroyed is also becoming. So becoming and destruction cannot coexist, but cannot exist apart. Hence they cannot exist independently at all.

7.   There is no becoming of the disappeared.
       There is no becoming of the nondisappeared.
       There is no destruction of the disappeared.
       There is no destruction of the nondisappeared.

This verse offers an epigrammatic summary of the previous argument: All phenomena, when analyzed closely, resolve into ephemeral moments, constantly disappearing to be succeeded by later stages of what are conventionally identified as the same objects. So everything that has ever existed has disappeared. Such a thing cannot be coming into existence. But no nondisappeared thing ever comes into existence. For as soon as it exists, it disappears. Similarly such things cannot be in the process of destruction. But nothing that is not ephemeral is destroyed either. Given this ephemeral nature of phenomena, establishing becoming and destruction as distinct, independent processes is impossible. This claim is made directly in XXI: 8:

8.   When no entities exist,
       There is no becoming or destruction.
       Without becoming and destruction,
       There are no existent entities.

In the next verse, Nāgārjuna connects this point directly to emptiness and to inherent existence, pointing out both that emptiness precludes the inherent establishment of becoming and destruction and that positing inherently existent phenomena would do no better:

9.   It is not tenable for the empty
      To become or to be destroyed.
      It is not tenable for the nonempty
      To become or to be destroyed.

The empty cannot come to be or be destroyed simply because there is no basis for the predication. With no entities, there is nothing to be brought into existence or to be destroyed. But if we posit nonempty phenomena, their independence and consequent permanence preclude their coming to be or destruction.

10.   It is not tenable
      That destruction and becoming are identical.
      It is not tenable
      That destruction and becoming are different.

They cannot be identical because they are contradictory predicates. But every destruction is a coming to be and vice versa. Hence when conceived of inherently, they can be neither identical nor different; when conceived of inherently, they cannot exist:

11.   If you think you see both
      Destruction and becoming,
      Then you see destruction and becoming
      Through impaired vision.

In the next two verses, Nāgārjuna addresses coming to be. He points out that if it is conceived of as truly existent then it must satisfy at least one of the alternatives represented in each of the following two tetralemmas. But it cannot:

12.   An entity does not arise from an entity.
      An entity does not arise from a nonentity.
      A nonentity does not arise from a nonentity.
      A nonentity does not arise from an entity.

The first alternative is precluded because inherently existent and distinct phenomena, Nāgārjuna has argued, cannot be related dependently. The second is precluded because that would involve production from nothing. The third would fail to count as inherently existent production, and from the standpoint of one who posits inherent existence as a guarantor of reality, would only amount to the production of the imaginary in any case. The final alternative again would not amount to real production of anything.

13.   An entity does not arise from itself.
         It is not arisen from another.
         It is not arisen from itself and another.
         How can it be arisen?

This verse simply recapitulates the argument of Chapter I in the service of the conclusion that arising cannot be conceived of as an independent phenomenon. Nāgārjuna now draws more general conclusions regarding the implication of the view that existence amounts to inherent existence for the extreme positions. He develops in the next two verses a nice reductio ad absurdum:

14.   If one accepts the existence of entities,
         Permanence and the view of complete nonexistence follow.
         For these entities
         Must be both permanent and impermanent.

If one thinks that any existent entity must exist inherently, then one is forced simultaneously to embrace the extremes of nihilism and reification. One must reify because any existent must be treated as inherently existent and hence permanent. But upon observing the impermanence of phenomena, one will be driven to nihilism since their impermanence would entail their lack of inherent existence and hence their complete nonexistence. An opponent, however, can be imagined to reply as follows:

15.   If one accepts the existence of entities
         Nonexistence and permanence will not follow.
         Cyclic existence is the continuous
         Becoming and destruction of causes and effects.

If Nāgārjuna is correct, this objection goes, there is a constant becoming and destruction of causally related phenomena. This, after all, is the heart of the Mādhyamika analysis of phenomenal reality. But if that is so, these phenomena that are becoming and being destroyed must exist. Otherwise, what comes into and passes out of existence? It is these entities, this opponent argues, that we must posit. And from positing such entities, neither their complete nonexistence nor their permanence follows. For they are by definition impermanently existent. Nāgārjuna replies in the next verse:

16.   If cyclic existence is the continuous
         Becoming and destruction of causes and effects,
         Then from the nonarising of the destroyed
         Follows the nonexistence of cause.

Given the pervasiveness of dependent arising, the impermanence of all causes and effects, and the emptiness of the relation of dependence itself, causes and effects themselves must be regarded as noninherently existent. For the person who equates existence with inherent existence, this forces the denial of the very becoming and destruction he has posited as the only inherently existent phenomena. The point against the objection asserted in the previous verse is this: The very fact that constant becoming and destruction characterizes reality entails that at no point can anything be identified as an entity in the robust sense—a thing with a nature that persists over time. The very phenomena the opponent wants to posit as existent in order to make sense of the series of becoming and destruction are, when that series is taken seriously, themselves nonexistent. But the kind of full existence the opponent feels compelled to posit is in any case not only impossible given this situation, but unnecessary as well. Nāgārjuna now turns to the soteriological implications of this view of becoming, destruction, and entitihood:

17.   If entities exist with entitihood,
         Then their nonexistence would make no sense.
         But at the time of nirvāṇa,
         Cyclic existence ceases completely, having been pacified.

If we thought that anything had inherent existence—whether entities, processes, or arising and its determinants—that could not possibly cease in nirvāṇa. So this view would render Buddhist soteriology incoherent and is therefore, since it purports to be a view of the nature of cyclic existence by contrast with nirvāṇa, untenable.

The next three verses sum up the results of this investigation regarding the possibility of conceiving of empirical reality as consisting of a series of momentary phenomena, each one of which gives rise to the next through an inherently real nexus of destruction and becoming. The structure of the argument is by now familiar:

18.   If the final one has ceased,
        The existence of a first one makes no sense.
        If the final one has not ceased,
        The existence of a first one makes no sense.

If the momentary phenomenon prior to a present momentary phenomenon has ceased prior to the arising of the present one, there is no basis for that arising. But if it has not ceased, then its destruction cannot be an occasion for the arising of the subsequent event. So the prior momentary phenomenon can neither have ceased nor not ceased.

19.   If when the final one was ceasing,
        Then the first was arising,
        The one ceasing would be one.
        The one arising would be another.

That is, if we say that the cessation of the previous momentary phenomenon is simultaneous with the arising of its successor, then being simultaneous but distinct, the two phenomena are separable and hence independent. If so, there is no basis for positing any connection between them. This is yet another application of the principle of the independence of separable phenomena.

20.   If, absurdly, the one arising
        And the one ceasing were the same,
        Then whoever is dying with the aggregates
        Is also arising.

Finally, we don't want to identify arising and ceasing, claiming that they are the same phenomenon, since they are by definition contraries. It would be tantamount, Nāgārjuna claims, to saying that a person who is dying is simultaneously being born. From the standpoint of one who wants to posit arising and destruction as the two complementary inherently existent bases of cyclic existence, it would hardly do to say that they are one and the same thing.

21.   Since the series of cyclic existence is not evident
       In the three times,
       If it is not in the three times,
       How could there be a series of cyclic existence?

And finally, if we cannot conceive of the domain of conventional phenomena as inherently existent in time, there is no sense in suggesting that it has some kind of transtemporal existence. The object of analysis here is the conventional world we inhabit. So, Nāgārjuna concludes, we cannot, upon analysis, resolve the domain of conventional phenomena into a series of constantly arising, constantly ceasing, yet individually inherently existent momentary phenomena, connected to one another and characterized by inherently real arising and ceasing. As this target ontology was among the subtlest of the pre-Mādhyamika views of the nature of reality, dependent arising, and impermanence (and is indeed not by any means a relic within Theravada Buddhism) and as it represents a plausible interpretation of fundamental Buddhist tenets, this refutation is an appropriate close to the portion of the text concerned directly with the analysis of the fundamental structure of conventional reality. With this in hand, Nāgārjuna turns in the final six chapters to topics concerned with the nature of ultimate reality: buddhahood, prominent incorrect views about the ultimate, the Four Noble Truths and emptiness, nirvāṇa, and the twelve limbs of dependent origination.

Chapter XXII

Examination of the Tathāgata

This is the first of the final set of chapters in the text, all of which
deal directly with topics concerning the ultimate truth and its relation to the conventional. The doctrine of the two truths, central to
all Mahāyāna Buddhist philosophy, is most explicitly enunciated in
Chapter XXIV. But it is present as a pervasive theme in the text.
There is a conventional world of dependently arisen objects with
properties, of selves and their properties and relations. And in that
world there is conventional truth: Snow is white. Grass is green.
Individual humans are distinct from one another and from their
material possessions. But there is also an ultimate truth about this
world: It is empty (of inherent existence). None of these objects or
persons exists from its own side (independently of convention).
From the ultimate point of view there are no individual objects or
relations between them. Just how these two truths are connected,
and how we are to understand them simultaneously, is the central
problem of Mādhyamika epistemology and metaphysics, and from
the standpoint of Mādhyamika, a satisfactory solution is essential
for Buddhist soteriological practice and ethics as well.

But discourse about the ultimate is perilous in a number of ways.
First, and most obviously, there is the ever-present danger of talking sheer nonsense. For the ultimate truth is, in some sense, ineffable in that all words and their referents are by definition conventional. The dualities generated by the use of terms that denote

individuals or classes as distinct from others or from their complements are unavoidable in discourse and nonexistent in the ultimate. So one must be very careful to kick away all ladders
promptly. At the same time, there are things that one can say
without lapsing into nonsense, by way of ostention, even from the
bottom rungs.

But the other grave danger is this: By distinguishing the conventional from the ultimate, it is tempting to disparage the former in
contrast to the latter, developing a sort of theory of one truth and
one falsehood. This is done if one reifies the entities associated
with the ultimate, such as emptiness or impermanence, or the Four
Noble Truths, or the Buddha. Then one treats these as real, intrinsically existent phenomena. The conventional then becomes the
world of illusion. It is to combat this tendency to treat the conventional world as illusory through treating such apparently transcendent entities as inherently existent that Nāgārjuna develops these
final chapters. Perhaps the most obvious candidate for reification
in a Buddhist context is the Buddha himself, and that is where
Nāgārjuna begins:

1.   Neither the aggregates, nor different from the aggregates,
        The aggregates are not in him, nor is he in the aggregates.
        The Tathāgata does not possess the aggregates.
        What is the Tathāgata?[102]

    This form of analytic demonstration of the nonexistence of the
self through an analysis of its possible relationship to the aggregates, often referred to as the "fivefold analysis," is developed with
great elegance by Candrakīrti in *Mādhyamakāvatāra*. Nāgārjuna
proposes four of five possible relations the self bears to the aggregates in this first verse, and the fifth is considered in the next two
verses. Here the self in question is the Buddha's self, but the
analysis is perfectly general as a refutation of any assertion of an
inherently existent personal self. That self cannot be the aggre-

---

102. *"Tathāgata"* is an epithet of the Buddha. It is an ambiguous compound,
meaning, depending upon how it is parsed, "thus gone" or "thus come," hence
indicating either the one gone along the path to enlightenment, or the one come to
teach the Buddhist doctrine.

gates for two reasons: First, the self posited is meant to be unitary, and the aggregates are plural. Second, the aggregates are constantly undergoing change, while the self that is posited is meant to endure as a single entity.

But the self can't be different from the aggregates either. For anything that happens to the aggregates happens to the self, and vice versa. If I hurt my body, I hurt *myself*. If you lose your vision, *you* become blind. And in the present case, buddhahood is presumably attained by a purification of the aggregates through practice. If the aggregates were entirely different from the self, it is not clear how purifying *them* would lead the *practicioner* to buddhahood.

The self cannot stand outside the aggregates as a basis for them, for if we strip away all of the aggregates, there is nothing left as an independent support. But nor is the self somehow contained in the aggregates as a hidden core, and for the same reason. When we strip away all of the aggregates in thought, nothing remains of the self.

2.   If the Buddha depended on the aggregates,
           He would not exist through an essence.
           Not existing through an essence,
           How could he exist through otherness-essence?

The fifth possibility is that the self, in this case the Buddha's self, is distinct from but dependent upon the aggregates. But from the standpoint of positing an inherently existent Buddha this is unsatisfactory. For if the Buddha were dependent, he would lack an essence and would be empty. And the situation can't be saved by suggesting that he has an essence through a relation to another since that presupposes essential difference, which presupposes that both the Buddha and the aggregates on which he is supposed to depend have individual essences. This is reinforced in the first two lines of the next verse:

3.   Whatever is dependent on another entity,
           Its selfhood is not appropriate.
           It is not tenable that what lacks a self
           Could be a Tathāgata.

The reifier in the last two lines of this verse and in the next asks how it is possible that a real Buddha could lack a self. What then would be the thing that practiced, that became enlightened and that preached the Dharma?

4.   If there is no essence,
       How could there be otherness-essence?
       Without possessing essence or otherness-essence,
       What is the Tathāgata?

5.   If without depending on the aggregates
       There were a Tathāgata,
       Then now he would be depending on them.
       Therefore he would exist through dependence.

That is, on the opponent's view, even if the Buddha had no dependence on the aggregates prior to attaining Buddhahood, in order to act as a Buddha, he must depend upon his consciousness, perception, body, and so forth. So if we suppose that the Buddha is now inherently existent and omniscient and compassionate and so forth, we must assume that he exists through dependence on his aggregates in some sense.

6.   Inasmuch as there is no Tathāgata
       Dependent upon the aggregates,
       How could something that is not dependent
       Come to be so?

We already know that the Buddha as a sentient being in saṃsāra, prior to entering nirvāṇa, could not exist dependent on the aggregates. This is a straightforward consequence of the argument for the nonexistence of a self distinct from the aggregates and from the fact that in order to depend upon the aggregates, the self would need to be distinct from them. And so, Nāgārjuna points out, it would be odd to think that an entity not dependent upon the aggregates in saṃsāra would come to be so upon entering nirvāṇa. It would, of course, be particularly odd for someone defending the target of this critique. Anyone holding such a position would hardly be expected to ascribe to the Buddha a *more* dependent status in nirvāṇa than in saṃsāra.

7.   There is no appropriation.
      There is no appropriator.
      Without appropriation
      How can there be a Tathāgata?

The appropriation here is the appropriation of aggregates as one's own. Without it, there can be no sense of individual identity. Since the opponent is positing the Tathāgata as an inherently existent individual, he must hold him to have his own aggregates.

8.   Having been sought in the fivefold way,
      What, being neither identical nor different,
      Can be thought to be the Tathāgata
      Through grasping?

But, as we have seen in the first two verses of this chapter, there is no way that the Buddha can be thought of as inherently existent in relation to those aggregates. So we can't divorce the Buddha from the aggregates. Nor can we understand the Buddha as inherently existing given that he must have aggregates.

9.   Whatever grasping there is
      Does not exist through essence.
      And when something does not exist through itself,
      It can never exist through otherness-essence.

So the Buddha does not exist inherently in virtue of his own essence. Nor does he exist inherently in virtue of some property of his aggregates or, for that matter, in virtue of anything else that is other, such as an inherently existent buddha-nature or state of nirvāṇa.

10.   Thus grasping and grasper
      Together are empty in every respect.
      How can an empty Tathāgata
      Be known through the empty?

So we must conceive of the Buddha and of all that pertains to him as empty of inherent existence. But the question then arises:

What can we say or know of such an empty Buddha? This is a fundamental question not only with regard to our knowledge of the nature of enlightenment, but also with regard to our ability to say anything coherent about emptiness itself and empty phenomena.

11. "Empty" should not be asserted.
     "Nonempty" should not be asserted.
     Neither both nor neither should be asserted.
     They are only used nominally.

This negative tetralemma is a crucial verse for understanding the relation between discourse on the conventional level and the understanding of emptiness or the ultimate truth. Nāgārjuna has been urging all along that ultimately all things are empty. It would be easy to interpret him to mean that from the ultimate standpoint, we can say of phenomena that they are empty. But here he quite deliberately undermines that interpretation, claiming instead that nothing can be literally said of things from such a standpoint. For ultimately there is no entity of which emptiness or nonemptiness can be predicated. Nor can we say that things are neither empty nor nonempty. For that would contradict the fact that from the standpoint of one using conventional language and cognition, it is correct to characterize phenomena as empty. The central claim in this verse is that all assertion, to the extent that it is true at all, is at best nominally true. Discourse about the ultimate character of things is not exempt from this generalization. Predication always requires an entity of which the predicate can be true; and the emptiness of phenomena guarantees that from the ultimate standpoint, there are no phenomena to be empty. The language is hence at best only ostensive.[103] The next verse generalizes this observation:

103. See Padhye (1988), esp. pp. 79–82, for further useful discussion of the import of this and other negative tetralemmas for Nāgārjuna's philosophy of language. Padhye correctly emphasizes that Nāgārjuna and his Prāsaṇgika-Mādhyamika followers reject any kind of Fregean or other realistic semantics that would require the independent existence of properties, including emptiness or nonemptiness, or of individuals, as the semantic values of predicates or subject terms, respectively, arguing for a more pragmatic view of linguistic meaning. Huntington (1989) emphasizes this point as well. I discuss this issue at greater length in connection with the interpretation of *Vigrahavyāvartanī* in Garfield (unpublished).

12. How can the tetralemma of permanent and impermanent, etc.,
     Be true of the peaceful?
     How can the tetralemma of finite, infinite, etc.,
     Be true of the peaceful?

13. One who grasps the view that the Tathāgata exists,
     Having seized the Buddha,
     Constructs conceptual fabrications
     About one who has achieved nirvāṇa.

Here Nāgārjuna returns to the problem of ascribing inherent
existence to the Buddha in the context of thinking about phenomena from the ultimate standpoint. The problem is that, as Nāgārjuna has argued above, the only grounds for asserting the inherent
existence of the Buddha would be on the grounds of the inherent
existence of the aggregates and some view about the relations of
the self to the aggregates. And we have seen that to be untenable.
Moreover, since upon achieving nirvāṇa, on most Buddhist doctrine, one ceases to identify a self and aggregates, it would follow
that upon achieving nirvāṇa one would cease to exist. This is doubly problematic. On the one hand, it forces one to see nirvāṇa as
complete annihilation, which doesn't make it look quite so attrac-
tive. On the other hand, it forces the conclusion that the Buddha is
either not in nirvāṇa (since he exists), which is paradoxical in that
buddhahood should guarantee nirvāṇa, or that he both exists (as a
genuine buddha) and does not exist (in virtue of being in nirvāṇa),
which is contradictory.

14. Since he is by nature empty,
     The thought that the Buddha
     Exists or does not exist
     After nirvāṇa is not appropriate.

Nāgārjuna here draws on the results of XXII: 11, 12 to point out
that one can evade all of these paradoxes by simply rejecting the
language of existence and nonexistence when these are read inherently. Empty things exist conventionally; but about their ultimate
status, nothing can be literally said. Of course we can say that the
Buddha is empty and, hence, neither really existent nor completely

nonexistent. But that, Nāgārjuna is arguing in this chapter, can be only understood in a purely negative sense. The ultimate nature of things is perhaps *shown* by it, to use a Wittgensteinian metaphor, but cannot be *said* in this language.[104]

15. Those who develop mental fabrications with regard to the Buddha,
     Who has gone beyond all fabrications,
     As a consequence of those cognitive fabrications,
     Fail to see the Tathāgata.

To see buddhahood for what it is—to see things as a buddha sees them—one must see things independently of the categories that determine an ontology of entities and a dichotomy of existence and nonexistence. That this is inconceivable to us, for Nāgārjuna, only indicates the fact that we are trapped in conventional reality through the force of the delusion of reification. But we can, through using the Mādhyamika dialectic, come to see the nature of our predicament, the possibility of transcending it, and even the nature of that transcendence. That, however, requires us to acknowledge the merely nominal character of conceptual imputation.

16.   Whatever is the essence of the Tathāgata,
        That is the essence of the world.
        The Tathāgata has no essence.
        The world is without essence.

This crucial final verse emphasizes again the lack of any fundamental nature of entities. Emptiness is the final nature of all things, from rocks to dogs to human beings to buddhas.[105] This fact entails, for Mahāyāna philosophers, the possibility of any sentient being to be fundamentally transformed—to attain enlightenment.

---

104. Nagao (1991) puts this point nicely: ". . . [F]or one whose point or departure is *śūnyatā*, even the claim that all is *śūnyatā* is absurd, for non-assertion or non-maintenance of a position is the real meaning of *śūnyatā*" (p. 42).

105. See also Kalupahana (1986), pp. 310–11, and Ng (1993), pp. 26–28, for a similar reading.

But this is so, paradoxically, because ultimately there is no fundamental transformation, because there is nothing to transform. In Chapters XXIV and XXV below, we will see the dramatic consequences of this line of reasoning.

Chapter XXIII

Examination of Errors

This chapter continues the investigation of the relation between cyclic existence and nirvāṇa by asking whether the fundamental defilements and the four basic cognitive errors, which according to orthodox Buddhist doctrine bind us to saṃsāra, themselves inherently exist and by asking how it is possible to abandon them and enter nirvāṇa. The fundamental defilements are desire, hatred, and confusion: the desire for things that are not desirable, the aversion to things to which it is not reasonable to be averse, confusion about the actual nature of entities. These, according to most strains of Buddhist philosophy, are the bases of afflicted action, which in turn leads to further grasping and error. The four basic errors or erroneous philosophical theses are: (1) There is a permanent self among the five personal aggregates. (2) There is real happiness in saṃsāra. (3) The body is pure—that is, that it is a real source of happiness. (4) There is a permanent self distinct from the aggregates.

If these defilements and errors were inherent properties of the self, that might serve as a ground for the inherent existence of saṃsāra and its phenomena, to the extent that saṃsāra is grounded in these phenomena. Moreover, though, if these defilements and errors were inherently existent, it is hard to see how nirvāṇa is possible since it requires their elimination. But on the other hand, if these defilements do not exist, it is hard to see why there is saṃsāra at all and why we are not already in nirvāṇa. And if they are merely illusions, why isn't the distinction between saṃsāra and nirvāṇa merely an illusion; why isn't suffering merely an illusion? In short, why isn't illusion merely an illusion? This chapter is devoted to answering these fundamental questions in Buddhist soteriological theory.

1. Desire, hatred, and confusion all
    Arise from thought, it is said.
    They all depend on
    The pleasant, the unpleasant, and errors.

Without reifying entities, a cognitive operation, there is no basis for desire for those entities, of aversion from them, and no confusion regarding their mode of existence. Seeing things as pleasant or unpleasant in themselves depends upon confusing our desire or aversion with respect to them with properties they have in themselves. The desire and aversion in turn depend upon our attributing pleasantness and unpleasantness to the entities. It is a tight and vicious circle of attribution and emotional reaction, all depending upon reification.

2. Since whatever depends on the pleasant and the unpleasant
    Does not exist through an essence,
    The defilements
    Do not really exist.

But it follows from this that the defilements, in virtue of depending on these attributions and upon our relation to pleasant and unpleasant things, all of which are themselves empty, are empty of inherent existence. Indeed, they are not only dependently arisen, but depend upon things or features of those things already shown to be empty.

3. The self's existence or nonexistence
    Has in no way been established.
    Without that, how could the defilements'
    Existence or nonexistence be established?

Moreover, the defilements are meant to be defilements of the self. But the self—the putative basis of those defilements—cannot exist inherently. So the defilements, being attributes of an empty phenomenon, cannot be nonempty. The following verse reiterates that position:

4.   The defilements are somebody's.
        But that one has not been established.
        Without that possessor,
        The defilements are nobody's.

In the first line, an interlocutor points out that if there are defilements at all there must be somebody whose defilements they are. Nāgārjuna replies that we have already shown that there is no subject for personal attributes in the many discussions of the relation between the self and its states previous to this (Chapters III, IV, VIII, IX, XII, XIII, XVI, XVII, and XVIII). So whatever analysis of defilement we develop, it will have to be one according to which they presuppose no defiled individual.

5.   View the defilements as you view yourself:
        They are not in the defiled in the fivefold way.
        View the defiled as you view your self:
        It is not in the defilements in the fivefold way.

This verse recalls and applies the fivefold analysis of the self developed in the previous chapter to the analysis of the defilements and the defiled. They are not identical to the aggregates, completely different from the aggregates, present as a basis of the aggregates, contained in the aggregates as a core, or separate from or dependent upon the aggregates. The arguments concerning the relation of the self to the aggregates can simply be applied directly either to the defilements or to the defiled.

6.   The pleasant, the unpleasant, and the errors
        Do not exist through essence.
        Which pleasant, unpleasant, and errors
        could the defilements depend upon?

Nor can we say that the defilements are inherently existent in virtue of being grounded in inherently existent pleasantness, unpleasantness, and error. While it is true that the latter are the basis of the defilements, they, too, Nāgārjuna will argue, are empty.

7.   Form, sound, taste, touch,
          Smell, and concepts of things: These six
          Are thought of as the foundation of
          Desire, hatred, and confusion.

8.   Form, sound, taste, touch,
          Smell, and concepts of things: These six
          Should be seen as only like a city of the Gandharvas and
          Like a mirage or a dream.

Sensory contact, perception, and cognition are the causal grounds of the defilements. But as was shown in Chapter III, they are empty as well.

9.   How could the
          Pleasant and unpleasant arise
          In those that are like an illusory person
          And like a reflection?

Since the self and others have been demonstrated to be empty and pleasantness and unpleasantness must be properties of one, the other, or both, there can be no inherently existent basis for pleasantness or unpleasantness. They themselves must also therefore be empty.

10.   We say that the unpleasant
          Is dependent upon the pleasant,
          Since without depending on the pleasant there is none.
          It follows that the pleasant is not tenable.

11.   We say that the pleasant
          Is dependent upon the unpleasant.
          Without the unpleasant there wouldn't be any.
          It follows that the unpleasant is not tenable.

Moreover, pleasant and unpleasant are mutually dependent. Nāgārjuna here claims that "pleasant" and "unpleasant" are not

absolute but rather comparative terms and, hence, essentially in-
terdefined. If this is so, then since their referents depend upon
each other for their satisfaction of these descriptions, neither property can exist inherently.

12.   Where there is no pleasant,
       How can there be desire?
       Where there is no unpleasant,
       How can there be anger?

And since these are the bases for desire and anger, desire and
anger, arising from empty phenomena, must themselves be seen as
empty.

13.   If to grasp onto the view
       "The impermanent is permanent" were an error,
       Since in emptiness there is nothing impermanent,
       How could that grasping be an error?

This verse adverts to the first of the four principal errors—that
one of the five aggregates, typically consciousness, is permanent.
The reason that it is held by Buddhists to be an error, of course, is
that all of the aggregates are analyzed as impermanent—hence the
formulation in the second line, whose definite description must be
read de re. But, Nāgārjuna argues, since there are no actual impermanent phenomena from the ultimate point of view, this can't
actually be seen as the false attribution of a property (permanence)
to a real entity that actually has a contrary property (impermanence). The point here is simply that in calling this an error, one
must be very careful not to commit a corresponding error—to
suggest that calling the impermanent *impermanent* constitutes the
assertion of an ultimate truth or of the presupposition of the ultimate reality of impermanent phenomena. That is at best a true
conventional assertion that indicates the ultimate nature of things.
This claim is made explicit in XXIII: 14:

14.   If to grasp onto the view
       "The impermanent is permanent" were an error,
       Why isn't grasping onto the view
       "In emptiness there is nothing impermanent" an error?

15. That by means of which there is grasping, and the grasping,
     And the grasper, and all that is grasped:
     All are being relieved.
     It follows that there is no grasping.

The argument above addresses the first and fourth of the principal errors directly. This verse hints at the generalization of this argument to the other two. If there is no permanent self, there is nothing to do the grasping that generates the view that there is happiness in saṃsāra or to grasp onto the body. Since all of these errors are rooted in grasping and since any inherently existent grasping would depend on an inherently existent grasper, these errors cannot be inherently existent. The next two verses emphasize the nonexistence of both the error and the one in error from the ultimate standpoint:

16. If there is no grasping
     Whether erroneous or otherwise,
     Who will come to be in error?
     Who will have no error?

17. Error does not develop
     In one who is in error.
     Error does not develop
     In one who is not in error.

And, Nāgārjuna points out, following the same pattern used in the analysis of motion and redeployed numerous times in the text, we can't think of error developing in one in whom error is arising. If the error is already arising in him, an independent error cannot be developing there. Moreover, as error develops, the person in whom it is developing changes, and no substrate for the development of error can be found. It follows that really existent error, conceived of as an independent phenomenon, is no more real than its putative subject (but of course no less real, either):

18. Error does not develop
     In one in whom error is arising.
     In whom does error develop?
     Examine this on your own!

The next two verses mobilize a by now familiar general argument against inherent existence specifically against the inherent existence of error: Either error has arisen or it hasn't. If it has, it depends on something and so is not inherently existent. If it has not, it has not come to be and so is either nonexistent or unexplained. Moreover, if error is to be conceived as inherently existent, it must arise from one of the four possible sources: self, other, both, or neither. And all four possibilities have been refuted for inherently existent entities in the general case in Chapter I:

19. If error is not arisen,
     How could it come to exist?
     If error has not arisen,
     How could one be in error?

20. Since an entity does not arise from itself,
     Nor from another,
     Nor from another and from itself,
     How could one be in error?

Nāgārjuna now returns to the objects of the four principal errors and points out that if they existed inherently, as the proponent of inherently existent error would have it, they would be truly existent and, hence, would be nondeceptive ultimate truths.

21. If the self and the pure,
     The permanent and the blissful existed,
     The self, the pure, the permanent,
     And the blissful would not be deceptive.

But why is the opponent forced to think of the objects of inherently existent error as inherently existent? That is, of course, an obviously incoherent position. But the view characterized as an error must have some ontological basis. And the self that is putatively in error has already been ruled out. So the only remaining possibility is that the error is the perception of an inherently real but at the same time deceptive object: a real but nonexistent object. It is this that Nāgārjuna claims is incoherent. Error then can neither be an objectless but inherently existent mental phenomenon,[106] nor can it be a subjectless perception of an inherently real but nonexistent object. So in no way can error be grounded in anything substantial.

22. If the self and the pure,
    The permanent and the blissful did not exist,
    The nonself, the impure, the permanent,
    And suffering would not exist.

But at this point Nāgārjuna draws quite a surprising conclusion. These observations apply not only to the putative objects of the errors, but also to those of Buddhist doctrine, at least when it is given a substantialist reading. Continuing his critique of the idea that assertions made from the standpoint of conventional truth about the ultimate nature of things are literally true from the ultimate standpoint, Nāgārjuna points out that the fact that there is no permanent self, no happiness in saṃsāra, and no pure body does not entail that an impermanent self, suffering, or an impure body are in any way inherently existent. That is, the objects of correct conventional understanding are no more inherently existent than those of incorrect understanding. The truth of even Nāgārjuna's own philosophical theory is not grounded in its reference to independently existent, substantially real entities.

23.   Thus, through the cessation of error
        Ignorance ceases.
        When ignorance ceases
        The compounded phenomena, etc., cease.

When all error is abandoned and we see the world aright, we are no longer ignorant of the true nature of things. But this is not because we then apprehend things and their true nature. Rather we apprehend that there are no things, per se, and that those posited from our side have no nature to understand.

106. For one thing, Nāgārjuna has argued that there is no inherently existent mind in which it could be located. For another, the idea of error, per se, though not error about anything, is patently incoherent.

24.   If someone's defilements
        Existed through his essence,
        How could they be relinquished?
        Who could relinquish the existent?

Nāgārjuna reminds the substantialist at the end that if the defilements or errors were inherent in the person and, hence, were part of his/her essence, they would be permanent and, hence, could not be relinquished. This would constitute a direct rejection of one of the most fundamental tenets of the Buddhist outlook—the possibility of liberation.

25.   If someone's defilements
        Did not exist through his essence,
        How could they be relinquished?
        Who could relinquish the nonexistent?

On the other hand, he reminds those who may have followed the argument this far, but who may be tempted either to nihilism about the defilements or to the subtler error of asserting that their dependence and emptiness is literally their ultimate nature, that the defilements must be conventionally real in order to be relinquished. They are, from the ultimate point of view, completely unreal; from that point of view, there is no relinquishment of anything at all. This, as we shall see, is an important harbinger of the doctrines of the identity of the two truths and of saṃsāra and nirvāṇa to be developed in the next two chapters, which represent the climax of the text.

Chapter XXIV

Examination of the Four Noble Truths

While Chapter XXIV ostensibly concerns the Four Buddhist Truths and the way they are to be understood from the vantage point of emptiness, it is really about the nature of emptiness itself and about the relation between emptiness and conventional reality. As such, it is the philosophical heart of *Mūlamadhyamakakārikā*. The first six verses of the chapter (XXIV: 1–6) present a reply to Nāgārjuna's doctrine of emptiness by an opponent charging the doctrine with nihilism. The next eight verses (XXIV: 7–14) are primarily rhetorical, castigating the opponent for his misunderstanding of Mādhyamika. The positive philosophical work begins with XXIV: 15. From this point Nāgārjuna offers a theory of the relationship between emptiness, dependent origination, and convention and argues not only that these three can be understood as corelative, but that if conventional things (or emptiness itself) were *nonempty,* the very nihilism with which the reificationist opponent charges Mādhyamika would ensue. This tactic of arguing not only against each extreme but of arguing that the contradictory extremes are in fact mutually entailing is, as we have seen in earlier chapters, a dialectical trademark of Nāgārjuna's philosophical method. In this chapter, it is deployed with exceptional elegance and acuity.

The opponent opens the chapter by claiming that if the entire phenomenal world were empty, nothing would in fact exist, a conclusion absurd on its face and, more importantly, contradictory to fundamental Buddhist tenets such as the Four Noble Truths (XXIV: 1–6) as well as to conventional wisdom:

1.   If all of this is empty,
     Neither arising, nor ceasing,
     Then for you, it follows that
     The Four Noble Truths do not exist.

The Four Noble Truths are: (1) All life in cyclic existence is suffering. (2) There is a cause of this suffering, namely, craving caused by ignorance. (3) There is a release from suffering. (4) The path to that release is the eightfold Buddhist path of right view, right concentration, right mindfulness, right speech, right effort, right action, right morality, right livelihood. The Four Noble Truths, preached by the Buddha in his first teaching after gaining enlightenment, are the fundamental philosophical tenets of Buddhism. If it were a consequence of Nāgārjuna's doctrine of emptiness that the Four Noble Truths were in fact false or, more radically, nonexistent, that would constitute in this philosophical context an immediate refutation of the position. This is not because these assertions are articles of faith, in the sense of revealed doctrine, but because anyone arguing within this framework has accepted the arguments for them.

2.   If the Four Noble Truths do not exist,
     Then knowledge, abandonment,
     Meditation, and manifestation
     Will be completely impossible.

Once we reject the Four Noble Truths, the essential ingredients of Buddhist practice become unintelligible. Knowledge of the ultimate nature of things becomes impossible since all of the knowledge gained in this tradition is knowledge of things that accords with the truths. Abandonment of error and craving, and eventually of cyclic existence, becomes unintelligible without the context of the analysis contained in the truths. Meditation loses its point. The eightfold path becomes a path to nowhere. This all amounts to a rejection of the entire Buddhist Dharma, one of the three jewels in which Buddhists take refuge, the others being the Buddha[107] and the Sangha, or the spiritual community of Buddhist practicioners and teachers.

3.   If these things do not exist,
       The four fruits will not arise.
       Without the four fruits, there will be no attainers of the fruits.
       Nor will there be the faithful.

4.   If so, the spiritual community will not exist.
       Nor will the eight kinds of person.
       If the Four Noble Truths do not exist,
       There will be no true Dharma.

These verses highlight these implications regarding the Dharma, but also point out that the rejection of the Four Noble Truths entails the nonexistence of the Sangha. For absent practice and the fruits of the path—that is, realization and accomplishment—there will be no practicioners and realizers.

5.   If there is no doctrine and spiritual community,
       How can there be a Buddha?
       If emptiness is conceived in this way,
       The three jewels are contradicted.

The whole point of the Dharma and the Sangha is to make it possible to attain buddhahood. The Dharma provides the philosophical insight and knowledge necessary for enlightenment; and the Sangha provides the teachers, the encouragement, the models, the opportunity for practice, and other support necessary for the strenuous and perseverant practice of the path. The attainment of buddhahood requires reliance on these two. So, if they are rejected, so is the possibility of buddhahood. So, the opponent charges, Nāgārjuna's doctrine of emptiness, in virtue of undermin-

107. Not only the historical Buddha, but also the possibility of buddhahood in general and one's own future buddhahood in particular, a point emphasized by the Most Ven. Prof. Samdhong Rinpoche in oral comments.

ing the Four Noble Truths, denies the existence of the three refuges and makes Buddhism itself impossible.

6.   Hence you assert that there are no real fruits.
       And no Dharma. The Dharma itself
       And the conventional truth
       Will be contradicted.

The implicit dilemma with which Nāgārjuna here confronts himself is elegant. For as we have seen, the distinction between the two truths or two vantage points—the ultimate and the conventional— is fundamental to his own method. So when the opponent charges that the assertion of the nonexistence of such things as the Four Noble Truths and of the arising, abiding, and ceasing of entities is contradictory both to conventional wisdom and to the ultimate truth (viz., that all phenomena are dependent, impermanent, merely arising, abiding momentarily and ceasing, and only existing conventionally, empty of inherent existence), Nāgārjuna is forced to defend himself on both fronts and to comment on the connection between these standpoints.

Nāgārjuna launches the reply by charging the opponent with foisting the opponent's own understanding of emptiness on Nāgārjuna. Though this is not made as explicit in the text as one might like, it is important to note that the understanding Nāgārjuna has in mind is one that, in the terms of Mādhyamika, reifies emptiness itself. This will be made more explicit in XXIV: 16:

7.   We say that this understanding of yours
       Of emptiness and the purpose of emptiness
       And of the significance of emptiness is incorrect.
       As a consequence you are harmed by it.

8.   The Buddha's teaching of the Dharma
       Is based on two truths:
       A truth of worldly convention
       And an ultimate truth.

This is the first explicit announcement of the two truths in the text. It is important to note that they are introduced as two *truths*, and that they are introduced as distinct. This will be important to bear in mind later. For it is tempting, since one of the truths is characterized as an ultimate truth, to think of the conventional as "less true."[108] Moreover, we will see later that while the truths are introduced as quite distinct here, they are in another sense identified later. It will be important to be very clear about the respective senses in which they are distinct and one. The term translated here as "truth of worldly convention" (Tib: *kun-rdzob bden-pa*, Skt: *saṃvṛti-satya*) denotes a truth dependent upon tacit agreement, an everyday truth, a truth about things as they appear to accurate ordinary investigation, as judged by appropriate human standards.[109] The term "ultimate truth" (Tib: *dam-pa'i don gyi bden-*

108. See, for instance, the comments of Murti (1985) on this verse:

The *paramārtha*, however, can be understood and realized only negatively, *only as we remove the saṃvṛti*, the forms which thought has already, unconsciously and beginninglessly, ascribed to the real. The real is to be *uncovered, discovered and realized* as the reality of appearances. In the order of our discovery, the removal of *saṃvṛti* must precede our knowledge of the *paramārtha*. (p. xxvi [emphasis in the original]).

As we shall see, this analysis of the distinction between the two truths as an appearance/reality distinction is explicitly rejected by Nāgārjuna in XXIV: 18, 19. I agree with Kalupahana (1986), who notes that "*artha* as well as *paramārtha* are truths (*satya*). The former is not presented as an un-truth (*a-satya*) in relation to the latter, as it would be in an absolutistic tradition. Neither is the former sublated by the latter." But Kalupahana goes a bit too far when he continues, "There is no indication whatsoever that these are two truths with different standing as higher and lower" (p. 69). For there is clearly an important sense in which, despite their ontic unity, the ultimate truth is epistemologically and soteriologically more significant than the conventional. Kalupahana also errs in my view when he characterizes the two truths as "two fruits" and, hence, as different but complementary moral ideals (p. 332). In his zeal to see Nāgārjuna as a non-Mahāyāna philosopher and as a Jamesian pragmatist, I fear that he distorts the central epistemological and metaphysical themes of the text.

109. It should be noted that both Sanskrit and Tibetan offer two terms, each of which in turn is often translated "conventional truth." Sanskrit presents "*saṃvṛti-satya*" and "*vyavahāra-satya*." The former is delightfully ambiguous. "*Saṃvṛti*" can mean *conventional* in all of its normal senses—everyday, by agreement, ordinary, etc. But it can also mean *concealing*, or *occluding*. This ambiguity is exploited by Mādhyamika philosophers, who emphasize that the conventional, in occluding its conventional character, covers up its own emptiness.

Candrakīrti's commentary to this verse distinguishes three readings, reflecting three distinct etymologies: "*Saṃvṛti*" can mean concealing; it can mean mutually dependent; it can mean transactional, or dependent on linguistic convention. The latter is captured exactly by the second term "*vyavahāra*," which simply means

pa, Skt: *paramārtha-satya*) denotes the way things are independent of convention, or to put it another way, the way things turn out to be when we subject them to analysis with the intention of discovering the nature they have from their own side, as opposed to the characteristics we impute to them.

9.   Those who do not understand
     The distinction drawn between these two truths
     Do not understand
     The Buddha's profound truth.

10. Without a foundation in the conventional truth,
     The significance of the ultimate cannot be taught.
     Without understanding the significance of the ultimate,
     Liberation is not achieved.

The goal of Mādhyamika philosophy is liberation from suffering. But that liberation, on Nāgārjuna's view, can only be achieved by insight into the ultimate nature of things—their emptiness—and indeed into the ultimate nature of emptiness, which we shall see to be emptiness again. But this insight can only be gained through reasoning and hence through language and thought. And the truth that is to be grasped can only be indicated through language and thought, which are thoroughly conventional and which can only be interpreted literally at the conventional level. It is important to see here

---

transactional—determined by convention. Tibetan presents not only *"kun-rdzob bden-pa,"* which literally means costumed, or disguised, picking up on one of the meanings of *"saṃvṛti,"* but *"tha-snyed bden-pa,"* which means nominal, or by agreement, picking up the other meaning. Because these two Tibetan terms are, according to most Tibetan interpretations of Mādhyamika, identical in extension, they are often treated as synonymous. This is a bit unfortunate for when we come to the parallel pair of terms for conventional existents, *"kun-rdzob yod-pa"* and *"tha-snyed yod-pa,"* this coextension breaks down in an important case: emptiness is a nominal *(tha snyed)* existent, but not a concealing *(kun-rdzob)* existent.

   See Nagao (1989), pp. 40–59, and (1991), pp. 13–16, for additional discussion of the Sanskrit etymologies and of the sense in which the conventional truth is a truth.

   Kalupahana (1986), however, argues (p. 88) that whenever Nāgārjuna uses the terms *"saṃvṛti"* or *"vyavahāra,"* he *"was referring to moral conventions of good or bad."* He argues that the relation between the two truths is a relation between an ideal life and conventional morality. This claim about usage, however, seems just plain erroneous.

that Nāgārjuna is not disparaging the conventional by contrast to the ultimate, but is arguing that understanding the ultimate nature of things is completely dependent upon understanding conventional truth. This is true in several senses: First, as we shall see, understanding the ultimate nature of things just is understanding that their conventional nature *is merely conventional.* But second, and perhaps less obscurely, in order to explain emptiness—the ultimate nature of all phenomena—one must use words and concepts and explain such things as interdependence, impermanence, and so forth. And all of these are conventional phenomena. So both in the end, where the understanding of ultimate truth is in an important sense the understanding of the nature of the conventional, and on the path, where the cultivation of such understanding requires the use of conventions, conventional truth must be affirmed and understood.[110]

11.   By a misperception of emptiness
      A person of little intelligence is destroyed.
      Like a snake incorrectly seized
      Or like a spell incorrectly cast.

110. See Streng (1973), pp. 92–98, and Huntington (1989), pp. 48-50, for a similar analysis. (But Huntington places a bit too much emphasis on specifically social convention in his analysis of the conventional truth, neglecting the role of what the Mādhyamikas call "primal ignorance," or the "innate disposition to reify," embodied in our ordinary cognitive tendencies, which may, in fact, be ontogenetically more fundamental than the specifically social conventions to which they give rise and that then reinforce them. See esp. pp. 52–54.) This analysis contrasts sharply with Murti's (1973) assertion that "the Absolute [ultimate truth] is transcendent to thought . . . phenomena in their essential form" (p. 9). This view of the ultimate truth as an absolute standing behind, or in opposition to, a relative truth of the conventional, as a Kantian noumenal world stands to a phenomenal world, is quite contrary to Nāgārjuna's doctrine of the emptiness of emptiness. See also Murti (1955) for an extended defense of this reading and Sprung (1973), esp. pp. 43–46, for another argument for a radical discontinuity between the two truths. Tola and Dragonetti (1981) agree with this view of Mādhyamika as nihilistic with regard to the conventional truth: "As a consequence of their argumentation and analysis, the Mādhyamikas deny the existence of the empirical reality, of all of its manifestations. . . . As a result . . . there remains (we are obliged to say) 'something' completely different. . . . That 'something' is the true reality" (p. 276). Crittenden (1981) is in substantial agreement with this view.
Curiously, even Nagao seems to succumb to this temptation to absolutize emptiness when he turns to his analysis of the ultimate truth, despite his emphasis on the identity of the two truths when he is elucidating the conventional. See Nagao (1989), pp. 71–72, 75–76.

The Mādhyamika doctrine of emptiness is subtle and is easily misinterpreted. In particular, it is often misinterpreted as a thoroughgoing nihilism about phenomena. This is so not only among classical Indian critics of Mādhyamika, in both Buddhist and non-Buddhist philosophical schools, but also among Western critics, who have sometimes regarded it as completely negative.[111] In this respect, Mādhyamika philosophy has suffered from the same fate as much Western sceptical philosophy, including that of the Pyrrhonians and of Hume and Wittgenstein, all of whom were at considerable pains to warn readers against interpreting them as denying the existence of ordinary entities, but all of whom have been repeatedly read as doing so. Nāgārjuna is here charging the opponent represented in the opening verses with interpreting the assertion that a phenomenon is empty as the assertion that it is nonexistent. Nothing, Nāgārjuna will argue, could be further from the truth.[112]

---

111. E.g., Stcherbatsky (1930), Robinson (1967), and Wood (1994).
112. Wood (1994) on p. 202 says that he is

unable to find anything in MK 24 to support [the non-nihilistic] interpretation of MK 24.7–11. . . . According to [the non-nihilistic interpretation], we would have to read MMK 24 as follows. According to Nāgārjuna, the doctrine that everything is void does not mean that everything is unreal or nonexistent; it only means that everything is empty in the sense that everything arises and perishes through a process of dependent co-origination (pratītya-samutpāda); and the critic must be taken as criticizing this position.

Wood then argues correctly that no Buddhist opponent would criticize the doctrine of dependent co-origination. This is in fact the cornerstone of Wood's nihilistic reading of the text, as it must be. For this chapter clinches the non-nihilistic interpretation. So, a few things deserve note: While Wood cannot find anything in this chapter to support such a reading, commentators including both Buddhapālita and Bhāvaviveka, as well as Candrakīrti and Tsong Khapa, not to mention a host of modern Western and Tibetan scholars, have found quite a bit there. Nāgārjuna's disciple Āryadeva also insists in Catuḥsātaka on a non-nihilistic reading of emptiness. In fact Wood does have the necessary gloss on the verses in question just right. But he misses the position attributed to the opponent entirely. The opponent need not be represented as denying that phenomena are codependently originated. Rather the opponent is failing to see that that dependent co-origination is emptiness. He hence sees the attribution of emptiness as the denial, rather than the assertion, of codependent origination. Hence the entire remainder of the chapter is devoted not to arguing for emptiness, nor to arguing for the reality of codependent origination, but rather to arguing for their identity. To miss this is to miss the entire point of the text.

12.   For that reason—that the Dharma is
             Deep and difficult to understand and to learn—
             The Buddha's mind despaired of
             Being able to teach it.

13.   You have presented fallacious refutations
             That are not relevant to emptiness.
             Your confusion about emptiness
             Does not belong to me.

Nāgārjuna here simply denies that his view sustains the nihilistic reading, while granting that if one treats emptiness as nonexistence, all of the absurd conclusions that the opponent enumerates indeed follow. But, Nāgārjuna continues in XXIV: 14, the interpretation of the entire Mādhyamika system depends directly on how one understands the concept of emptiness. If that is understood correctly, everything else falls into place. If it is misunderstood, nothing in the system makes any sense:

14.   For him to whom emptiness is clear,
             Everything becomes clear.
             For him to whom emptiness is not clear,
             Nothing becomes clear.[113]

15.   When you foist on us
             All of your errors
             You are like a man who has mounted his horse
             And has forgotten that very horse.

Here is the idea behind this image, a standard trope in classical Indian rhetoric: A man with a herd of horses thinks that he is missing one and accuses you of having stolen it. As he rides around and counts his horses, he always comes up one short. But you point out to him that the one he is accusing you of stealing is in fact the very one he is riding but has forgotten to count. Likewise, Nāgārjuna is saying, the opponent who confuses the Mādhyamika

113. The Tibetan term translated as "clear" here is *"rung-ba"* which literally means *suitable*, or *appropriate*. But while that makes sense in Tibetan, it clearly doesn't in English, and the context indicates "clear" as the word that best captures the meaning.

analysis in terms of emptiness with nihilism is charging Nāgārjuna
with a nihilism that is in fact his own. Nāgārjuna will argue, that is,
that while the opponent claims to preserve the reality of the three
jewels, the Four Noble Truths, and dependently arisen phenomena
against Nāgārjuna's nihilism, Nāgārjuna himself can explain the
reality of these things, though it will turn out that on the opponent's view they must be nonexistent![114] At this point the positive
philosophical program of this chapter begins.

16.   If you perceive the existence of all things
        In terms of their essence,
        Then this perception of all things
        Will be without the perception of causes and conditions.

There are two related assertions contained in this critical verse:
First, at the conventional level, the opponent, in virtue of thinking
that to exist is to exist inherently, will be unable to account for
dependent arising and hence for anything that must be dependently arisen. As Nāgārjuna will make explicit later on, this will
include such things as suffering, its causes, nirvāṇa, the path
thereto, the Dharma, the Sangha, and the Buddha, as well as more
mundane phenomena.

But secondly and more subtly, since the opponent is seeing actual existence as existence as a discrete entity with an essence, it
would follow that for the opponent the reality of emptiness would

114. But see Wood (1994), pp. 115–16, for a dramatically different reading (of the
parallel verse in *Vigrahavyāvartanī*—but the points all go over) of this verse. Wood
interprets emptiness as complete nonexistence and reads Nāgārjuna as a thoroughgoing nihilist. So he interprets Nāgārjuna as asserting that if one sees conventional
phenomena as real in any way, one is in trouble and that philosophical problems
vanish only if one sees all apparent phenomena as illusions. In offering this interpretation, Wood notes that Nāgārjuna often characterizes phenomena as like dreams or
mirages. That is indeed so, but his interpretation of that simile is itself problematic.
For a thing to be like a mirage or a dream is for it to exist in one way (as, e.g., a
mirage), but to not exist in the way that it appears (as water). To put the point another
way: Mirages *really are* mirages, but are *not* really water, though they might *appear* to
be. So conventional phenomena, according to the simile, *really are* empty, dependently arisen, nominally real phenomena, but are *not* substantial, inherently existent
phenomena, though they might *appear* to be. So, pace Wood, it is not Nāgārjuna, but
his opponent who is the nihilist here. See also Padhye (1988), esp. pp. 61–66, for a
good critical discussion of the nihilistic reading.

entail that emptiness itself is an entity, an inherently existing entity at that. To see emptiness in this way is to see it as radically different from conventional, phenomenal reality. It is to see the conventional as illusory and emptiness as the reality standing behind it. If Nāgārjuna were to adopt this view of emptiness, he would indeed have to deny the reality of the entire phenomenal, conventional world. This would also be to ascribe a special, nonconventional, nondependent hyperreality to emptiness itself. Ordinary things would be viewed as nonexistent, emptiness as substantially existent. (It is important and central to the Mādhyamika dialectic to see that these go together—that nihilism about one kind of entity is typically paired with reification of another.) This view is not uncommon in Buddhist philosophy, and Nāgārjuna is clearly aware that it might be suggested by his own position. So Nāgārjuna's reply must begin by distancing himself from this reified view of emptiness itself and hence from the dualism it entails. Only then can he show that to reify emptiness in this way would indeed entail the difficulties his imaginary opponent adumbrates, difficulties not attaching to Nāgārjuna's own view.[115] This brings us to the central verses of this chapter:

17.   Effects and causes
       And agent and action
       And conditions and arising and ceasing
       And effects will be rendered impossible.

Again, this verse is to be read at two levels: At the conventional level, the opponent, through reifying phenomena in order to preserve their conventional reality, will deny the possibility of any

115. So, for instance, when Wood (1994) writes on p. 161 that "[he does] not think that there is a non-nihilistic sense of the phrase 'does not exist,' " he is succumbing to the very view that Nāgārjuna criticizes here—the view that to exist is to exist inherently and that to not exist inherently is not to exist at all. The non-nihilistic sense of "does not exist" is in play when Nāgārjuna, in providing a reductio on the opponent's view, is taking inherent existence as the meaning of "existence." Given that understanding, Nāgārjuna can quite easily say that, e.g., the self does not exist while retaining his commitment to its conventional existence. He can also say that no inherently existent phenomena exist at all without denying the conventional existence of conventional phenomena.

kind of dependence, impermanence, or action. But more importantly, if Nāgārjuna's analysis of these things as empty meant that they were nonexistent and that only emptiness exists, then Nāgārjuna himself would be denying the empirical reality of these phenomena. That is, not only would an inherently existent phenomenal world be devoid of change, dependency, and so forth, but inherently existent emptiness would render the phenomenal world completely nonexistent.

This defines the straits between which the middle path must be found, as well as the presupposition that generates both extremes: The extreme of reification of the phenomenal world depends upon viewing emptiness nihilistically; the extreme of reification of emptiness requires us to be nihilistic about the phenomenal world. A middle path must reify neither and hence must regard emptiness, as well as all empty phenomena, as empty. Both extremes presuppose that to exist is to exist inherently. They only disagree about whether this inherent existence is properly ascribed to conventional phenomena or to their ultimate nature. Nāgārjuna will deny exactly that presupposition, arguing that to exist is to exist conventionally and that both conventional phenomena and their ultimate natures exist in exactly that way. The next verse is the climax of the entire text and can truly be said to contain the entire Mādhyamika system in embryo. It is perhaps the most often quoted and extensively commented on verse in all of Mahāyāna philosophy:

18.   Whatever is dependently co-arisen
        That is explained to be emptiness.
        That, being a dependent designation,
        Is itself the middle way.

19.   Something that is not dependently arisen,
        Such a thing does not exist.
        Therefore a nonempty thing
        Does not exist.

These two verses demand careful scrutiny and are best discussed together. In XXIV: 18, Nāgārjuna establishes a critical three-way relation between emptiness, dependent origination and verbal convention, and asserts that this relation itself is the Middle Way toward which his entire philosophical system is aimed. As we shall see, this is the basis for understanding the emptiness of emptiness itself. Nāgārjuna is asserting that the dependently arisen is emptiness. Emptiness and the phenomenal world are not two distinct things. They are, rather, two characterizations of the same thing. To say of something that it is dependently co-arisen is to say that it is empty. To say of something that it is empty is another way of saying that it arises dependently.[116]

Moreover, whatever is dependently co-arisen is verbally established. That is, the identity of any dependently arisen thing depends upon verbal conventions. To say of a thing that it is dependently arisen is to say that its identity as a single entity is nothing more than its being the referent of a word. The thing itself, apart from conventions of individuation, has no identity. To say of a thing that its identity is a merely verbal fact about it is to say that it is empty. To view emptiness in this way is to see it neither as an entity nor as unreal—it is to see it as conventionally real.[117]

Moreover, "emptiness" itself is asserted to be a dependent designation (Tib: *brten nas gdags-pa*, Skt: *prajñaptir-upādāya,*). [118] Its referent, emptiness itself, is thereby asserted to be merely dependent and nominal—conventionally existent but ultimately empty. This is hence a middle path with regard to emptiness.[119] To view

116. Padhye (1988), pp. 66–67, also emphasizes this corelativity of emptiness and dependent arising.

117. His Holiness the Dalai Lama, in oral remarks (Columbia University 1994), says:

Since dependent co-origination is used as a premise to argue for the lack of inherent existence of things, it can't be independent of it. Lack of inherent existence must always be understood as negative and as a feature of conventional reality. . . . In *Mūlamadhyamakakārikā* these two truths—dependent co-origination and emptiness—are taught as two perspectives on the same reality.

118. See Nagao (1991), pp. 190–94, for a useful discussion of alternative renderings of this compound and of the interpretive issues raised in translating it. Nagao himself opts for "a designation based upon (some material)." I find this both awkward and misleading; it commits Nāgārjuna univocally to "some material" as the designative basis for emptiness, submerging the metalinguistic reading. Both seem to me to be clearly intended by the text.

119. Compare to Murti (1973):

Relativity or mutual dependence is a mark of the unreal. . . . For the Mādhyamika, reciprocity, dependence, is the lack of inner essence. *Tattva,* or the Real, is something in itself, self-evident, and self-existent. Reason, which understands things through distinction and relation is a principle of falsity, as it distorts and thereby hides the Real. Only the Absolute as the unconditioned is real. . . . (p. 16)

the dependently originated world in this way is to see it neither as nonempty nor as completely nonexistent. It is, viewed in this way, conventionally existent, but empty. So we have a middle path with regard to dependent origination.[120] To view convention in this way

---

This represents as clear a statement as one would like of the position that the conventional/ultimate distinction is a version of an appearance/reality or phenomenon/noumenon distinction, a position I read Nāgārjuna as at pains to refute. As Murti says later in this essay (p. 22), "I have interpreted *śūnyatā* and the doctrine of the Two Truths as a kind of Absolutism, not Nihilism. Nāgārjuna's 'no views about reality' should not be taken as advocating a 'no-reality view.' "

Nagao (1991) concurs with Murti on this point: "The Twofold Truth is composed of paramārtha (superworldly or absolute) and saṃvṛti (worldly or conventional). These two lie sharply contrasted, the former as the real truth, and the latter as the truth concealed by the veil of falsehood and ignorance" (p. 46). Now while Nagao, to be sure, is less disparaging of the conventional truth than is Murti, noting the alternative etymologies of *"saṃvṛti-satya"* and allowing that ". . . the Twofold Truth opens a channel by which language recovers itself in spite of its falsehood and ignorance," he emphasizes that "the 'silence' of paramārtha is true 'Wisdom' " (p. 46) Hence in the end, he agrees with Murti on the critical interpretive claim that the two truths are radically distinct from one another and that the conventional truth is not in fact a truth in any straightforward sense. See also Napper [1993] and Hopkins [1983] for a similar interpretation.

There are two things to say about this interpretation: First, as Nāgārjuna would be quick to point out, absolutism is not the only alternative to nihilism. Mādhyamika is an attempt to forge a middle path between precisely those two extremes. And second, to say that a rejection of absolutism is a rejection of the reality of the world tout court is to presuppose exactly the equation of existence with inherent existence that is the target of Nāgārjuna's critique. To the extent that "reality" is interpreted to be absolute reality, Nāgārjuna indeed advocates a "no-reality view." But to the extent that we accept the Mādhyamika reinterpretation of "reality" as conventional reality, no such consequence follows.

Streng (1973) agrees:

Because Nāgārjuna's ultimate affirmation is *pratītyasamutpāda*, any conventional affirmation that might suggest an absolute, in the form of a dogma or doctrine, is avoided. Even *śūnya, asvabhāva, Tathāgata* or *pratyaya* cannot be transformed into absolutes. . . .

. . . The highest awareness, which is needed for release from *svabhāva*, is not the result of moving from the finite to the infinite, but the release from ignorance about the dependent co-origination of anything at all. *Paramārthasatya*, then, is living in full awareness of dependent co-origination. . . . (p. 36)

120. Nagao (1989) puts this point nicely:

When the birth-death cycle itself is empty, when there is nothing that exists permanently as its own essence; when, without self-identity all the functions of beings depend upon others, then dependent co-arising is emptiness and emptiness is dependent co-arising. . . .

is to view it neither as ontologically insignificant—it determines the character of the phenomenal world—nor as ontologically efficacious—it is empty. And so we also have a middle way with regard to convention. Finally, given the nice ambiguity in the reference of "that," (*de ni*), not only are "dependent arising" and "emptiness" asserted to be dependent designations, and their referents hence merely nominal, but the very relation between them is asserted to be so dependent and hence to be empty.

This last fact, the emptiness of the relation between the conventional world of dependently arisen phenomena and emptiness itself, is of extreme importance at another stage of the Mādhyamika dialectic and comes to salience in Nāgārjuna's *Vigrahavyāvartanī* and in Candrakīrti's *Prasannapadā*. For this amounts to the emptiness of the central ontological tenet of Nāgārjuna's system and is what allows him to claim, despite all appearances, that he is positionless. That is, Nāgārjuna thereby has a ready reply to the following apparent reductio argument (reminiscent of classical Greek and subsequent Western challenges to Pyrrhonian scepticism): You say that all things are, from the ultimate standpoint, nonexistent. That must then apply to your own thesis. It therefore is really nonexistent, and your words, only nominally true. Your own thesis, therefore, denies its own ground and is self-defeating. This objection would be a sound one against a view that in fact asserted its own inherent existence, or grounded its truth on an inherently existing ontological basis. But, Nāgārjuna suggests here, that is not the case for his account. Rather everything, including this very thesis, has only nominal truth, and nothing is either inherently existent or true in virtue of designating an inherently existent fact. This is hence one more point at which ladders must be kicked away.[121]

These morals are driven home in XXIV: 19, where Nāgārjuna emphasizes that everything—and this must include emptiness—is

---

... The real is suchness where there is an identification of emptiness and dependent co-arising whereby empty non-being "hollows out" every trace of inner selfhood. (p. 15)

See also Ng (1993), esp. pp. 16–18.

121. See Garfield (unpublished) and Streng (1973), chap., 4 for a similar interpretation of these verses and the correlative arguments.

dependently arisen. So everything—including emptiness—lacks inherent existence. So nothing lacks the three coextensive properties of emptiness, dependent-origination, and conventional identity.

With this in hand, Nāgārjuna can reply to the critic: He points out (XXIV: 20–35) that, in virtue of the identity of dependent origination and emptiness on the one hand and of ontological independence and intrinsic reality on the other, such phenomena as arising, ceasing, suffering, change, enlightenment, and so on—the very phenomena the opponent charges Nāgārjuna with denying—are possible only if they are empty. The tables are thus turned: It appeared that Nāgārjuna, in virtue of arguing for the emptiness of these phenomena, was arguing that in reality they do not exist precisely because for the reifier of emptiness, existence and emptiness are opposites. But, in fact, because of the identity of emptiness and conventional existence, it is the reifier who, in virtue of denying the emptiness of these phenomena, denies their existence. And it is hence the reifier of emptiness who is impaled on *both* horns of the dilemma he presented to Nāgārjuna: Contradicting the ultimate truth, the opponent denies that these phenomena are empty; contradicting the conventional, he is forced to deny that they even exist! And so Nāgārjuna can conclude:

20.   If all this were nonempty, as in your view,
        There would be no arising and ceasing.
        Then the Four Noble Truths
        Would become nonexistent.

The argument for this surprising turnabout reductio is straightforwardly presented in the subsequent verses:

21.   If it is not dependently arisen,
        How could suffering come to be?
        Suffering has been taught to be impermanent,
        And so cannot come from its own essence.

The first noble truth is the truth of the existence of suffering. The opponent charges Nāgārjuna with denying the existence of suffering through asserting its emptiness. But, Nāgārjuna points out, since emptiness is dependent origination, when the opponent denies its emptiness, he denies that suffering is dependently originated. But he agrees that all phenomena are dependently originated. He thus is forced to deny the existence of suffering. But for Nāgārjuna, since existence amounts to emptiness, the assertion of the emptiness of suffering affirms, rather than denies, its existence.

22.   If something comes from its own essence,
        How could it ever be arisen?
        It follows that if one denies emptiness
        There can be no arising (of suffering).

The second noble truth is that suffering has a cause. But, again, if the opponent asserts the nonemptiness of suffering, he asserts that it does not arise from causes and conditions. Yet Nāgārjuna's analysis shows that it must, in virtue of its emptiness, be so arisen and thus accords with the second truth.

23.   If suffering had an essence,
        Its cessation would not exist.
        So if an essence is posited,
        One denies cessation.

Similarly, the third noble truth is the truth of cessation. But inherently existent things cannot cease. Empty ones can. Nāgārjuna's analysis thus explains the third truth; the reifier contradicts it.

24.   If the path had an essence,
        Cultivation would not be appropriate.
        If this path is indeed cultivated,
        It cannot have an essence.

25.   If suffering, arising, and
        Ceasing are nonexistent,
        By what path could one seek
        To obtain the cessation of suffering?

The fourth truth is the truth of the path. Again, the path only makes sense, and cultivation of the path is only possible, if suffering is impermanent and alleviable and if the nature of mind is empty and hence malleable. The path, after all, is a path from suffering and to awakening. If the former cannot cease and the latter does not depend on cultivation, the path is nonexistent. But it is the analysis in terms of emptiness that makes this coherent. An analysis on which either the phenomena were inherently existent or on which emptiness was and the phenomena were therefore nonexistent would make nonsense of the Four Noble Truths. Nāgārjuna now turns to the implications for this line of argument for the three jewels, the Sangha, the Buddha, and the Dharma:

26.　　　If nonunderstanding comes to be
　　　　Through its essence,
　　　　How will understanding arise?
　　　　Isn't essence stable?

If ignorance is real and thus for the opponent inherently existent, there is no possibility of replacing it with insight. Therefore the cultivation of Buddhist practice is impossible, or at least pointless.

27.　　　In the same way, the activities of
　　　　Relinquishing, realizing, and meditating
　　　　And the four fruits
　　　　Would not be possible.

28.　　　For an essentialist,
　　　　Since the fruits through their essence
　　　　Are already unrealized,
　　　　In what way could one attain them?

So the essentialist has a dilemma if he wants to maintain the possibility of a community of practicioners (the Sangha) and of a path for them to practice: Either the ignorance in which they find themselves and that serves as the impetus to practice is inherently existent, in which case practice is bound to be inefficacious, or the understanding they hope to achieve is inherently existent, in which case there is no need to practice since it is already present and no use in practicing since its existence is independent of practice.

29.   Without the fruits, there are no attainers of the fruits,
           Or enterers. From this it follows that
           The eight kinds of persons do not exist.
           If these don't exist, there is no spiritual community.

The consequence of this is that there is no Sangha. The existence of the Sangha is entirely dependent upon the existence of the path and of the possibility of the fruits of the path—increasing degrees of realization since the Sangha is, by definition, the community of practicioners of the path.

30.   From the nonexistence of the Noble Truths
           Would follow the nonexistence of the true doctrine.
           If there is no doctrine and no spiritual community,
           How could a Buddha arise?

But it would also follow that there is no Dharma—no true Buddhist doctrine since that is grounded on the existence of the Four Noble Truths. And finally, as Nāgārjuna emphasizes in XXIV: 31, 32, since the attainment of buddhahood depends upon the study and practice of the Dharma within the context of the spiritual community, the opponent's view, unlike Nāgārjuna's, has the consequence that no buddha can arise. Moreover, if the Buddha and enlightenment were each inherently existent, they would be independent and could hence arise independently, which is absurd. To be a buddha is to be enlightened, and vice versa:

31.   For you, it would follow that a Buddha
           Arises independent of enlightenment.
           And for you, enlightenment would arise
           Independent of a Buddha.

32.   For you, one who through his essence
           Was unenlightened,
           Even by practicing the path to enlightenment
           Could not achieve enlightenment.

Nāgārjuna has hence demonstrated that any reification, whether of the conventional or of the ultimate, ends up, paradoxically, denying the existence of the very things it reifies. And any reification renders the most fundamental Buddhist philosophical insights and practices incoherent. A thoroughgoing analysis in terms of emptiness, on the other hand—one that includes the understanding of the emptiness of emptiness—renders the entire phenomenal world as well as emptiness itself comprehensible as nominally existent, empirically actual, and dependently arisen—real but essenceless. At this stage, Nāgārjuna shifts to the charge leveled by the opponent in XXIV: 2 that no practice is intelligible in the context of emptiness and argues that, on the contrary, practice is intelligible only in that context. The argument is a reprise of earlier moves, and so is rather straightforward:

33.   Moreover, one could never perform
         Right or wrong actions.
         If this were all nonempty what could one do?
         That with an essence cannot be produced.

   Nāgārjuna now turns to the moral dimensions of the extreme positions and their consequences for the Buddhist doctrine of karma, specifically with regard to the consequences for one's own life of one's actions. Nonempty phenomena, such as the opponent wishes to posit, are seen, on analysis, to be static. But practice and action require dependence, change, and a regular relation between one's actions and one's future state. So in the preceding verse, Nāgārjuna notes that in a static, nonempty world, we can't even make sense of the possibility of action. He then points out (XXIV: 34) that even were action possible, in virtue of the impossibility of change and dependence in an essentialist universe, there would be no consequences of those actions. For to be a consequence is to be dependent, hence to be empty, hence from the standpoint of the essentialist—whether reificationist or nihilist—nonexistent.

34.   For you, from neither right nor wrong actions
         Would the fruit arise.
         If the fruit arose from right or wrong actions,
         According to you, it wouldn't exist.

35.   If, for you, a fruit arose
         From right or wrong actions,

> Then, having arisen from right or wrong actions
> How could that fruit be nonempty?

The reificationist develops a strict dichotomy between things that exist inherently and things that are completely nonexistent. That dichotomy exhausts the ontological domain. But neither possibility for understanding the nature of practice, the practicioner, or the fruits of practice makes sense of action. If the relevant phenomena are granted inherent existence, their essence precludes development and change. If, on the other hand, they lack essence and hence, for the reifier, are completely nonexistent, there literally is no practice, in any sense. But if they are conceived of as empty and hence empirically and conventionally real, yet essenceless and dependent, the possibility and purpose of practice fall out straightforwardly. So it is the reifier, not Nāgārjuna, who makes action and soteriology impossible, and Nāgārjuna and not the reifier who rescue them from ontological oblivion.

36.   If dependent arising is denied,
        Emptiness itself is rejected.
        This would contradict
        All of the worldly conventions.

Recall the other horn of the dilemma in XXIV: 6. The opponent charged Nāgārjuna not only with contradicting fundamental Buddhist tenets, but with contradicting the conventional truth as well. Nāgārjuna has responded up to this point to the first charge, turning it back on the opponent. He now does the same with the second.

Nāgārjuna suggests that to assert the nonemptiness of phenomena and of their interrelations when emptiness is properly understood is not only philosophically deeply confused, but is contradictory to common sense. We can make sense of this argument in the following way: Common sense neither posits nor requires intrinsic reality in phenomena or a real causal nexus. Common sense holds the world to be a network of dependently arisen phenomena. So common sense only makes sense if the world is asserted to be empty. Hence it is the opponent, not Nāgārjuna, who disagrees with the conventional truth.

The standpoint of emptiness is hence not at odds with the conventional standpoint, only with a particular philosophical understanding of it—that which takes the conventional to be more than merely conventional. What is curious—and, from the Buddhist standpoint, sad—about the human condition, on this view, is the naturalness and seductiveness of that philosophical perspective.[122]

This, of course, is the key to the soteriological character of the text: Reification is the root of grasping and craving and hence of all suffering. And it is perfectly natural, despite its incoherence. By understanding emptiness, Nāgārjuna intends one to break this habit and extirpate the root of suffering. But if in doing so one falls into the abyss of nihilism, nothing is achieved. For then action itself is impossible and senseless, and one's realization amounts to nothing. Or again, if one relinquishes the reification of phenomena but reifies emptiness, that issues in a new grasping and craving— the grasping of emptiness and the craving for Nirvāṇa—and a new round of suffering. Only with the simultaneous realization of the emptiness, but conventional reality, of phenomena and of the emptiness of emptiness, argues Nāgārjuna, can suffering be wholly uprooted.

Let us consider now more carefully what it is to say that emptiness itself is empty. The claim, even in the context of Buddhist philosophy, does have a somewhat paradoxical air. For emptiness is, in Mahāyāna philosophical thought, the ultimate nature of all phenomena. And the distinction between the merely conventional nature of things and their ultimate nature would seem to mark the distinction between the apparent and the real. While it is plausible to say that what is merely apparent is empty of reality, it seems

---

122. This point requires emphasis. For Nāgārjuna is not merely speaking to and correcting philosophers. He is no Berkeley, suggesting that his own position is that of common sense and that only a philosopher would reify. In fact, it is fundamental to any Buddhist outlook, and certainly to Nāgārjuna's view, that one of the root delusions that afflicts all non-buddhas is the innate tendency to reify. But that tendency is raised to high art by metaphysics. Nāgārjuna intends his attack to strike both at the prereflective delusion and at its more sophisticated philosophical counterpart. But in doing so, he is not denying, and is in fact explaining, the nonmetaphysical part of our commonsense framework—that part that enables us to act and to communicate and, especially for Nāgārjuna, to practice the Buddhist path.

nihilistic to say that what is ultimately real is empty of reality, and as we have seen, the Mādhyamika are quite consciously antinihilistic. But again, when we say that a phenomenon is empty, we say, inter alia, that it is impermanent,[123] that it depends upon conditions and that its identity is dependent upon convention. Do we really want to say of each phenomenon that its emptiness—the fact that it is empty—is itself impermanent; itself dependent on something else; itself dependent upon conventions? It might at least appear that even if all other properties of conventional entities were so, their emptiness would be an eternal, independent, essential fact.

It may be useful to approach the emptiness of emptiness by first asking what it would be to treat emptiness as nonempty. When we say that a phenomenon is empty, we mean that when we try to specify its essence, we come up with nothing. When we look for the substance that underlies the properties, or the bearer of the parts, we find none. When we ask what it is that gives a thing its identity, we stumble not upon ontological facts but upon conventions. For a thing to be nonempty would be for it to have an essence discoverable upon analysis, for it to be a substance independent of its attributes, or a bearer of parts, for its identity to be self-determined by its essence. A nonempty entity can be fully characterized nonrelationally.

For emptiness to be nonempty would be for it to be a substantial entity, an independent existent, a nonconventional phenomenon. On such a view, emptiness would be entirely distinct from any conventional phenomenon. It would, on such a view, be the object of correct perception, while conventional phenomena would be

123. To be sure, both in the *Abidharma* literature and in most Māhāyana metaphysical literature, space is regarded as permanent, despite being a conventional phenomenon. There are two things to say about this apparent counterexample: First, on general metaphysical grounds the claim is suspect. Whether one argues along Kantian lines, or from general relativity theory, space apparently shares, from the transcendental point of view, the impermanence of all other phenomena. But second, and for the purposes of understanding this text, more importantly, Nāgārjuna never asserts the permanence of space and repeatedly associates emptiness with impermanence. I would thus argue that other Māhāyana literature to the contrary notwithstanding, nothing in Nāgārjuna's presentation of Mādhyamika entails the permanence of space or indeed of any other entity.

the objects of delusive perception. While conventional phenomena would be dependent upon conventions, conditions, or the ignorance of obstructed minds, emptiness, on such a view, would be apparent precisely when one sees through those conventions, dispels that ignorance, and overcomes those obstructions. Though such a position might appear metaphysically extravagant, it is hardly unmotivated. For one thing, it seems that emptiness does have an identifiable essence—namely the lack of inherent existence. So if to be empty is to be empty of essence, emptiness fails on that count to be empty. Moreover, since all phenomena, on the Mādhyamika view, are empty, emptiness would appear to be eternal and independent of any particular conventions and, hence, not dependently arisen. The two truths, on such an ontological vision, are indeed radically distinct from one another.

But this position is, from Nāgārjuna's perspective, untenable. The best way to see that is this: Suppose that we take a conventional entity, such as a table. We analyze it to demonstrate its emptiness, finding that there is no table apart from its parts, that it cannot be distinguished in a principled way from its antecedent and subsequent histories, and so forth. So we conclude that it is empty. But now let us analyze that emptiness—the emptiness of the table—to see what we find. What do we find? Nothing at all but *the table's* lack of inherent existence. No conventional table, no emptiness of the table. The emptiness is dependent upon the table and is, therefore, itself empty of inherent existence, as is the emptiness of *that* emptiness, and so on, ad infinitum. To see the table as empty, for Nāgārjuna, is not to somehow see "beyond" the illusion of the table to some other, more real entity. It is to see the table *as conventional; as dependent.* But the table that we see when we see its emptiness is the very same table, seen not as the substantial thing we instinctively posit, but rather as it is. Emptiness is hence not different from conventional reality—it is the fact that conventional reality is conventional. Hence it must be dependently arisen since it depends upon the existence of empty phenomena. Hence emptiness itself is empty. This is perhaps the most radical and deep step in the Mādhyamika dialectic, but it is also, as we shall see, the step that saves it from falling into metaphysical extravagance and brings it back to sober prag-matic scepticism.[124]

37.   If emptiness itself is rejected,
         No action will be appropriate.
         There would be action which did not begin,
         And there would be agent without action.

Without viewing the world as empty, we can make no sense of any human activity. Action would be pointless since nothing could be accomplished. Any existent action would have to have been eternal, and anyone who is an agent would be so independently of any action since agency would be an essential attribute.

38.   If there is essence, the whole world
         Will be unarising, unceasing,
         And static. The entire phenomenal world
         Would be immutable.

Without viewing the world as empty, we can make no sense of impermanence or dependent origination and hence no sense of change.

39.   If it (the world) were not empty,
         Then action would be without profit.
         The act of ending suffering and
         Abandoning misery and defilement would not exist.

Perhaps most important from the standpoint of Buddhist phe-nomenology and, though not hard to see, easy to overlook: We are driven to reify ourselves, the objects in the world around us, and—in more abstract philosophical moods—theoretical constructs, val-ues, and so on because of an instinctual feeling that without an intrinsically real self, an intrinsically real world, and intrinsically real values, life has no real meaning and is utterly hopeless. Nāgārjuna emphasizes at the close of this chapter that this gets

124. That is, scepticism in the Pyrrhonian, or Humean sense: See Garfield (1990).

things exactly backward: If we seriously and carefully examine what such a reified world would be like, it would indeed be hopeless. But if instead we treat ourselves, others, and our values as empty, there is hope and a purpose to life. For then, in the context of impermanence and dependence, human action and knowledge make sense, and moral and spiritual progress become possible. It is only in the context of *ultimate nonexistence* that *actual existence* makes any sense at all.

40.   Whoever sees dependent arising
        Also sees suffering
        And its arising
        And its cessation as well as the path.

Nāgārjuna closes as he opens, with the Four Noble Truths, this time connecting them not negatively, as in the beginning, to emptiness, but positively, to dependent arising. Understanding the nature of dependent arising is itself understanding emptiness and is itself the understanding of the Four Noble Truths.

It is absolutely critical to understanding the dialectical structure not only of this chapter but of the entire text to see that this doctrine of the emptiness of emptiness that is the central thesis of Mādhyamika philosophy emerges directly from XXIV: 18. For the emptiness of emptiness, as we have just seen, simply amounts to the identification of emptiness with the property of being dependently arisen and with the property of having an identity just in virtue of conventional, verbal designation. It is the fact that emptiness is no more than this that makes it empty, just as it is the fact that conventional phenomena in general are no more than conventional and no more than their parts and status in the causal nexus that makes them empty.

Paradox may appear to loom at this point. For, one might argue, if emptiness is empty, and to be empty is to be merely conventional, then the emptiness of any phenomenon is a merely conventional fact. Moreover, to say that entities are merely conventional is merely conventional. Hence it would appear optional, as all conventions are. Hence it would seem to be open to say that things are in fact nonconventional and therefore nonempty. This would be a deep incoherence indeed at the heart of Nāgārjuna's system. But the paradox is merely apparent. The appearance of paradox derives from seeing "conventional" as functioning logically like a negation operator—a subtle version of the nihilistic reading Nāgārjuna is at pains to avoid, with a metalinguistic twist. For then, each iteration of "conventional" would cancel the previous occurrence, and the conventional character of the fact that things are conventional would amount to the claim that really they are not, or at least that they might not be. But in Nāgārjuna's philosophical approach, the sense of the term is more ontological than logical: To say of a phenomenon or of a fact that it is conventional is to characterize its mode of subsistence. It is to say that it is without an independent nature. The fact that a phenomenon is without independent nature is, to be sure, a further phenomenon—a higher order fact. But that fact, too, is without an independent nature. It, too, is merely conventional. This is another way of putting the strongly nominalistic character of Mādhyamika philosophy.

So a Platonist, for instance, might urge (and the Mādhyamika would agree) that a perceptible phenomenon is ultimately unreal. But the Platonist would assert that its properties are ultimately real. And if some Buddhist-influenced Platonist would note that among the properties of a perceptible phenomenon is its emptiness and its conventional reality, s/he would assert that these, as properties, are ultimately real. This is exactly where Nāgārjuna parts company with all forms of realism. For he gives the properties a nominalistic construal and asserts that they, including the properties of emptiness and conventionality, are, like all phenomena, merely nominal, merely empty, and merely conventional. And so on for their emptiness and conventionality. The nominalism undercuts the negative interpretation of "conventional" and thereby renders the regress harmless.

So the doctrine of the emptiness of emptiness can be seen as inextricably linked with Nāgārjuna's distinctive account of the relation between the two truths. For Nāgārjuna, as is also evident in this crucial verse, it is a mistake to distinguish conventional from ultimate reality—the dependently arisen from emptiness—at an ontological level. Emptiness just is the emptiness of conventional phenomena. To perceive conventional phenomena as empty is just to see them as conventional and as dependently arisen. The difference—such as it is—between the conventional and the ultimate is a difference in the way phenomena are conceived/perceived. The point must be formulated with some delicacy and cannot be formulated without a hint of the paradoxical about it: Conventional phenomena are typically represented as inherently existent. We typically perceive and conceive of external phenomena, ourselves, causal powers, moral truths, and so forth as independently existing, intrinsically identifiable, and substantial. But though this is, in one sense, the conventional character of conventional phenomena—the manner in which they are ordinarily experienced—to see them this way is precisely not to see them *as conventional*. To see that they are merely conventional, in the sense adumbrated above and defended by Nāgārjuna and his followers, is thereby to see them as empty, and this is their ultimate mode of existence. These are the two truths about phenomena: On the one hand, they are conventionally existent and the things we ordinarily say about them are in fact true, to the extent that we get it right on the terms of the everyday. Snow is indeed white, and there are indeed tables and chairs in this room. On the other hand, they are ultimately nonexistent. These two truths seem as different as night and day—being and nonbeing. But the import of this chapter and the doctrine we have been explicating is that their ultimate nonexistence and their conventional existence are the same thing. Hence the deep identity of the two truths. And this is because emptiness is not other than dependent arising and, hence, because emptiness is empty.

Finally, at this stage we can see why Chapter I opens the text. The discussion of the emptiness of conditions and their relation to their effects is not only essential groundwork for this central argument, but in fact anticipates it and brings its conclusion to bear implicitly on the whole remainder of the text, allowing us, once we see that, to read the entire text as asserting not only the emptiness of phenomena, but that emptiness understood as empty. To see this, note that this entire account depends upon the emptiness of dependent origination itself. Suppose for a moment that one had the view that dependent arising were nonempty (not a crazy view and not *obviously* incompatible with, and arguably entailed by, certain Buddhist doctrines). Then from the identification of emptiness with dependent arising would follow the nonemptiness of emptiness. Moreover, if conventional phenomena are empty, and dependent arising itself is nonempty and is identified with emptiness, then the two truths are indeed two in every sense. Emptiness-dependent arising is self-existent, while ordinary phenomena are not, and one gets a strongly dualistic, ontological version of an appearance-reality distinction. So the argument for the emptiness of emptiness in Chapter XXIV and the identity of the two truths with which it is bound up depend critically on the argument for the emptiness of dependent origination developed in Chapter I.

Having developed this surprising and deep thesis regarding the identity of the two truths, Nāgārjuna turns in the next chapter to the nature of the relation between saṃsāra and nirvāṇa and the nature of nirvāṇa itself.

Chapter XXV

Examination of Nirvāṇa

This chapter continues the study of the nature of what are often thought of as ultimate realities and that of their relation to the conventional world. It follows quite naturally on the preceding chapter, which considered the relation between emptiness and the conventional world. For insight into emptiness is, from the standpoint of Mādhyamika philosophy, an important precondition for entry into nirvāṇa. And just as the ultimate truth is related to the conventional as an understanding of the way things really are as opposed to the way they appear to be, nirvāṇa is related to saṃsāra as a state of awareness of things as they are as opposed to a state of awareness of things as they appear to be. But given the results of Chapter XXIV, and the surprising identification in entity of the conventional with the ultimate and the doctrine of the emptiness of emptiness, one might well wonder about the status of nirvāṇa. Is it no different from saṃsāra? If it is, how, and how is it related to saṃsāra? If not, why pursue it, or better, why aren't we already there? Is nirvāṇa empty? If not, how does it escape the Mādhyamika dialectic? If it is, can it really be different from saṃsāra?

Nāgārjuna begins the examination with a challenge from the reificationist, raised by the previous chapter:

1.   If all this is empty,
      Then there is no arising or passing away.

By the relinquishing or ceasing of what
Does one wish nirvāṇa to arise?

Nirvāṇa is defined as a state one achieves when delusion and
grasping cease, and when one relinquishes saṃsāra and its entities.
But if there is neither self, nor object, nor delusion, nor grasping,
who relinquishes what, and in what manner? Moreover, if there is
no arising or passing away from the ultimate point of view, how can
nirvāṇa arise or saṃsāra pass away? Nāgārjuna replies, using the
same dialectical strategy deployed in the previous chapter:

2.   If all this is nonempty,
        Then there is no arising or passing away.
        By the relinquishing or ceasing of what
        Does one wish nirvāṇa to arise?

Nirvāṇa would be precluded not by the emptiness of saṃsāra,
but rather by its inherent existence. For then it could not pass
away. Nor could an inherently grasping grasper relinquish grasping, or an inherently existent delusion be alleviated. The achieve-
ment of nirvāṇa requires dependence, impermanence, and the possibility of change, all of which are grounded in emptiness.

3.   Unrelinquished, unattained,
        Unannihilated, not permanent,
        Unarisen, unceased:
        This is how nirvāṇa is described.

It is important that these predicates are all negative in character,
and that they are all expressed, both in Sanskrit and in the Tibetan
translation, with explicitly negative particles (Skt: *a*, Tib: *med-pa*).
The point is that no ascription of any predicate to nirvāṇa, for
Nāgārjuna, can be literally true. For such a predication would
purport to be an assertion that nirvāṇa is an ultimately existent
phenomenon with a determinate property, and there are no ultimately existent phenomena, not even nirvāṇa. Because nirvāṇa
can only be spoken of by contrasting it in some sense with saṃsāra
and because there is no conventionally existent perceptible entity

that could serve as a referent for the term, there is the terrible
temptation when speaking of nirvāṇa to think that, to the extent
that one is saying anything true of it in any sense, one is literally
asserting an ultimate truth about an inherently existent thing or
state. One forgets that once one transcends the bounds of convention, there is no possibility of assertion.[125]

The discussion in XXV: 4–18 is framed by the tetralemma that
would follow from considering nirvāṇa to be something independent about which something could be said; or as a proper subject
for a theory; or as a genuine alternative to saṃsāra, from which it
is inherently different. If it were so, it would have to either be
existent, nonexistent, both, or neither. (Note that here Nāgārjuna
uses the terms "existent"/"non-existent" in both their adjectival
and nominal forms [Tib: *dngos/dngos-min//dngos-po/dngos-med*,
Skt: *bhāva/bhāvo//abhāva/abhāvo*] deliberately calling attention to
their correlation. I have generally translated the Tibetan "*dngos-
po*" as "entity" throughout this text. But for the purposes of this
discussion in order to highlight the structure of the text, I switch in
the next few verses to "existent.") Nāgārjuna will now argue that
none of these alternatives is possible.

4.   Nirvāṇa is not existent.
        It would then have the characteristics of age and death.
        There is no existent entity
        Without age and death.

Nirvāṇa is negatively characterized as release from saṃsāra and
the constant flux, aging, death, and rebirth it comprises. But that
means that since all entities have these characteristics, nirvāṇa cannot be thought of as an existent entity. And here we must be very
careful: The point isn't that nirvāṇa can't be thought of as inherently
existent. For inherently existent entities, if there were such things,
would not have these characteristics. In this discussion, Nāgārjuna
is rejecting the notion that nirvāṇa can be thought of as existent in
any sense at all—even as a conventional entity. That is why we must
be so careful in our discourse—very careful indeed—for, as we shall

125. See Streng (1973), chap. 5.

see in a moment, neither do we want to say that nirvāṇa is nonexistent. But moreover, Nāgārjuna will want in another sense to identify nirvāṇa and saṃsāra (see XXV: 19, 20 below), and there is clearly a sense in which we can say that samsaric phenomena exist and a sense in which we can say that they do not. (Again, see the discussion of the positive tetralemma in XVIII: 8 above.) The point here is that though things seen from the standpoint of saṃsāra and from the standpoint of nirvāṇa are not different in entity, from the standpoint of saṃsāra they can be characterized and appear *as entities*. But from the standpoint of nirvāṇa, no characterization is possible since that involves the dualities and dichotomies introduced by language, including the positing of entities and characteristics, as well as their contraries and complements. These have only conventional and nominal existence, and no existence at all from the standpoint of nirvāṇa. (See also the discussion of XXVII: 30 below.) In a sense this discussion can be seen as a useful commentary on chapter IX of the *Vimilakīrti-nirdeśa-sūtra* and, in particular, on the dramatic concluding remarks by Manjuśri and nonremarks by Vimalakīrti on the subject of nonduality and insight into emptiness: Manjuśri indicates that the distinction between the conventional and ultimate is itself dualistic and hence merely conventional. To realize it is hence to enter into nondual awareness of emptiness. He then asks Vimalakīrti to comment on nonduality. Vimalakīrti remains silent.[126]

5. If nirvāṇa were existent,
    Nirvāṇa would be compounded.
    A non-compounded existent
    Does not exist anywhere.

126. His Holiness the Dalai Lama in oral remarks (Columbia University 1994) notes that "The ultimate nature of things—emptiness—is also unknowable, in that one cannot comprehend it as it is known in direct apprehension in meditation." Nayak (1979) writes:

Being firmly entrenched in *śūnyatā* and realizing that language has only a conventional use, an *ārya* or a philosopher regards silence or noncommitment as the highest good or *paramārtha*. And the attainment of *paramārtha* in this sense, not in the sense of a transcendent reality, constitutes an essential feature of *nirvāṇa* or liberation. (p. 478)

All empirical phenomena are compounded. But being compounded involves phenomena in the round of saṃsāra. For since the recognition of compounds as unitary phenomena demands conventions of aggregation, to be compounded is, ipso facto, to have a merely conventional existence. And it is the treatment of merely conventional, nominally existent phenomena as inherently existent entities that generates saṃsāra. That is because from the standpoint of Buddhist soteriological theory, the foundation of suffering—the basic condition of saṃsāra—is craving and the foundation of craving is the root delusion of taking to be inherently existent—and so worthy of being craved—that which is merely conventionally, or nominally existent. We are hence trapped in saṃsāra exactly to the extent that we mistake the conventionally existent as inherently existent. So given the contrast between nirvāṇa and saṃsāra and the fact that everything in saṃsāra is compounded, nirvāṇa cannot be compounded. So it is not existent, even conventionally.

6.   If nirvāṇa were existent,
       How could nirvāṇa be nondependent?
       A nondependent existent
       Does not exist anywhere.

Saṃsāra and dependent arising go hand in hand. For a phenomenon to be dependent is for it to be impermanent and for it to be subject to destruction. (See the discussion in Chapter XV.) Nirvāṇa is supposed to be beyond all this. It is, by definition, liberation from all that characterizes saṃsāra. So again, nirvāṇa cannot be a conventionally existent entity. (It is important to see that there is a sense in which nirvāṇa is dependent and a sense in which it is independent, and these are not contradictory: Nirvāṇa is achieved in dependence upon the practice of the path and the accumulation of wisdom and merit. But once attained, inasmuch as from the standpoint of nirvāṇa there are no entities at all, there is nothing on which nirvāṇa can be said to depend. In this sense it is nondependent.) But all of this raises the obvious possibility that nirvāṇa is simply not real at all—that it is completely nonexistent. This possibility is considered and rejected in the next two verses:

7.   If nirvāṇa were not existent,
      How could it be appropriate for it to be nonexistent?
      Where nirvāṇa is not existent,
      It cannot be a nonexistent.

To say that nirvāṇa possesses the positive property of nonexistence is not coherent either. For then there would be nothing to which the predicate "nonexistent" could in fact apply. Note the difference between saying, in the sense relevant here, "nirvāṇa is nonexistent" and "Santa Claus does not exist." The latter, Nāgārjuna would certainly agree, is not only coherent but true. But in explaining the semantics of the latter, we can posit a concept of Santa Claus and interpret the sentence as asserting that that concept is not instantiated. But when, in trying to characterize nirvāṇa, one is tempted to say that it is a nonexistent, this is in response to the difficulty we have just noted in asserting that nirvāṇa in fact exists. The temptation is to assert then that it is real, but has some kind of ghostly reality as a substratum of the property "nonexistent." But that is simply incoherent—an attempt to have it both ways. So the predicate "does not exist" cannot, in this case, even be applied. If there is no nirvāṇa at all, there is no such basis of predication. Even this apparently negative discourse about nirvāṇa is then blocked, to the degree that it is taken literally as positive attribution of a negative predicate.

8.   If nirvāṇa were not existent,
      How could nirvāṇa be nondependent?
      Whatever is nondependent
      Is not nonexistent.

Moreover, Nāgārjuna reminds us, one of the reasons that we rejected the view that nirvāṇa is an entity in the first place is that it is nondependent. The latter assertion is, of course, intended in a merely negative sense—a denial of the possibility of characterizing nirvāṇa as dependent, or of recognizing dependent phenomena or dependency from the standpoint of nirvāṇa. But to the extent that we can make sense of nonexistence as a positive attribute, it would have to be the attribute of something. And as we have seen—

especially in Chapters VII, XXII, and XXIV—entities can only be conceived as dependent. So if something is nondependent, it can't also be a real nonexistent! In the next two verses, Nāgārjuna reframes the problem about the ontological status of nirvāṇa in preparation for consideration of the final two tetralemma possibilities for nirvāṇa—that it is both existent and nonexistent and that it is neither existent nor nonexistent:

9.   That which comes and goes
      Is dependent and changing.
      That, when it is not dependent and changing,
      Is taught to be nirvāṇa.

10.   The teacher has spoken of relinquishing
      Becoming and dissolution.
      Therefore, it makes sense that
      Nirvāṇa is neither existent nor nonexistent.

Nirvāṇa is here again explicitly characterized only by contrast with saṃsāra. While it therefore cannot be an entity of the kind with which saṃsāra is populated, it is, as the release from saṃsāra, not completely nonexistent. So it can neither be conceived of conventionally or ultimately as a thing, nor coherently asserted not to exist. In fact, as XXV: 9 emphasizes with eloquence, the very same world is saṃsāra or nirvāṇa, dependent upon one's perspective. When one perceives the constant arising and ceasing of phenomena, one perceives saṃsāra. When all reification is abandoned, that world and one's mode of living in it, becomes nirvāṇa.[127] Nāgārjuna now considers the possibility that nirvāṇa is both existent and nonexistent:

11.   If nirvāṇa were both
      Existent and nonexistent,
      Passing beyond would, impossibly,
      Be both existent and nonexistent.

This would entail that it is contradictory. And it is absurd to assign anything contradictory properties. Moreover, having seen

---

127. See *Yuktiṣaṣṭika* 11 for another presentation of this view.

that each of the conjuncts is individually impossible, their conjunction, even were it not a conjunction of contradictories, could certainly not be coherent. In particular, we don't want to say that one does and does not pass into nirvāṇa upon release from saṃsāra.

12.　　If nirvāṇa were both
　　　　Existent and nonexistent,
　　　　Nirvāṇa would not be nondependent.
　　　　Since it would depend on both of these.

But since both existent and nonexistent entities are dependent, as Nāgārjuna has argued in XXV: 6, 8, if nirvāṇa were both existent and nonexistent it would be doubly dependent. It would depend both on existent and nonexistent phenomena.

13.　　How could nirvāṇa
　　　　Be both existent and nonexistent?
　　　　Nirvāṇa is uncompounded.
　　　　Both existents and nonexistents are compounded.

Moreover, not only are existents compounded—that is made up of parts or given rise to by causes—but genuine nonexistents are compounded as well—their nonexistence is determined by the nature of other things; if real, they would be composed of parts. A nonexistent elephant is composed of a nonexistent trunk, tusks, and so forth.

14.　　How could nirvāṇa
　　　　Be both existent and nonexistent?
　　　　These two cannot be in the same place.
　　　　Like light and darkness.

This verse simply sums up the results of the previous three: There is simply no way to avoid manifest contradiction if one takes this horn of the tetralemma. Nāgārjuna now considers the final possibility—that nirvāṇa is neither existent nor nonexistent:[128]

128. See also Padhye (1988), pp. 109–14, for a concise discussion of Nāgārjuna's treatment of the tetralemma of existence/nonexistence with respect to nirvāṇa.

15.   Nirvāṇa is said to be
           Neither existent nor nonexistent.
           If the existent and the nonexistent were established,
           This would be established

But this can't be so either. For really to assert this as the nature of nirvāṇa would be to suppose that both of these possibilities made sense with respect to it, but that neither happened to be realized. But it makes no sense for nirvāṇa to exist. And it makes no sense for it not to exist. So of each, the negation can't be assigned any coherent meaning. And conjoining two pieces of nonsense only yields further nonsense.

16.   If nirvāṇa is
           Neither existent nor nonexistent,
           Then by whom is it expounded
           "Neither existent nor nonexistent"?

If this could be coherently asserted, it would have to be asserted either by one in nirvāṇa or one not. But, as is emphasized in the next verse, this has never been asserted by anyone certifiably in nirvāṇa. And if it is asserted by someone in saṃsāra, we have no particular reason to believe it.

17.   Having passed into nirvāṇa, the Victorious Conqueror
           Is neither said to be existent
           Nor said to be nonexistent.
           Neither both nor neither are said.

18.   So, when the victorious one abides, he
           Is neither said to be existent
           Nor said to be nonexistent.
           Neither both nor neither are said.

None of the four tetralemma possibilities can be asserted. Just as in Chapter XXII, we see that when things are plausibly posited by an interlocutor as ultimates, Nāgārjuna resorts to a negative tetralemma. This emphasizes that all discourse is only possible from the conventional point of view. When we try to say something coherent about the nature of things from an ultimate standpoint, we end up talking nonsense.[129] But recall the discussion of emptiness and convention in chapter XXIV: We can develop an understanding of emptiness in relation to conventional reality, of emptiness as empty: Emptiness seen that way simply is the lack of essence of the conventional. Its own emptiness is the fact that it itself is no more than that. Seeing the conventional as conventional, we argued, is to see it as it is ultimately. At this point, Nāgārjuna makes a similar move with regard to nirvāṇa and draws one of the most startling conclusions of the *Mūlamadhyamakakārikā:* Just as there is no difference in entity between the conventional and the ultimate, there is no difference in entity between nirvāṇa and saṃsāra; nirvāṇa is simply saṃsāra seen without reification, without attachment, without delusion. The reason that we cannot say anything about nirvāṇa as an independent, nonsamsaric entity, then, is not that it *is* such an entity, but that it is ineffable and unknowable.[130] Rather it is because it is only saṃsāra seen as it is, just as emptiness is just the conventional seen as it is:

19.   There is not the slightest difference
        Between cyclic existence and nirvāṇa.
        There is not the slightest difference
        Between nirvāṇa and cyclic existence.

20.   Whatever is the limit of nirvāṇa,
        That is the limit of cyclic existence.
        There is not even the slightest difference between them,
        Or even the subtlest thing.

To distinguish between saṃsāra and nirvāṇa would be to suppose that each had a nature and that they were different natures. But each is empty, and so there can be no inherent difference. Moreover, since nirvāṇa is by definition the cessation of delusion and of grasping and, hence, of the reification of self and other and of confusing imputed phenomena for inherently real phenomena,

129. See Nagao (1991), pp. 42–43, for a similar account.
130. This reading contrasts with that of Inada (1970), who asserts that nirvāṇa, in fact, is transcendent, belonging to a wholly different ontological realm. I find his reading very difficult to reconcile with XXV: 19, 20 or indeed, with any of Chapters XXII, XXIV, or XXV.

it is by definition the recognition of the ultimate nature of things. But if, as Nāgārjuna argued in Chapter XXIV, this is simply to see conventional things as empty, not to see some separate emptiness behind them, then nirvāṇa must be ontologically grounded in the conventional. To be in saṃsāra is to see things as they appear to deluded consciousness and to interact with them accordingly. To be in nirvāṇa, then, is to see those things as they are—as merely empty, dependent, impermanent, and nonsubstantial, but not to be somewhere else, seeing something else.[131]

Another way of distinguishing between saṃsāra and nirvāṇa is to think of them somehow as different places, as Earth and Heaven are often conceived in Western religious traditions and then to think that upon attaining nirvāṇa one leaves this place—disappears—and goes there. Of course, if one thinks at all about the career of the historical Buddha Sakyamuni, that would entail that upon attaining enlightenment, he would have disappeared. This would make something of a hash of the Buddhist canon. But Nāgārjuna is emphasizing that nirvāṇa is not someplace else. It is a way of being here.

Here is another way to put the somewhat paradoxical point: Nāgārjuna surely thinks that in nirvāṇa, unlike saṃsāra, one perceives emptiness and not entities; one perceives the ultimate truth and not the conventional truth.[132] But emptiness is only the empti-

---

131. Compare Streng (1973):

...[A] problem occurs when we act inappropriately to the empty (non-svabhāva) set of conditions that allow saṃskṛta to arise. This inappropriateness is our acting as if we could discern a self-existent thing either in the conditioned 'thing' or in some identifiable 'element' of our experience. . . . Contrariwise, the insight that leads to the cessation of these inappropriate acts is an awareness that the conditions and relations by which we define our experience are empty. (p. 30)

Nayak (1979) puts it this way: "*Nirvāṇa* is thus nondifferent from critical insight par excellence which is free from all essentialist picture-thinking" (p. 489).

132. Though it is standard doctrine that a buddha, in virtue of being omniscient (setting aside the vexed and controversial question of the nature of this omniscience—a matter of considerable debate within Buddhist philosophy), perceives all conventional phenomena and knows all conventional truths, as well as all ultimate truths. But a buddha does not know conventional truths and perceive conventional phenomena in the same way that a nonenlightened being does. A buddha knows them and perceives them as conventional and sees them at the same time as empty, through an immediate knowledge of the unity of the two truths. A non-buddha, by contrast, even if s/he knows that conventional phenom-

ness of all entities, and the ultimate truth is merely the essenceless essence of those conventional things. So nirvāṇa is only saṃsāra experienced as a buddha experiences it. It is the person who enters nirvāṇa, but as a state of being, not as a place to be.[133]

21. Views that after cessation there is a limit, etc.,
     And that it is permanent, etc.,
     Depend upon nirvāṇa, the final limit,
     And the prior limit.

The kind of metaphysical speculations that the Buddha discouraged in the famous discussion of the unanswerable questions regarding the origins and limits of the world and what lies beyond the universe in space and time, are grounded, Nāgārjuna asserts, in the view that cyclic existence—the entire phenomenal world—can be conceived as an entity against which stand other entities or other regions. This is the same kind of picture that motivates the view that nirvāṇa is someplace or something beyond cyclic existence or that nirvāṇa is bounded or eternal. But there is no vantage point from which the universe is one place among many. That is why talking about what lies beyond it is nonsense and why reifying or characterizing nirvāṇa temporally is one example of that nonsense.

22. Since all existents are empty,
     What is finite or infinite?
     What is finite and infinite?
     What is neither finite nor infinite?

23. What is identical and what is different?
     What is permanent and what is impermanent?
     What is both permanent and impermanent?
     What is neither?

---

ena are empty, through studying Mādhyamika philosophy, perceives them as inherently existent and only reasons her/himself into the knowledge that these phenomena are really empty and that these truths are merely conventional.

133. Kalupahana (1986) reads this verse differently. He translates it as follows: "Whatever is the extremity of freedom and the extremity of the life-process, between them not even a subtle something is evident." He then takes the purport to be the denial of any entity such as a "seed of release" mediating between the states of *saṃsāra* and *nirvāṇa* (p. 367)

Again Nāgārjuna uses negative tetralemmas to emphasize that while of conventional entities a good deal can be said, so long as we take the predications to be asserted in a conventional, relative sense, the moment we try to conceive of things as they are ultimately, as empty, such assertion has to stop. That is not, again, to say that things are nonempty. Far from it. But it is to say that literal description applies only within the bounds of conception and that attempts to develop a metaphysics of the ultimate are doomed.[134]

24. The pacification of all objectification
     And the pacification of illusion:
     No Dharma was taught by the Buddha
     At any time, in any place, to any person.

In many Buddhist teachings many conventional phenomena are described and are subjected to analysis, including the mind, mental phenomena, and a wide range of external phenomena. But this is always a conventional analysis intended to demonstrate the emptiness of these phenomena, their impermanent character, and so forth, for soteriological purposes. The goal is to dispel illusion and to end deluded ontological fabrication and the various epistemological, psychological, and moral ills Nāgārjuna has argued are grounded therein. But it is important, Nāgārjuna concludes, not to reify that doctrine, or any of the entities that appear as prima facie referents of the words used to expound it (the Buddha, the spiritual community, etc.,). In fact, it is important to see that nirvāṇa does not, on this account, amount to an entity; it is not achieved or described by entities. Rather it is a way of engagement with nonentities by nonentities.

134. Padhye (1988) points out (pp. 68–70) that Nāgārjuna should also be read here and in this chapter as a whole as emphasizing that, in virtue of the emptiness of all phenomena in *saṃsāra* and of the self that experiences them, *nirvāṇa*, which is defined simply as that self's liberation from positing those phenomena, must be equally empty. For it, too, can only be understood as a characteristic of that empty self and of its relation to empty phenomena.

Chapter XXVI

Examination of the Twelve Links

Given an analysis of the nature of nirvāṇa, one might well ask how to achieve it. In this chapter, Nāgārjuna provides a straightforward answer. The twelve links of dependent origination are regarded by all Buddhist schools as providing an analysis of the nature of interdependence in the context of human existence. The tone of this chapter is decidedly positive, marking the turning of a dialectical corner in the preceding two chapters. Having elucidated the Mādhyamika account of the nature of conventional and ultimate reality, Nāgārjuna does not need at this point so much to emphasize the emptiness of the twelve links. Rather he can assume that to provide an account of them as dependently arisen is, ipso facto, to demonstrate that fact. Their emptiness is therefore simply presupposed. This chapter is thus a straightforward exposition of how, in light of the interdependence of the twelve links, to enter into and to exploit the cycle in the service of liberation.

1.   Wrapped in the darkness of ignorance,
        One performs the three kinds of actions
        Which as dispositions impel one
        To continue to future existences.

One is caught in cyclic existence for a reason, Nāgārjuna asserts, because one acts. There are three general kinds of actions distinguished in Buddhist action theory—physical, verbal, and mental. These actions in turn have immediate psychological consequences for the agent. That is, they give rise to new psychological dispositions. In the framework of Buddhist action theory, these dispositions are themselves conceived of as actions existing in a potential form, and of course when actualized, they emerge as new actions of body, speech, or mind. These in turn lead to a variety of new such consequences and to the continuation of cyclic existence.[135] Transmigration—the continuation of saṃsāra—for Nāgārjuna is then simply a dependent consequence of one's actions.

2.   Having dispositions as its conditions,
       Consciousness enters transmigration.
       Once consciousness has entered transmigration,
       Name and form come to be.

Continuing through the traditional presentation of the twelve links, Nāgārjuna notes that consciousness is a consequence of dispositions and depends upon them and that "name and form" follow as a consequence of consciousness. These, therefore, are obviously also dependent phenomena.

There are two ways to think of the twelve links, generating two parallel circles of explanation: One can approach them from the standpoint of transmigration, which provides a standard Buddhist explanation of the cycle of life. Or one can think of them as providing a phenomenological analysis of the nature of experience. In the former sense, we could say at this point in the story that actions performed in the past and dispositions inherited from one's previous history lead to new actions whose consequences are cyclic existence. In particular, the actions and dispositions from one's prior life, on this view, lead to the generation of a new consciousness, which upon entering the womb, gives rise to a body that will get a particular name.

Or, from a phenomenological perspective, we can see dispositions to attend to or to interpret particular phenomena in certain

135. The term *"las"* (Skt: *karma*) hence refers both to action and to the consequences of action for the individual.

ways (perceptual or conceptual "sets") and actions upon them leading to our becoming aware of external or internal phenomena (consciousness), which leads to our representing them as having determinate locations and denominations (name and form). These two levels of analysis are obviously quite compatible, and while the former plays a central role in Buddhist cosmological and soteriological theory, the latter is important in Buddhist psychology and practice.

3.   Once name and form come to be,
        The six sense spheres come into being.
        Depending on the six sense spheres,
        Contact comes into being.

From the ontogenetic side, the development of the body gives rise to the development of the sense faculties, which make sensation—contact between sense objects and functioning sense organs—possible. From the phenomenological point of view, we can say that the domain of perceptibles and the structure of perceptual experience and knowledge depends upon our ability to represent and individuate objects, and that sensory contact is sensory contact in the first place only in virtue of its role in experience, which is in turn dependent upon the entire perceptual process. To put the matter crudely, an amputated sense organ in contact with an object is hardly in contact in the appropriate way.

4.   That is only dependent
        On eye and form and apprehension.
        Thus, depending on name and form,
        And which produces consciousness—

The first two lines emphasize that contact—that is, the initial relation between the sense organ and its object—has three necessary and sufficient conditions: sense organ, the object, and the cognitive state to which the sense organ gives rise (apprehension/ *dran byed*). The last two lines are continuous with the next verse:

5.   That which is assembled from the three—
        Eye and form and consciousness,

> Is contact. From contact
> Feeling comes to be.

It is important to note that this occurrence of "consciousness" (*rnam-par shes-pa*) in fact refers to the apprehension of the previous verse, which is in Buddhist psychology a form of consciousness. But it should *not* be confused with the consciousness whose condition is contact, on pain of a hopeless explanatory tangle. Contact, as we have seen, is dependent upon the existence of the organ, the object, and the functioning of the sense faculty. Dependent upon that contact is sensation. The exposition here is perfectly traditional. It only derives its punch from the context: In light of the connection that has been developed between the dependence that is central to this model and emptiness, the entire Theravada model of the nature of the phenomenal world comes to look like an analysis in terms of emptiness.

6.   Conditioned by feeling is craving.
       Craving arises because of feeling.
       When it appears, there is grasping,
       The four spheres of grasping.

Pleasurable sensations lead to craving; painful ones lead to craving for their end. That craving leads to grasping—an attempt to appropriate and make one's own the source of pleasure or the means for the alleviation of pain, and to excessive valuation of the grasped object. The four spheres probably denote the four realms—the desire, the form, the formless, and the pure, entities in each of which could be the objects of grasping.

7.   When there is grasping, the grasper
       Comes into existence.
       If he did not grasp,
       Then being freed, he would not come into existence.

The identity of the individual as a grasper—and hence as a deluded actor in the world and an agent of the continuation of saṃsāra—depends upon this grasping. As Nāgārjuna argued in Chapters VI and XVI, without grasping, there is no grasper.

8.   This existence is also the five aggregates.
       From existence comes birth,
       Old age and death and misery and
       Suffering and grief and . . .

9.   Confusion and agitation.
       All these arise as a consequence of birth.
       Thus this entire mass of suffering
       Comes into being.

But moreover, the account that emerges so far of the nature of human existence—one involving a body, sensations, perception, dispositions, and consciousness—is just the account of personal existence in terms of the five aggregates into which standard Buddhist psychology analyzes the person. So this account so far is an account of the conditions that give rise to human existence. But human existence gives rise to human births, and these eventually give rise to aging, to pain and suffering, and eventually to death and the consequent grief of one's loved ones. This part of the story, of course, is central to making the case for the first two noble truths.

We are born with dispositions to reify, to crave, and to grasp, all of which, on this analysis, lead directly to suffering—to the pain of wanting what we cannot have, of not wanting what we do have, of grasping onto permanence in an impermanent world, of cherishing our own existence and interests in a world where they are minor affairs, and of grasping for independence and freedom in a conditioned universe.

10.   The root of cyclic existence is action.
       Therefore, the wise one does not act.[136]

136. " *'du byed*" (Skt.: *saṃskāra*). This term is often translated in this text as "disposition." It can also mean "to compound" or "compounded phenomenon." Here it must function as a verb. Both Streng (1967) and Inada (1970) prefer the reading "to compound" or "to construct." But given Nāgārjuna's theory of action, as we have seen, dispositions and actions are of a kind. And what generates the karma that creates and maintains cyclic existence is action. Hence, I read the term here as denoting action and disposition together, via its primary meaning, "disposition." This receives further support from the use of the nominal *"byed-po,"* which is cognate with the compound " *'du byed*" and is most naturally translated as "agent."

> Therefore, the unwise is the agent.
> The wise one is not because of his insight.

The place to pick up the tangle in order to unravel it, from the standpoint of practice, Nāgārjuna suggests, is with action and disposition, here comprised together under the single term "action" (*'du byed*), which in this context conveys not only the unity of action and disposition as seen from the soteriological point of view, but also their role in creating or bringing about future existence. These are most easily controlled through philosophical reflection, through meditation, and through assiduous practices of various virtues. By changing the way that we act physically, verbally, and mentally, we thereby change the way that we perceive, think, and act and thereby change what we see and the consequences of our actions.

11.   With the cessation of ignorance
            Action will not arise.
            The cessation of ignorance occurs through
            Meditation and wisdom.

But in order really to modify our actions and dispositions to act, we need wisdom—in this context an understanding of the real nature of things, which for Nāgārjuna means the view of all things as empty. This view, Nāgārjuna asserts, must be internalized through meditation, so that it becomes not merely a philosophical theory that we can reason our way into, but the basic way in which we take up with the world. Accomplishing that, he asserts, leads to the cessation of that activity responsible for the perpetuation of the suffering of saṃsāra.

12.   Through the cessation of this and that
            This and that will not be manifest.

It is important, however, to bear in mind that Nāgārjuna is discussing actions and dispositions together as a unitary phenomenon and thinking of them—as the translations of Inada and Sprung bring to the fore—as that which constructs or creates our future existence. dGe 'dun-grub agrees with this reading, as does Je Tsong Khapa. I am indebted to the Ven. Sherab Gyatso for convincing me of this.

The entire mass of suffering
Indeed thereby completely ceases.

And this is not only the analysis Nāgārjuna offers of the world and of our experience of it, but his final soteriological recommendation given the doctrine of the emptiness of all phenomena. Human existence and experience are indeed governed by the twelve links of dependent origination. But since they are essentially dependent, they are essentially empty and, hence, are impermanent and subject to change. The twelve links provide an anatomy and an etiology of suffering. But by understanding their impermanence and dependency, we also see the cure for that condition. For by cultivating a clear and accurate philosophical view of the nature of things—the view so explicitly articulated in Chapter XXIV, by internalizing that view, and by taking up with the world in accordance with it, we can cease the reification of the "this" and the "that," grasping for which binds us to suffering. Nāgārjuna argues that if we can achieve that, we can achieve the nirvāṇa characterized in Chapter XXV—a nirvāṇa not found in an escape from the world but in an enlightened and awakened engagement with it.

Chapter XXVII

Examination of Views

The final chapter of the text, like the previous chapter, applies the results of the climactic analyses of Chapters XXIV and XXV. It is noteworthy that all of the classic erroneous views discussed and refuted in this chapter are refuted earlier in the text. Indeed, Chapters XXIV and XXV are immediately preceded by a chapter on errors. One might therefore think that this chapter is otiose, or at least misplaced. For here Nāgārjuna considers a range of alternative metaphysical views conflicting with Nāgārjuna's analysis in terms of emptiness. These views are all well-known and considered false by all schools of Buddhist philosophy. So why does Nāgārjuna return to them as a collection at the close of the text?

The previous chapter demonstrated the positive payoff of the analysis of emptiness and its relation to conventional phenomena. Nāgārjuna there argued that one can exploit emptiness and an understanding of emptiness in following the path to nirvāṇa. But the pursuit of the path entails the elimination of error. In fact, it can negatively be characterized, as we saw in the nirvāṇa chapter, specifically as the elimination of error. So it is important for Nāgārjuna to show that the analysis developed in XXIV and XXV can not only promote positive movement toward nirvāṇa but also the eradication of the erroneous views that bind us to saṃsāra. That is the burden of this final chapter. It is also important dialectically to see that Nāgārjuna is demonstrating that the root of all of these erroneous views is the view that the self or the external world exist inherently. If, he will argue, one grants either of those claims, one is stuck with one or more of these errors. It therefore follows that any view, including any view of any other Buddhist school—including all of the schools that castigate these views on independent grounds—that posits inherently existent entities will succumb to these errors. Nāgārjuna thus concludes by arguing not only that his position is capable of leading to nirvāṇa, but that it is the only position capable of doing so.

1. The views "in the past I was" or "I was not"
   And the view that the world is permanent, etc.,
   All of these views
   Depend on a prior limit.

Nāgārjuna summarizes the diagnosis he will offer of the error underlying these metaphysical views: Any view that the self is permanent or nonexistent or that the world is permanent or nonexistent presupposes that one can think coherently about the beginning of time or of identity. For to think of things as permanent requires us either to posit a beginning of time from which they existed or to assert that time has no beginning. To think that there was a past at which the self did not exist or in which the world did not exist presupposes that we can mark a point at which the world came into existence or at which there is a definite separation between a world without the self and a world with the self—an initial moment of personal existence.

2. The view "in the future I will become other" or "I will not do so"
   And that the world is limited, etc.,
   All of these views
   Depend on a final limit.

Similarly, such views require us to be able to talk coherently about the end of the world or the end of personal existence—to be able to speak of a future time where nothing exists, or of the end of time, or of an unlimited future existence or of a definite moment when the self ceases to exist, whereas before it had existed. Nāgārjuna begins by discussing arguments regarding the self, opening with a set of arguments for the permanence of the self:

3.   To say "I was in the past"
          Is not tenable.
          What existed in the past
          Is not identical to this one.

It is a fundamental confusion to think that because I can say that I or someone or something else existed in the past that there is a real identity between what exists now and what existed then. Identity requires that we share all properties, and that is trivially impossible over time. But any assertion of the permanence of the self requires that we be able to identity it over time.

4.   According to you, this self is that,
          But the appropriator is different.
          If it is not the appropriator,
          What is your self?

Suppose that one through introspection or analysis takes some putative entity—one's body, one's stream of consciousness, or whatever—to be one's self. There will be in that act a duality of appropriator and the thing appropriated as the self or as part of the self. But at different times what is appropriated and what is appropriating differ. Both subject and object will necessarily be distinct. But in order to posit the appropriating entity as the self, it must retain its identity over time. The sequence of appropriators hence fails to provide a candidate for a continuing self. But, Nāgārjuna points out, there is no other candidate.

5.   Having shown that there is no self
          Other than the appropriator,
          The appropriator should be the self.
          But it is not your self.

The self that is posited by the advocate of a permanent self is a substantial entity capable of grasping, not a mere evanescent activity. So it cannot be the appropriator. Moreover, Nāgārjuna points out in the next verse, the same argument applies, mutatis mutandis, to the act of appropriation. To identify that with the self would be to identify agent and action:

6.   Appropriating is not the self.
      It arises and ceases.
      How can one accept that
      Future appropriating is the appropriator?

Two problems are developed in this verse: First of all, the self that the reificationist wishes to posit is a permanent, enduring self. But appropriating is a momentary action that arises and ceases constantly with new objects of appropriation. A sequence of such actions is hardly a substantial subject. This is a straightforwardly Humean argument. Second, Nāgārjuna points out, even if one argued that the self was substantial and also identical to that sequence, there is a further difficulty: The self that is posited by this interlocutor is an enduring subject of these acts of appropriation. But some of the members of the sequence have yet to come into existence. If the self exists entirely at all moments of time, as an unchanging substantial subject, it cannot be identified with a sequence, some of whose members are not presently existent.

7.   A self that is different
      From the appropriating is not tenable.
      If it were different, then in a nonappropriator
      There should be appropriation. But there isn't.

This is a very obscure argument as it is put in the text, but given the context we can flesh it out: The target position here is one according to which the existence of appropriation as a real, persistent feature of cyclic existence is used as the basis for attributing personal identity to a continuing self. That self is not supposed to be the appropriating itself, but rather a separate entity independent of it. Nāgārjuna points out, though, that it is, and for the proponent of this view, it must be possible not to appropriate—otherwise nirvāṇa would be impossible. So, there will be a

nonappropriator who once was an appropriator. But if appropriation is the basis of the identity of the one who has been liberated
with the one who was not, that appropriation should persist in the
nonappropriator, which would be contradictory.

8.   So it is neither different from the appropriating
       Nor identical to the appropriating.
       There is no self without appropriation.
       But it is not true that it does not exist.

Thus we cannot use the existence of appropriation as a basis on
which to construct a permanent self. For that self cannot be both
permanent and identified with such a constantly changing activity.
But still, that is all there is to the self. This raises the possibility
that it would be correct to say that the self does not persist at all—
that there is no existent person in any sense. It is to this view that
Nāgārjuna now turns. He first announces the conclusion—that it is
not correct to say that the person who now exists did not exist in
the past. There is a sense in which that person is identical with his/
her past stages:

9.   To say "in the past I wasn't"
       Would not be tenable.
       This person is not different
       From whoever existed in previous times.

10.   If this one were different,
       Then if that one did not exist, I would still exist.
       If this were so,
       Without death, one would be born.

If there were a genuine difference in entity between the current
stage and the previous stages of a person, they would be independent. If that were so, the current stage—since if it depends on
anything, depends on the previous stage—would come into existence depending on nothing. That is, it would be possible for none
of my previous stages to exist, but for me, as the person with my
past, to pop into existence ex nihilo. Or, on the other hand, it
would be possible, if the current stage and previous stages were

completely different and independent, for the current stage to come into existence without the previous stage having passed out of existence, which is absurd.

11.   Annihilation and the exhaustion of action would follow;
        Different agents' actions
        Would be experienced by each other.
        That and other such things would follow.

We could make no sense of the actual empirical fact of conventional personal identity; action done at one moment would be done by one person, and that person would experience none of its consequences. To the extent that we could make sense of them at all, the phenomena of memory and experiencing the consequences of one's previous actions would become interpersonal affairs, which seems at least a bit odd.

12.   Nothing comes to exist from something that did not exist.
        From this errors would arise.
        The self would be produced
        Or, existing, would be without a cause.

Moreover, since the past, as per the discussion of time in Chapter XIX and the discussion of dependent origination in VII, does not actually exist, we would have the consequence of an existent (the present person) being brought into existence dependent upon something that no longer exists (some past person). Anything that exists has some past.

13.   So, the views "I existed," "I didn't exist,"
        Both or neither,
        In the past
        Are untenable.

While Nāgārjuna has not explicitly considered the "both" or "neither" horns of the tetralemma, we have seen enough of these arguments by this stage to know how to complete the picture. Since neither a continually existent nor a discontinuous self makes sense, both can't make sense since that would just be double nonsense. And the "neither" option is not open since there is no third alternative. Nāgārjuna now points out that the argument applies straightforwardly to the future existence of the self:

14.   To say "In the future I will exist or
        Will not exist,"
        Such a view is like
        Those involving the past.

Another possible avenue to a permanent self is the classical Indian view (not unlike certain Judeo-Christian views) that the human soul partakes of the divine, and that its divinity is what engenders its eternality:

15.   If a human were a god,
        On such a view there would be permanence.
        The god would be unborn.
        For any permanent thing is unborn.

16.   If a human were different from a god,
        On such a view there would be impermanence.
        If the human were different from the god,
        A continuum would not be tenable.

But if the human is at all different from a god, as is eminently plausible (i.e., nobody seriously argues that humans simply *are* gods), then the permanence of the divine in no way entails the permanence of the person. There is another possibility, however, namely that the person is part divine and part mortal:

17.   If one part were divine and
        One part were human,
        It would be both permanent and impermanent.
        That would be irrational.

The problem with this option is that either we say that the person is both permanent and impermanent, which is contradictory, or that the divine part is permanent and the mortal part imperma-nent. But if the person is a mereological sum of these two parts, then since there is an impermanent part, the whole is constantly changing and the inherent identity of the person from moment to moment is still lost.

18.   If it could be established that
        It is both permanent and impermanent,
        Then it could be established that
        It is neither permanent nor impermanent.

That is, the "both" and "neither" horns of the tetralemma stand or fall together. Permanence and impermanence are mutually exclusive and exhaustive alternatives. They can neither be co-present nor co-absent. (The option of asserting them in different voices—conventional and ultimate—is not open to the opponent here, who is trying to defend an inherently existent self.)

19.   If anyone had come from anyplace
        And were then to go someplace,
        It would follow that cyclic existence was beginningless.
        This is not the case.

As Nāgārjuna has argued, if there were to be true identity through time, so that the person who exists now is literally identical to one who existed in the past and to one who will exist in the future, this would have to be in virtue of sharing some essence. But this would make real change impossible. The person, once in saṃsāra, would be there essentially—the state of being in saṃsāra would hence be inherently existent. (Here Nāgārjuna is using the term "beginningless" as a synonym for "inherently existent.") If saṃsāra were inherently existent, it would have to be eternal and unchanging. Nirvāṇa would be unattainable, and saṃsāra would be utterly hopeless. But given the possibility of transformation, it follows that such literal identity must be abandoned.

20.   If nothing is permanent,
        What will be impermanent,
        Permanent and impermanent,
        Or neither?

Finally, given that there are no permanent entities, no entities, from the ultimate point of view, can serve as inherent bases of predication. That is, the views that Nāgārjuna has been considering regarding the nature of the self, which purport to give its ultimate nature, must all be seen as incoherent on that ground alone—namely, that they propose an ultimate analysis. Nāgārjuna now turns his attention to views not about the self, per se, but about the world as a whole:

21.   If the world were limited,
           How could there be another world?
           If the world were unlimited,
           How could there be another world?

Nāgārjuna begins by questioning the sense of the question regarding the limits of the world: It seems to be like a question about the size of a table. But it is not. It is not, that is, a question about whether there is anything beyond the world. For suppose that the world is limited. That suggests that there is something beyond it. But that just means that we haven't come to the end of the world. The whole world includes that stuff that lies beyond. Or suppose that the world is unlimited. That suggests that there is nothing beyond the world. But that just means that everything that is in the world is, in fact, in the world, which is trivial. The question regarding the limits of the world, so Nāgārjuna suggests, is nonsensical.

22.   Since the continuum of the aggregates
           Is like the flame of a butterlamp,
           It follows that neither its finitude
           Nor its infinitude makes sense.

In this discussion, Nāgārjuna is focusing on the temporal limits of the world. Again, the question regarding whether the world has temporal limits presupposes that it is a single entity that either exists forever or that passes out of existence. But the world, Nāgārjuna suggests, is more like a flame. It is a series of distinct flickering events. While each event is momentary, the sequence continues. But there is no entity that persists and can be said to be eternal or momentary.

23.   If the previous were disintegrating
        And these aggregates, which depend
        Upon those aggregates, did not arise,
        Then the world would be finite.

We could say that the world is finite if its current state simply ceased and nothing else arose. But absent that, there is no basis for positing an end, and dependent origination argues against positing an end to the world in time.

24.   If the previous were not disintegrating
        And these aggregates, which depend
        Upon those aggregates, did not arise,
        Then the world would be infinite.

On the other hand, the world would be infinite if it reached a stage where its current state became permanent. But again, given the nature of dependent arising, this is not a likely eventuality.

25.   If one part were finite and
        One part were infinite,
        Then the world would be finite and infinite.
        This would make no sense.

Nāgārjuna now makes use of the argument mobilized at XXVII: 17. The world cannot have these contradictory properties any more than an individual can.

26.   How could one think that
        One part of the appropriator is destroyed
        And one part is not destroyed?
        This position makes no sense.

27.   How could one think that
        One part of the appropriation is destroyed
        And one part is not destroyed?
        This position makes no sense.

The appropriator here is the self; the appropriation, the existence of the world. Nāgārjuna in these two verses is summing up and drawing together the conclusions of the two main arguments in the chapter. We want to say on the one hand that neither the world nor the self is permanent. Both are thoroughly characterized by impermanence. On the other hand, we want to say of both that they endure in time and of each that there is no fixed boundary to its identity. But it can't be that either has both of these properties.

28.   If it could be established that
        It is both finite and infinite,
        Then it could be established that
        It is neither finite nor infinite.

This verse echoes XXVII: 18. If either the self or the world could be conceived as both finite and infinite, finitude and infinitude would make no sense at all. They are contradictory properties and cannot characterize the same thing at the same time. Moreover, they are exhaustive alternatives.

29.   So, because all entities are empty,
        Which views of permanence, etc., would occur,
        And to whom, when, why, and about what
        Would they occur at all?

But if we bear in mind the emptiness of all phenomena, on the subject and on the object side, these views do not even arise as possibilities. The self and all of the phenomena in the world itself, being empty, are dependently arisen, conventional phenomena. Their emptiness itself is dependently arisen and empty. There is no candidate for permanence. There is no candidate for ultimate impermanence. And to the extent that we grasp and live this truth, there is no one to stand over and against the world as "I" against "it."

30.   I prostrate to Gautama
        Who through compassion
        Taught the true doctrine,
        Which leads to the relinquishing of all views.

The most common interpretation of this final verse has the phrase "all views" (Tib: *lta-ba thams-cad*, Skt: *sarva-dṛṣṭi*) referring to all false views, that is, all views according to which things have inherent existence.[137] These, after all, are the views under examination and refutation in this chapter. And it is the clear purport of this chapter that these views are the principal hindrances to enlightenment and the causes of attachment to cyclic existence. On this reading, Nāgārjuna exempts his own view and therefore the Mādhyamika understanding of the Buddhist doctrine, which Nāgārjuna here reminds us was taught compassionately explicitly to enable the rejection of these views. *That* doctrine, or standpoint, on this reading, is not to be relinquished. Indeed, one might say, it is not even a "view" in the relevant sense since a view must be a view of something, and the analysis in terms of emptiness reveals a world with no entities to view. This interpretation is urged unanimously by all of the commentaries with which I am familiar and by many of the scholars with whom I have consulted.

137. This, for instance, is the view urged unanimously by Je-Tsong Khapa (pp. 477–84), mKhas-grub-rje (pp. 112–17), and dGe-'dun-grub (p. 237) and by most of the Geluk-pa scholars with whom I have consulted. Whether Candrakīrti or Āryadeva read the text this way is unclear. On the other hand, many Nyingma scholars adopt the alternative reading I suggest here. In conversation, H.H. the Dalai Lama has suggested to me that the Geluk-pa interpretation may make the most sense from the standpoint of philosophy and for the purposes of characterizing an inferential understanding of emptiness, but that the Nyingma understanding may provide a better expression of the nature of the direct understanding of emptiness and may be more useful for guiding meditative practice. The Ven. Prof. Geshe Yeshes Thap-Khas, on the other hand (oral commentary), suggests that the two interpretations are both intended—the first as the teaching regarding the conventional truth, and appropriate for those not yet advanced in meditative practice, and the second as a teaching regarding the nature of the direct realization of emptiness experienced by a buddha at enlightenment, and by advanced practitioners in meditative equipoise directly realizing emptiness. Huntington (1989), pp. 119–22, presents a clear and compelling discussion of such direct realization. He writes of the difference between a dualistic and nondualistic awareness of the world:

> The difference is one of attitude, for all else remains as it was. Similarly, when the bodhisattva cultivates non-dualistic knowledge he both sees and sees through the natural interpretations that structure his world. He sees nothing new or different, but he knows, directly and incorrigibly, that all the elements of experience are dependent upon one another and upon the nature of the perceiving consciousness in a very profound and significant way. (p. 122)

But there is a second reading available, not instead of, but in addition to, the standard reading.[138] There is a startling grammatical and poetic parallel between this closing verse and the dramatic dedicatory verses. Both have the form, if translated literally, almost preserving Tibetan word order, "To him who . . . To that [great one/Gautam] I prostrate" (*gang gis . . . dam-pa/go-dam de la phyag-'tshal lo*). The echo at the end of the opening is apparent, and it draws attention to Nāgārjuna's denial in the dedication of the possibility of any predication from the ultimate point of view— of the inability to say anything positive that is literally true about the ultimate nature of things. When this is joined with our reading of such verses as XVIII: 7,9; XXII: 11, 12, 15; XXIV: 18; and XXV: 23—all of which emphasize in different ways the impossibility of literal statements about the ultimate and the merely ostensive character of language about it, despite the need for such conventional assertion to enable one to approach ultimate truth—we can see a double entendre in this verse. For, if one reads it not from the conventional point of view as in the previous interpretation, but as an echo of the dedication, one can see Nāgārjuna's own view and the Buddhist Dharma itself included under "all views" and, hence, necessarily to be relinquished once it is understood and used. And compare especially XIII: 8:

8.   The victorious ones have said
      That emptiness is the relinquishing of all views.
      For whomever emptiness is a view,
      That one has accomplished nothing.

We can now return to this verse with more of Nāgārjuna's analysis available: For the practicioner who directly realizes emptiness, nothing is present to consciousness but emptiness itself. For such a

138. Both the Most Ven. Khamtrul Rinpoche and the Most Ven. Samdhong Rinpoche emphatically support the second reading as the primary meaning of the verse and as the final expression of the emptiness of emptiness (personal communication). Inada (1970) waffles. In his commentary (p. 164), he endorses the "all views" reading. But in his translation (p. 171), he inserts "false" parenthetically before "views." These are clearly not consistent moves. Ng (1993) also agrees with the "false view" reading. See pp. 18–20.

consciousness, there literally is no object since there is in such a consciousness no reification of the kind that gives rise to subject-object duality. Moreover, since such a consciousness is directed only upon what can be found ultimately to exist and since nothing can be so found, there is literally nothing toward which such a consciousness can be directed. But this very fact is what is ostended by the dictum that emptiness is itself empty: Emptiness is not the real object as opposed to the unreal objects of ordinary perception, not the object that appears when false appearance is shed. In fact, to the extent that it appears as an object at all, it does so as falsely as any table. If so, the best we can then say is that from such a standpoint the words "emptiness is empty" ascribe no property to any object at all. From that standpoint, there is no view to be expressed, where a view is something that can be given assertoric voice. For a view is possible if, and only if, (1) there is some*thing* to view and (2) there is some *way* in which it is viewed.

That is, first, if it were possible to have a (true) view about emptiness, emptiness would have to be a thing—an object of awareness. But if we supposed that it is, a dilemma emerges: Emptiness must then exist either conventionally or ultimately. The latter, as we have seen, is impossible since then it would fail itself to be empty and not only would a central tenet of Mādhyamika philosophy be contradicted, but the remainder would be rendered incoherent as well. But positing emptiness as a conventional existent and as the object of a correct view is no better, for things that appear conventionally appear *as* entities—as phenomena that exist independently and substantially. And all such appearance is, from the standpoint of Mādhyamika, in an important sense, *false* appearance. To put this point another way, true predication is always predication from a perspective in which the subject of the predicate exists and within which the predicate can be instantiated. For conventional entities, the conventional standpoint provides such a perspective. But for emptiness, neither the conventional nor the ultimate standpoint can do the job: In the conventional standpoint, there is no emptiness; in the ultimate standpoint there are no entities at all.

Now let us consider the second entailment—that concerning the manner in which emptiness would need to be viewed. Views are views of things under descriptions and, hence, are views of things as having some nature. I view this paper as paper, as white, as a bearer of print, as a product of a tree, and so forth. And again, so long as I am characterizing a conventional entity as it is viewed from the conventional perspective, there is no problem here. But when we attempt to extend this analysis to emptiness itself, problems arise. For the attribution of properties—descriptions under which things can be viewed—again requires the existence of the substrata and the possibility of their serving as property bearers, as well as the dualism between substratum and property this presupposes. The perspective from which this continued existence and this dualism are available is the conventional perspective for it is only conventions that bring ontology into play. But again, in that perspective, we don't find emptiness; we find all kinds of entities, but we find them *as entities* and, hence, as nonempty. But from the perspective in which we find emptiness, we don't find any entities or any characteristics, not even emptiness itself or the fact of its emptiness. Hence again, since we can't view emptiness even as empty, in view of its very emptiness, we can't have a view of emptiness. This point is made pithily in a verse quoted by Nāgārjuna in his autocommentary to the *Vigrahavyāvartanī:* "By their nature, the things are not a determinate entity. For they have only one nature, i.e. no nature" (*Aṣṭasāhasrikā Prajñāpāramitā-sūtra*).

This reading of the concluding verse, and by implication of the related verses we have noted (particularly XIII: 8), would not entail any self-refutation or any denial of the need at the conventional level for the assertion of Buddhist doctrine or the critique articulated by Nāgārjuna in *Mūlamadhyamakakārikā*. On the contrary, this interpretation would be consistent with the raft metaphor popular in Buddhist philosophy (one discards the raft after one has crossed the river; it would be foolish to continue to carry it overland; similarly, Buddhist teachings are soteriological in intent and are to be discarded after their goal has been attained) or the laxative metaphor of the *Ratnakuta-sūtra* mobilized by Candrakīrti in his comments on XIII: 8 and Sextus (one wants the medicine to be expelled along with the pathogenic bowel contents) used to discourage grasping even to the Dharma. Hence Nāgārjuna acknowledges that, having announced in the dedication that nothing can be said truly about the final nature of things and having defended this thesis exhaustively in the text, his words and those of the Buddha cannot even be taken as literally true about the final nature of things. Hence in order to realize that nature, one must relinquish even a literal, nonostensive reading of these texts.[139]

139. The Ven. Prof. Geshe Yeshes Thap-Khas (oral commentary) points out that emptiness as it appears in direct realization does not appear as an entity (*ngospo*). From the ultimate point of view there are no entities. Since a view is always a view of an entity, in direct realization of emptiness, there is a necessary relinquishing of all views, including all Buddhist and all Mādhyamika views. But, he argues, it does not follow that one not directly realizing emptiness can relinquish all views or, in particular, that one should relinquish true ones. Insofar as direct realization of emptiness is a primary goal of Buddhist practice, he argues, and especially of the practice of Buddhist philosophy, it is hence appropriate to read this verse in this way as well as in the more conventional way.

The Ven. Geshe Yeshe Topden (also in oral commentary) puts this a bit differently: Emptiness, he argues, when it is known inferentially, is known as a positive phenomenon and appears as an inherently existent entity, even though the subject of such a cognition knows that it is not so (compare a mirage that appears as water even to someone who knows that it is merely a mirage). And in order to realize emptiness in this way, one must make use of the Mādhyamika view while rejecting all false views. To one who directly apprehends emptiness, however, he claims, emptiness, while an object of such an awareness, is not a positive phenomenon, but a mere negation of all positive phenomena and is not different in entity from the mind cognizing it. In such an awareness, he claims, since emptiness does not appear as qualified in any way and since such an awareness is nonconceptual, there is no view of emptiness. So, he argues, even the Mādhyamika view is to be relinquished at the stage of direct realization. Nonetheless, the verse indicates first, on his reading, the necessity to relinquish all false views, and then, in direct realization to relinquish the Mādhyamika view.

Mukherjee (1985) makes a similar point:

A significant point that the Mādhyamikas never fail to make out is that reason and concepts have a place in *Vyavahāra*. It is possible to select a pattern, hold a position without clinging to it, i.e., without being dogmatic. It teaches one to look at a view as something relative and shows that the error of clinging is not essential to reason. . . . Did not the Buddha himself use words, concepts without clinging to them? . . .

By being free of clinging one attains a level that is transcendent to all the views, but at the same time he remains fully cognisant of the other levels in their minutest details without losing sight of the undivided reality. He sees these levels as not yet perfect; he sees them as various stages on the way to the perfect." (pp. 221–22)

See also Kalupahana (1986), p. 80. But Kalupahana also says that these final lines "clearly show that Nāgārjuna was aware that the Buddha did not speak 'metaphysically' but only 'empirically' " (p. 391). That conclusion certainly does not follow. To refuse to give a metaphysical theory of the nature of phenomena and to

One must realize the ultimate truth dependent upon the conventional, but abandon all of these necessarily conventional designations as characterizations of an ultimate nature that is ultimately uncharacterizable.[140]

The anticipation of Wittgenstein's close of the *Tractatus* is remarkable:

6.54   My propositions serve as elucidations in the following way: anyone who understands me eventually recognizes them as nonsensical, when he has used them—as steps—to climb beyond them. (He must, so to speak, throw away the ladder after he has climbed up it.)

7   What we cannot speak about we must pass over in silence.

Nāgārjuna may well have intended (and of course we have no way of knowing what he intended, nor would it make much difference to interpretation at this point) both readings—the standard reading at the conventional level, according to which the truth of his own standpoint contrasts with all other false views, and this latter reading at the ultimate level, at which his own view must itself be seen as a merely conventional ostention of an ineffable ultimate truth.[141] And if the doctrine of the two truths and their identity is correct, these readings are mutually entailing. To assert

---

refuse to characterize what cannot be spoken of coherently does not by itself constitute an eschewal of metaphysics. Nor does it indicate that the arguments offered in this text are empirical. Manifestly, a great deal of metaphysics (albeit of a highly critical and negative kind) and very little empirical discussion occur in this text.

140. Wood (1994) argues, following his nihilistic interpretation of Nāgārjuna, that here and in *Vigrahavyāvartanī* Nāgārjuna is, in virtue of denying the existence of even his own view, completing a nihilistic program that denies existence of any kind to anything. As should be clear by now, I think that this nihilistic reading is untenable. Nonetheless, it is surely the case that Wood is correct in claiming that Nāgārjuna wishes to treat emptiness in exactly the way that he treats other phenomena—as empty—and that any theory about it that presupposes it has an essence must be false. I part company with Wood only when he goes on to interpret emptiness as complete nonexistence. A careful reading of *Vigrahavyāvartanī* reveals, as Wood notes, that Nāgārjuna denies that he has a proposition (*pratijñā*), but not that he utters words. Nāgārjuna is working to show the merely conventional character of his utterance and that its utility does not entail the existence of any convention-independent reality as its semantic value. But that is a far cry from nihilism. See Garfield (unpublished) for a more sustained discussion of emptiness and positionlessness.

141. Streng (1973) agrees. See chap. 6.

from the conventional standpoint that all phenomena are empty and that all views according to which they are not are to be relinquished is to recognize from the ultimate standpoint that there are no phenomena to be empty and that no view attributing any characteristic to anything can be maintained. Even the emptiness of emptiness is empty. . . .

May whatever merit has been achieved through this work and through its study be dedicated to the liberation of all sentient beings from cyclic existence.

References

While not all of these texts are explicitly cited in my discussion, all
have influenced my views and my treatment of the text in some
ways. With some I am in almost complete agreement; with others I
take issue in whole or in part. But all have been helpful to me in
thinking about Nāgārjuna's argument. This is not, however, by any
means meant to be a complete bibliography of useful works on
Nāgārjuna—only an indication of what influenced me. The English translations of canonical texts are given where available.

Earlier Translations of *Mūlamadhyamakakārikā*

Inada, Kenneth K. (1970). *Nāgārjuna: A Translation of his Mulamād-
hyamikakārikā With an Introductory Essay.* Tokyo: The Hokuseido
Press.
Kalupahana, David J. (1986). *Nāgārjuna: The Philosophy of the Middle
Way.* Albany: State University of New York Press.
Streng, Frederick (1967). *Emptiness: A Study in Religious Meaning.* Nash-
ville: Abdingdon Press.

Other Works by Nāgārjuna

Ratnāvalī (Precious Garland of Advice for the King), trans. J. Hopkins. In
Hopkins and H.H. the Dalai Lama (1975), *The Buddhism of Tibet.*
London: Wisdom Publications.
Śūnyatāsaptati (Seventy Stanzas on Emptiness), trans. C. Lindtner. In
Lindtner (1986), *Master of Wisdom.* Oakland: Dharma Press.

Vigrahavyāvartanī (Replies to Objections), trans. K. Bhattacharya, E. H. Johnston, and A. Kunst in Bhattacarya, Johnston and Kunst (1985), *The Dialectical Method of Nāgārjuna: Vigrahavyāvartanī.* New Delhi: Motilal Banarsidass.

Yuktiṣaṣṭika (Sixty Stanzas of Reasoning), trans. C. Lindtner. In Lindtner (1986), *Master of Wisdom.* Oakland: Dharma Press.

Primary Canonical Texts

Āryadeva, *Catuḥśātaka* (Four Hundred Stanzas), trans. K. Lang. In Lang (1986), *Āryadeva's Catuḥśātaka: On the Bodhisattva's Cultivation of Merit and Knowledge.* Copenhagen: Akademisk Forlag.

Candrakīrti, *Mādhyamakāvatāra* (Entrance into the Middle Way), trans. C. W. Huntington and Geshe Namgyal Wangchen. In Huntington and Wangchen (1989), *The Emptiness of Emptiness.* Honolulu: University of Hawaii Press.

———, *Prasannapadā* (Lucid Exposition of the Middle Way), trans. M. Sprung and T. R. V. Murti. In Sprung (1979), *Lucid Exposition of the Middle Way.* Boulder: Prajña Press.

———, *Prasannapadā* (Lucid Exposition of the Middle Way), trans. J. May in May (1959), *Candrakīrti Prasannapadā Mādhyamakavṛtti.* Paris: Adrien Maisoneuve.

———, *Mādhyamakāvatārabhasya* (Tibetan translation: *dBu ma 'jug pa'i rang 'grel bzhugs*) (1992). Sarnath: Kagyu Relief Society, Central Institute of Higher Tibetan Studies.

dGe 'dun grub, *dBu ma rtsa shes rtsa 'grel bzhugs* (Commentary on *Mūlamādhyamakakārikā*) (1987). Sarnath: Ge Lugs Pa Students' Welfare Publishing, Central Institute of Higher Tibetan Studies.

mKhas grub-rje, *sTong thun chen mo*, trans. J. Cabezon. In Cabezon (1992), *A Dose of Emptiness.* Albany: State University of New York Press.

Tsong Khapa, *Tsa she tig chen rigs pa'i rgya mtsho* (1973). Sarnath: Ge Lugs Pa Students' Welfare Publishing, Central Institute of Higher Tibetan Studies.

———, *The Speech of Gold in the Essence of True Eloquence (1984).* Trans. R. Thurman. Princeton: Princeton University Press.

Vimalakīrtinirdeśa-sūtra, trans. R. Thurman in Thurman (1976), *The Holy Teachings of Vimalakīrti.* State College: Penn State University Press.

References   363

Recent Scholarship and Western Texts

53Ames, W. L. (1986). "Buddhapālita's Exposition of the Mādhyamika." *Journal of Indian Philosophy* 14 (4): 313–48.

Anderson, T. (1985). "Wittgenstein and Nāgārjuna's Paradox." *Philosophy East and West* 35 (2): 157–170.

Betty, L. S. (1983). "Nāgārjuna's Masterpiece—Logical, Mystical, Both or Neither?" *Philosophy East and West* 33 (2): 123–38.

Bhattacharyya, B. (1979). "The Concept of Existence and Nāgārjuna's Doctrine of Śūnyatā." *Journal of Indian Philosophy* 7: 335–44.

Broido, M. (1988). "Veridical and Delusive Cognition: Tsong Kha-Pa On The Two Satyas." *Journal of Indian Philosophy* 16: 29-63.

Bugault, G. (1983). "Logic and Dialectics in the Mādhyamikakārikās." *Journal of Indian Philosophy* 11 (1): 7–76.

Crittenden, C. (1981). "Everyday Reality as Fiction—A Mādhyamika Interpretation." *Journal of Indian Philosophy* 9: 323–33.

Dargyay, L. (1990). "What is Non-existent and What is Remanent in Śūnyatā." *Journal of Indian Philosophy* 18: 81–91.

Della Santina, P. (1986). *Mādhyamika Schools in India*. New Delhi: Motilal Banarsidass.

Eckel, M. D. (1978). "Bhāvaviveka and the Early Mādhyamika Theories of Language." *Philosophy East and West* 28 (3): 323–37.

Evans, R. D., and B. K. Matilal (1986). *Buddhist Logic and Epistemology*. Dordrecht: Reidel Publishing.

Garfield, J. L. (1990). "Epoché and Śūnyatā: Scepticism East and West." *Philosophy East and West* 40 (3): 285–308.

———(1994)."Dependent Co-origination and the Emptiness of Emptiness: Why did Nāgārjuna begin with Causation?" *Philosophy East and West* 44: 219–50.

———(unpublished MS). "Emptiness and Positionlessness: Do the Mādhyamika Really Relinquish All Views?"

Ghose. R. M. (1987). *The Dialectics of Nāgārjuna*. Allahabad: Vohra Press.

Gudmunsen, C. (1977). *Wittgenstein and Buddhism*. London: MacMillan.

Gyatso, L. (1993). *The Harmony of Emptiness and Dependent Arising*. Dharamsala: Library of Tibetan Works and Archives.

Hopkins, J. (1983). *Meditation on Emptiness*. Boston: Wisdom Publications.

Hume, D. (1967). *A Treatise of Human Nature*. Ed. L. A. Selby-Bigge. Oxford: Oxford University Press.

Huntington, C. W. (1983a). "A Non-Referential View of Language and

Conceptual Thought in the Work of Tsong Kha-Pa." *Philosophy East and West* 33 (4): 325–40.

———(1983b). "The System of the Two Truths in the *Prasannapadā* and in the *Mādhyamakāvatāra:* A Study in Mādhyamaka Soteriology." *Journal of Indian Philosophy* 11 (1): 77–107.

———(1989). *The Emptiness of Emptiness.* Honolulu: University of Hawaii Press.

Kant, I. (1929). *Critique of Pure Reason.* trans. N. Kemp-Smith. New York: St. Martin's Press.

Lindtner, C. (1986). *Master of Wisdom.* Oakland: Dharma Press.

Lopez, D. (1987). *A Study of Svātantrika.* Ithaca: Snow Lion Press.

Matilal, B. K. (1973). "A Critique of the Mādhyamika Position." In Sprung, ed. (1973). *The Problem of Two Truths in Buddhism and Vedanta.* Dordrecht: D. Reidel Publishing.

———(1977). *The Logical Illumination of Indian Mysticism.* Oxford: Clarendon.

Mukherjee, B. (1985). "The Middle Way." In S. Rinpoche, ed. (1985). *Mādhyamika Dialectics and the Philosophy of Nāgārjuna.* Sarnath: CIHTS Press.

Murti, T. R. V. (1955). *The Central Philosophy of Buddhism.* London: Allen & Unwin.

———(1973). "Saṃvṛti and Paramārtha in Mādhyamika and Advaita Vedanta." In Sprung, ed. (1973). *The Problem of Two Truths in Buddhism and Vedanta.* Dordrecht: D. Reidel Publishing.

———(1985). Preface to S. Rinpoche, ed., *Mādhyamika Dialectic and the Philosophy of Nāgārjuna.* Sarnath: Central Institute of Higher Tibetan Studies.

Nagao, G. (1989). *The Foundational Standpoint of Mādhyamika Philosophy.* Trans. J. Keenan. Albany: State University of New York Press.

———(1991). *Mādhyamika and Yogacāra.* Albany: State University of New York Press.

Napper, E. (1989). *Dependent Arising and Emptiness.* Boston: Wisdom Publications.

Nayak, G. C. (1979). "The Mādhyamika Attack on Essentialism: A Critical Appraisal." *Philosophy East and West* 29 (4): pp. 478–90.

Newland, G. (1992). *The Two Truths.* Boston: Wisdom Publications.

Ng, Yu Kwan (1993). *T'ien-t'ai Buddhism and Early Mādhyamika.* Honolulu: University of Hawaii Press.

Padhye, A. M. (1988). *The Framework of Nāgārjuna's Philosophy.* New Delhi: Sri Satguru.

Rabten, Geshe, and S. Batchelor (1983). *Echoes of Voidness*. London: Wisdom Publications.

Ramanan, V. (1975). *Nāgārjuna's Philosophy*. New Delhi: Motilal Banarsidass.

Robinson, R. (1957). "Some Logical Aspects of Nāgārjuna's System." *Philosophy East and West* 6: 291–308.

————(1972). "Did Nāgārjuna Really Refute all Philosophical Views?" *Philosophy East and West* 22 (3): 325–31.

Ruegg, D. S. (1977). "The Uses of the Four Positions in the Catuṣkoṭi and the Problem of the Description of Reality in Mahāyāna Buddhism." *Journal of Indian Philosophy* 5 (1): 1–71.

————(1983). "On the Thesis and Assertion in the Mādhyamika/dBu Ma." In Steinkellner and Taschner, eds. (1983), *Contributions on Tibetan Buddhist Religion and Philosophy*, 205–241. Weiner Studien sur Tibetologie und Buddhismuskunde, Heft II. Vienna: Arbeitskreis für Tibetische und Buddhistische Studien, University of Vienna.

————(1986). "Does the Mādhyamika Have a Thesis and Philosophical Position?" In Evans and Matilal (1986), *Buddhist Logic and Epistemology*, 229–37. Dordrecht: D. Reidel Publishing.

Samdhong Rinpoche, ed. (1985). *Mādhyamika Dialectics and the Philosophy of Nāgārjuna*. Sarnath: CIHTS Press.

Siderits, M. (1988). "Nāgārjuna as an Anti-Realist." *Journal of Indian Philosophy* 16: 311–25.

————(1989). "Thinking on Empty: Mādhyamaka Anti-Realism and Canons of Rationality." In S. Biderman and B. A. Schaufstein, eds. *Rationality in Question*. Dordrecht: Brill.

————(unpublished). "Matilal on Nāgārjuna."

Sogyal Rinpoche (1992). *The Tibetan Book of Living and Dying*. San Francisco: Harper.

Sprung, M. (1973). "The Mādhyamika Doctrine of Two Realities as a Metaphysic." In Sprung, ed. (1973). *The Problem of Two Truths in Buddhism and Vedanta*. Dordrecht: D. Reidel Publishing.

Sprung, M., ed. (1973). *The Problem of Two Truths in Buddhism and Vedanta*. Dordrecht: D. Reidel Publishing.

Steinkellner, E., and H. Taschner, eds. (1983). *Contributions on Tibetan Buddhist Religion and Philosophy*. Wiener Studien sur Tibetologie und Buddhismuskunde, Heft 11. Vienna: Arbeitskreis für Tibetische und Buddhistische Studien, University of Vienna.

Streng, F. (1973). "The Significance of Pratītyasamutpāda for Understanding the Relationship between Saṃvṛti and Paramārthasatya in Nāgārjuna." In Sprung, ed. (1973).

Tola, F., and Dragonetti, C. (1981). "Nāgārjuna's Conception of 'Void-ness' (Śūnyatā)." *Journal of Indian Philosophy* 9: 273–82.

Tuck, A. P. (1990). *Comparative Philosophy and the Philosophy of Schol-arship: On the Western Interpretation of Nāgārjuna.* New York: Oxford University Press.

Waldo, I. (1975). "Nāgārjuna and Analytic Philosophy," *Philosophy East and West* 25 (3): 287–98.

———(1978). "Nāgārjuna and Analytic Philosophy II." *Philosophy East and West* 28 (3): 281–90.

Walsh, M., trans. (1987). *Thus Have I Heard: The Long Discourses of The Buddha.* London: Wisdom Publications.

Warder, A. K. (1973). "Is Nāgārjuna a Māhāyanist?" In Sprung, ed. (1973).

Williams, P. (1980). "Tsong Khapa on *Kun-rdzob bDen-pa.*" In M. Aris and T. Aung, eds., *Tibetan Studies in Honour of Hugh Richardson.* New Delhi: Vikas. (1980).

———(1982). "Silence and Truth." *Tibet Journal* 2: 67–80.

———(1983). "A Note on Some Aspects of Mi bskyod rdo rje's Critique of dGe lugs pa Mādhyamika." *Journal of Indian Philosophy* 11 (2): 125–46.

———(1989). *Mahāyāna Buddhism: The Doctrinal Foundations.* London: Routledge.

Wittgenstein, L. (1922). *Tractatus Logico-Philosophicus.* Trans. B. F. McGuinness. London: Routledge & Kegan Paul.

———(1953). *Philosophical Investigations.* Trans. G. E. M. Anscombe. New York: MacMillan.

Wood, T. (1994). *Nāgārjunian Disputations: A Philosophical Journey Through an Indian Looking-Glass.* Monographs of the Society for Asian and Comparative Philosophy, no. 11. Honolulu: University of Hawaii Press.

Index

Note: Tibetan terms are indexed alphabetically according to Wylie transcription, and *not* by root letter.